IMMIGRATION'S NEW FRONTIERS

This volume could not have been possible without the generous support of the CARNEGIE CORPORATION OF NEW YORK.

IMMIGRATION'S NEW FRONTIERS

EXPERIENCES FROM THE EMERGING GATEWAY STATES

EDITED BY

Greg Anrig, Jr., and Tova Andrea Wang

A CENTURY FOUNDATION REPORT

THE CENTURY FOUNDATION PRESS • NEW YORK

The Century Foundation sponsors and supervises timely analyses of economic policy, foreign affairs, and domestic political issues. Not-for-profit and nonpartisan, it was founded in 1919 and endowed by Edward A. Filene.

LIBRARY OF CONGRESS CATALOGING-IN-PUBLICATION DATA

Immigration's new frontiers : experiences from the emerging gateway states / edited by Greg Anrig, Jr., and Tova Andrea Wang.
    p. cm.
  Includes bibliographical references and index.
    ISBN-13: 978-0-87078-506-1 (alk. paper)
    ISBN-10: 0-87078-506-0 (alk. paper)
1. Immigrants—Government policy—United States—States. 2. United States—Emigration and immigration—Government policy. 3. United States—Emigration and immigration—History—21st century. I. Anrig, Greg, 1960– II. Wang, Tova Andrea. III. Title.
    JV6483.I564   2006
    325.73—dc22   2006034651

Cover design and illustration: Claude Goodwin

10 9 8 7 6 5 4 3 2 1

CONTENTS

CHAPTER 1

INTRODUCTION

Greg Anrig, Jr., and Tova Wang

For all of the passion that the debate over comprehensive immigration reform has aroused, just about everyone agrees that the status quo is a mess. More than 11 million individuals from other countries reside in the United States without documentation, with the vast majority of them working "off the books" without valid Social Security numbers and other mandated documentation. Whatever one believes about the role of immigrants in U.S. society, it is antithetical to America's commitment to the rule of law for such a large and rapidly growing population to continue to live in what amounts to the shadows of the nation's communities.

In the absence of federal legislation—as of this writing, Congress remains deadlocked over immigration reform—states and localities have been left to fend for themselves in addressing a range of problems posed to them by both documented and undocumented immigration. The number of states with sizable immigrant populations is much larger than in the past. Before 1995, about three-fourths of the nation's immigrants settled in just six states: California, Texas, Illinois, Florida, New York, and New Jersey. In the decade since, that share has declined to roughly two-thirds, with twenty-two other states experiencing extremely rapid growth in their immigrant populations over that period. In those "new destination" states, the lion's share of the immigrants are recent arrivals who generally have limited English skills and low incomes. Those factors, as well as the lack of experience that those states have in dealing with immigrants, have posed significant public policy and political challenges for officials in the "laboratories of democracy."

1

   To learn more about how new destination state and local governments have responded to the recent influx of immigrants, The Century Foundation commissioned papers examining the experience in five of
those states: North Carolina, Iowa, Georgia, Minnesota, and Nebraska.
The goal of the effort was to provide readers who care about immigration reform with a stronger understanding of the extent to which the absence of a functional federal system has created enormous difficulties for
other levels of government. In many cases, states and localities are attempting to resolve within their jurisdictions problems that simply cannot be addressed adequately at anything other than the national level.
For example, states and localities have neither the legal mandate nor the
resources to detain those individuals who do not have documentation
or punish the employers who hire them; they are prohibited from providing Medicaid health insurance to impoverished undocumented immigrants who receive emergency room treatment when they become sick
or ill; and they are left to their own devices to determine how to apply
state driver's license laws to an undocumented population. Such issues
have become all the more difficult as a combination of racial tensions,
job competition, disruption in particular neighborhoods, and political
grandstanding have often impeded problem-solving efforts.
   The stories the chapter authors tell about the five states in this report
convey unique narratives. The differences in experience reflect such dis-
tinctions among the states as the home countries and settlement patterns
of the immigrant populations, the local economic conditions, gover-
nance traditions, the current political environment, and the role of particular groups and leaders. But for all those variations, readers will find
that the case studies share three overriding themes. First, all of the states
initially approached their influx of new immigrants from the standpoint
of accommodation—in some cases actively welcoming them and recruiting more to enter the states to help their economies—while supporting
policies geared toward making their lives better. Second, all of the states
became more ambivalent toward their immigrants over time, adopting a
more combative posture and policies that discouraged their acceptance
into mainstream society. Often that reaction was assisted by outside
forces deeply involved in the debate at the national level—particularly
interest groups and activists opposed to reforms that would provide
a path for undocumented workers to become legal residents. Third,
and most important, none of the states has managed to find effective
solutions to any of the major public policy challenges posed by undocumented immigration. To the extent that any reforms have been implemented at all, they are at best stop-gap measures. Time and again, the

case studies in this report demonstrate that states and localities are ill-equipped to resolve problems posed by undocumented immigration. If there is to be a workable solution, the federal government will have to provide it.

Here are just a few examples of the ways in which the states in this report have struggled to come to grips with the policy challenges posed by the new immigration:

▲ *Law enforcement in North Carolina.* One of the most vexing questions that all states with large immigrant populations have been wrestling with is the criteria to be used in issuing drivers' licenses. Shortly after the September 11 terrorist attacks, the federal government criticized a number of states for making it too easy for undocumented immigrants to obtain drivers' licenses. North Carolina, which was on that list, responded by setting up a program called Operation Stop Fraud, intended to stop efforts by undocumented immigrants to use invalid documents to get a license. Then, in 2004, the state legislature passed a law reducing the number and types of identification that could be presented. Even more restrictive bills are pending. At the same time, at least one North Carolina county has chosen to become proactive in rounding up undocumented immigrants. In Mecklenburg County, for example, a U.S. Immigration and Customs Enforcement official trained ten county deputies to screen individuals for immigration violations and gave them the authority to detain those without proper documentation and turn them over to the federal government for deportation. It remains to be seen whether others will follow suit.

▲ *Health Care in Iowa.* In most states, Medicaid—the health insurance program financed in part through the federal government and administered by the states to protect low-income citizens and some nursing home residents—is the most expensive and rapidly growing budget item. But because undocumented immigrants are not eligible for Medicaid, they impose significant uncompensated costs on hospitals and other health care providers when they are treated for an illness or injury. Some states, including Iowa, have created a network of clinics outside the established medical system, geared mainly toward providing free or low-cost care to undocumented immigrants and their children. Iowa also has a state program called Hawk-I, which was initially focused on providing services to low-income children who are not eligible for Medicaid that was later expanded to include children regardless of the immigration status of their parents. Some of the clinics around the state have bilingual staff and published materials. Still, the health problems of the immigrant Latino population are especially severe, particularly the high incidence of tuberculosis and Type II diabetes.

▲ *Housing in Georgia.* Many immigrants who work as day laborers bunk in homes with large numbers of other undocumented workers staying in the same place. That often creates tensions in the communities where they live as well as violates housing codes. In Georgia, for example, overcrowding is so common that Latinos commonly use the phrase *camas calientes*, which means "hot beds," to refer to housing where so many people share living quarters that the beds never have a chance to get cold. Communities that enforce housing codes outlawing overcrowding invariably lead to more overcrowding in other, usually even more dilapidated, areas. Some localities have attempted to discourage immigrants from settling by restricting advertising in foreign languages. At the same time, many cases have been reported of unscrupulous realtors carrying out bait-and-switch deals in which they fool immigrants into thinking they have bought one property when they actually have gained ownership of another that they have not even seen. Enforcement to stop such housing fraud is minimal.

▲ *Education in Minnesota.* An influx of immigrant children into public schools has created significant pressures on classroom size and costs in some localities and in many cases has posed always difficult questions about how to address language barriers. Minnesota has been among the most aggressive states in developing English programs tailored to students from other countries. For example, the Minneapolis school district has a Kindergarten Language Development Model, in which students are taught in their native language for part of the day and in English during the remainder. For some new residents, such as the Hmong children who have recently arrived from refugee camps in Thailand, there is a Transitional Language Center led by bilingual teachers. At the same time, however, those programs have faced significant cutbacks in funding. Most alarming is the high drop-outs rates for students from immigrant families.

▲   *Workers' Rights in Nebraska.* A large share of immigrant workers in Nebraska, which has one of the lowest unemployment rates in the country, is employed in the meatpacking industry. In part because immigrants are recognized as important contributors to the state's economy, Nebraska in 2003 enacted a landmark bill that was intended to protect them against abuses called the "Non-English Speaking Workers Protection Act." Prompted by media reports conveying unsanitary and unsafe conditions in meatpacking plants, Nebraska's law is uniquely favorable toward immigrants, in contrast to the generally hostile policies implemented in other states. Its provisions include requiring employers to provide workers with written statements outlining the terms and conditions of their jobs, and to make available to those workers a bilingual employee who can explain the document and refer them to various community services. It also includes a "Meatpacking Industry Workers' Bill of Rights," the first of which is the right to organize. Despite its unquestionable importance, assessments of its impact have found that enforcement is highly uneven and that it has not fundamentally changed working conditions in the industry.

These examples are representative of the new challenges that local governments are facing. In case after case, inexperienced states and localities are improvising policies to adjust to significant and unprecedented inflows of new immigrants. In some instances, those efforts are intended to make like easier for immigrants, though more recently the trend has been to be much less accommodating. But almost regardless of whether the responses are welcoming or hostile, they almost invariably are halting and far from adequate to achieve whatever goal officials are trying to define. The fundamental problem, over and over, is that undocumented immigration is a consequence of failed federal policy. If there is to be a workable solution, it will only come from the federal government.

CHAPTER 2

NORTH CAROLINA'S RESPONSE TO LATINO IMMIGRANTS AND IMMIGRATION

Paula D. McClain[1]

INTRODUCTION

Latino immigration into the United States is changing the demographic character of much of the United States. Nowhere is that change more evident than in the American South. A number of southern states, such as North Carolina, Alabama, and Georgia, reported substantial increases in the size of their Latino populations from 1990 to 2000,[2] with North Carolina registering the highest rate of increase, 394 percent, during the period.[3] Moreover, the increase of the Latino population of 383,465 in 2000 to 506,206 in 2004 represents a 1,066 percent increase in the North Carolina Latino population since 1970, when there were only 43,414 Latinos in the state.[4] Latinos account for 27.5 percent of the state's population growth from 1990 to 2004, and now make up 7 percent of the state's population.[5]

With few exceptions, Latinos are an entirely new population in the South. Likewise, the South has had little experience with large numbers of immigrants in general, and no experience with immigrant populations of Latin American origin. This massive settlement of Latinos into the Deep South has been estimated to be no more than fifteen years old.[6] These new Southern locations are what Roberto Suro and Audrey Singer refer to as "New Latino Destinations."[7] Yet the picture of Latino movement into North Carolina can be characterized by two different phases of movement and by two different groups of Latinos.

Between 1985 and 1990, the largest group of Latino migrants to the state was comprised of American Latinos from California, Texas, Florida, and New York.[8] During this period, it is estimated that approximately 69 percent of Latino migrants into the state were U.S. born, 10 percent were naturalized citizens, and only 18 percent were not U.S. citizens.[9] After 1990, the picture changed dramatically with a substantial portion of Latinos coming directly into the state, primarily from Mexico. Yet, research suggests that these new immigrants to the South are not coming from the Mexican states with long histories of sending migrants to the United States, but from states whose residents are new to the immigrant stream, for example, Veracruz, Oaxaca, Guerrero, and Puebla.[10] Of the estimated 600,913 Latinos in the state,[11] between 300,000 and 400,000 are estimated to be illegal or undocumented.[12] Although immigration from other countries, particularly Asian countries, is present in the state, the numbers are very small. Asians constitute only 1.4 percent of the state population and the majority of this group is from India, mostly people seeking work in the high-tech section of the Research Triangle (Raleigh/Durham/Chapel Hill).[13] Thus, when immigration is discussed in North Carolina, the focus is on Latino immigration.

This tremendous influx of a new population into North Carolina presents challenges for state and local governments, as well as for the general state population. How are these actors handling these changed—and continually changing—demographics? This chapter will explore various aspects of these responses, particularly responses from state government. The chapter is organized in the following manner. The first section examines the reasons behind this substantial increase in Latino immigration into the state, and examines where Latino immigrants are settling. The chapter also develops a socioeconomic portrait of these immigrants that suggests possible responses from the state of North Carolina aimed at assisting these individuals.

An examination of the attitudes of the North Carolina residents toward the new immigrants is explored in the second section. The response of the state must be viewed within the context of the broader political environment, which also suggests that the state, in addition to creating policies and initiatives geared to assist, also will move in the direction of developing policies and laws that are directed at limiting the access of Latino immigrants to government services and state-funded programs. Politicians pay attention to public opinion, particularly when it might be consonant with their own beliefs about a particular policy issue. Thus, it is possible that the executive branch of government in North Carolina, that is, the governor's office and state agencies, may move in a different direction than the legislative branch, and these approaches might come into conflict at times.

The third section examines selected responses from the executive and legislative branches to Latino immigration. Institutions and issues covered are the Governor's Office of Hispanic/Latino Affairs and the Advisory Council on Hispanic/Latino Affairs, drivers' licenses, health care, day laborers, and education. The activities and legislation of the North Carolina General Assembly are reviewed. The section also contains a brief discussion of the actions of one law enforcement agency in Mecklenburg County. The fourth section highlights issues that might be on the horizon as possible immigration related issues—Latino drunk driving and gang activity. The final section is the conclusion, which draws the various parts of the chapter together.

LATINO IMMIGRATION IN TO NORTH CAROLINA

Why the tremendous increase in Latino immigration into the South in general and North Carolina in particular? Several reasons are posed in the immigration literature. First, globalization of the economy and new United States trade policies, such as the 1994 North American Free Trade Agreement (NAFTA), resulted in the migration of labor and capital resulting in the creation of newer economies, both domestically and internationally. Historic industries in the South, such as agriculture, steel, textiles, furniture, and clothing, saw their fortunes decline in a new economy that favored more technical businesses and new food processing plants for poultry, hogs, and seafood.[14] This shift in the southern economy required large numbers of unskilled and inexpensive laborers.[15] For example, the expanding poultry industry in the southeastern states created a need for unskilled workers.[16] Faced with this expanded labor need, the poultry industry started actively to recruit immigrant workers from Mexico and Central America.[17] In addition, other southern industries, such as meat processing, carpet manufacturing, oil refining, agriculture, and forestry also required large numbers of unskilled, low-wage workers and also began to recruit from Mexico and Central America, but primarily from Mexico.[18]

Second, the push of the ongoing economic crisis in Mexico worked in tandem with the pull of economic changes in the South. The continuing Mexican economic crisis has driven many legal as well as undocumented immigrants into the southern part of the United States.[19] Interviews with Latino immigrants in Durham are illustrative of the economic push from Mexico.[20] One Mexican woman said—"Principalmente por nuestra economía. Está muy difícil la situación en México y ese fue el motivo de haber venido a los Estados Unidos." ("Principally for our economy, the situation in Mexico is very difficult, and this was the motive that we came to the United States.")

The patterns of settlement in the South have varied. Many Latino immigrants have settled in southern towns and rural areas, but large numbers also have chosen urban areas as well. Those who settle in urban areas tend to be employed in nonunion, low-wage jobs, such as service work, cleaning hotels, working for other types of cleaning companies, working for construction and landscaping firms, and building maintenance.[21] Those who settle in rural areas tend to fill the low-skilled jobs in poultry, carpet, furniture, and meat and seafood processing industries as well as agricultural jobs.[22]

These patterns of settlement are present in North Carolina. Latinos, primarily Mexican immigrants, have come into western North Carolina to work as seasonal labor on the apple and Christmas tree farms in the mountains (for example, Henderson County) and the vegetable and tobacco farms along the coasts (for example, Sampson County).[23] Many have stayed and settled in these areas. Poultry processing and meatpacking are also attracting Latino workers. North Carolina is one of the top five poultry producers in the United States, with turkey production in the southeast part of the state and chicken broiler production more geographically dispersed throughout the state.[24] The largest turkey producer is located in Duplin County, with other producers in Sampson, Pender, Bladen, Lenoir, and Onslow counties.[25] Broiler production facilities are located in, among others, Chatham, Duplin, Montgomery, Randolph, and Union counties. Meatpacking plants are located in several counties, including Johnston, where Smithfield is located. Seafood processing plants are located in counties along the eastern shore of the state.[26]

Latinos are present in all one hundred counties in North Carolina. The county with the largest proportion of Latinos is Duplin with 18.3 percent, followed by Sampson (14.4 percent), Montgomery (13.6 percent), Lee (12.2 percent), Chatham (11.4 percent), Durham (10.7 percent), and Greene (10.4 percent). (See Figure 2.1, page 11, for the fifteen counties with the highest concentration of Latino populations.) Latino immigrants are also attracted to counties such as Durham and Mecklenburg, which include the cities of Durham and Charlotte. While these counties do not have poultry processing plants,

FIGURE 2.1. NORTH CAROLINA LATINO POPULATION CONCENTRATION BY COUNTY, 2004: TOP FIFTEEN COUNTIES

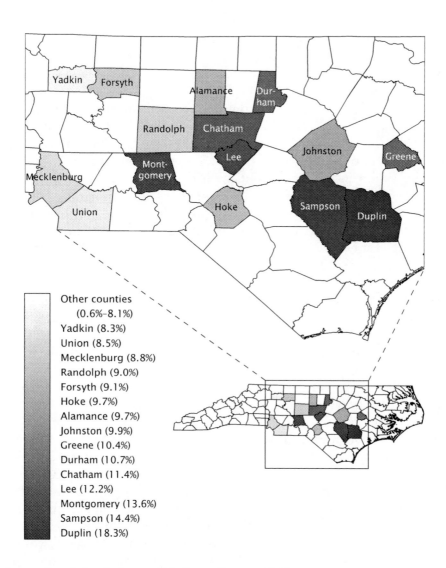

Other counties
   (0.6%–8.1%)
Yadkin (8.3%)
Union (8.5%)
Mecklenburg (8.8%)
Randolph (9.0%)
Forsyth (9.1%)
Hoke (9.7%)
Alamance (9.7%)
Johnston (9.9%)
Greene (10.4%)
Durham (10.7%)
Chatham (11.4%)
Lee (12.2%)
Montgomery (13.6%)
Sampson (14.4%)
Duplin (18.3%)

Source: Population Estimates, U.S. Census Bureau, 2004.

other industries, such as construction, landscaping, and service jobs, also need low-skilled labor and have proved attractive to Latino immigrants. In fact, the top job for Latino males is not in the poultry plants; the top occupations of Latino male immigrants are construction laborers; painters, construction and maintenance; miscellaneous agricultural workers; roofers and carpenters.[27] The top occupations for Latina female immigrants are maids and household cleaners; janitors and building cleaners; butchers and other meat, poultry, and fish; cashiers; and retail salespersons.[28]

These occupations suggest that the overwhelming majority of Latino immigrants into North Carolina are low-skilled, have low education levels, and are poor individuals. Recent data indicate that the median years of school completed by Latino immigrants is 7.5 years, the per capita income is $8,649, with the median household income standing at $32,000, and 26.3 percent of Latino immigrant families are in poverty.[29] In a series of articles throughout 2002 chronicling the lives of area residents living in poverty, the *Herald Sun* (Durham) provided a picture of life for Latinos in Durham City. Fully 26 percent of the more than 16,000 Latinos in Durham live below the federal poverty level, and, in order to make a good living, it is necessary for them to work more than one job.[30] In fact, the incidence of poverty is growing the most rapidly among the Latino portion of the population in North Carolina.[31]

These figures paint a portrait of a population whose members are without health insurance and draw heavily on the public health system; most likely living in substandard housing for which they might pay above market rental rates; avoiding the use of banks because of their immigration status, which makes them more susceptible to criminal victimization; drawing heavily on services for non-English speakers in the public school system; and gathering at specific locations in the hopes of being hired for a one-day job, among other things. The tremendous increase in the Latino population in the state and the resultant needs imply that state government might respond in ways geared to assisting this group. As will be discussed, many of the policy responses and initiatives of the North Carolina state government have been of this type. Yet there are other possible responses as well. Often, governments respond to policy issues based on the attitudes of constituents and the pressure those attitudes generate on government to do something about a particular situation. Therefore, it is important to get a sense of what North Carolinians feel about Latino immigration into North Carolina.

PUBLIC REACTIONS TO IMMIGRATION

Research on the effects of Latino immigration on North Carolina residents is limited, but enough exists to begin to sketch a broader context for the formation of public attitudes toward Latino immigration. In the previous section, the reasons for Latino immigration into North Carolina were discussed, and the industries in need of low-skilled labor were outlined. What was not discussed is the possible effect of Latino labor on native North Carolinians. Some studies do exist, and one of the earliest was conducted by David Griffith in the late 1980s. More recently, Griffith found that, in the agricultural sector, the workforce shifted from being predominantly white and African American in the early 1980s to being predominantly Mexican by 1988.[32] He found the same pattern in the poultry and meatpacking plants—Mexicans began to fill jobs that were previously held by African Americans. In interviews, Griffith found that plant managers readily admitted to a preference for Mexican over African American workers. Mexicans had networks that allowed for the recruitment of workers quickly and for lower wages than those paid to black American workers. [33] Alas, he found the same pattern in the seafood processing plants. During the 1980s, African American workers were pushed out of work by imported Mexican labor.

While Griffith's study was of rural North Carolina counties, a look at data from Durham, North Carolina, provides a picture of possible job competition or job replacement in an urban area. While data on specific job competition is limited, the data presented in Table 2.1 (see page 15) charts the shift from 1990 to 2000 in the absolute numbers of blacks in selected low-skilled occupational categories. The percentages of blacks in those categories may give us a sense of whether Latinos are displacing blacks in some low-paying, unskilled job categories. In 1990, black males were 62.7 percent of construction trade workers, and Latinos were less than 1 percent. By 2000, however, black male workers had dropped to 27.3 percent, and Latinos were now the majority, 56.9 percent, of the construction trade workers. Looking at female employment in this job category suggests that when the construction trades began to open up to women, Latinas have done far better than black women, 68.8 percent to 14.6 percent, respectively.

A similar pattern is present in black male and female employment in building and grounds, cleaning, and maintenance occupations. In 1990, black males and females were 89.2 percent and 86.1 percent of this category, and there were no Latino males and females employed in this category. By 2000, however, black male and female employment had dropped to 46.7 percent and 66.2 percent respectively, while Latino males and females were now 32.2 percent and 26.6 percent, respectively. These numbers are astonishing, especially in light of the fact that blacks are slightly more than 43 percent of Durham's population and Latinos are a little more than 8 percent.[34] Clearly, it is possible that blacks moved on to higher paying and more skilled jobs, but while these data by no means are definitive on the question, they are suggestive of possible job competition.

As early as 1996, statewide survey data began to pick up the emergence of tensions and conflicts among North Carolina residents as the size of the Latino population grew. In a recent survey, nearly half of the sample (42 percent) were uncomfortable with the increasing presence of Latinos, about two-thirds (67 percent) thought their neighbors would not approve of Latinos moving into the neighborhood, and more than half (55 percent) were uncomfortable being around people who did not speak English.[35] Interestingly, there were differences in the attitudes of black and white North Carolinians at this earlier point in time. Fewer blacks had negative attitudes about the influx of Latinos than did whites, 38 percent to 44 percent, respectively. Although still a majority, significantly fewer blacks had negative attitudes about Latinos moving into their neighborhoods than did whites (54 percent to 69 percent, respectively), and fewer blacks, although still a majority (51 percent), than whites (57 percent) were uncomfortable with people who do not speak English.[36]

Unfortunately, 1996 was the last year these particular questions were asked, so it is not possible to track these numbers over time. Nevertheless, statewide surveys conducted by Elon University indicate increasing concern with Latino immigration. In February 2006, 62.4 percent of North Carolina residents surveyed felt that Latino immigration into the state was a very important issue to them and 24.8 percent considered it somewhat important. By April 2006, 70.8 percent considered the issue of Latino immigration to be very important and 22.5 percent considered it somewhat important. In both months, the proportion of North Carolina residents who did not consider the issue to be important was only 7.8 percent in February and 5.6 percent in April.[37] When asked why immigration was an issue, 70.3 percent indicated that it was a problem because of the services they used, such as school and health care, cost the state too much. In other responses, wide majorities indicated that immigration was an issue for them because it takes away jobs from North Carolinians (53.3 percent), they believe that immigrants do not pay their fair share in taxes (72.2 percent), that they have broken the law, regardless of their situation (69.2 percent), and that most Latino immigrants are in the state illegally (51.9 percent).[38]

TABLE 2.1. RACE AND SEX, BY OCCUPATION FOR THE EMPLOYED CIVILIAN POPULATION SIXTEEN YEARS AND OVER, DURHAM[1]

OCCUPATION[2]	TOTAL MALE 1990	TOTAL MALE 2000	TOTAL FEMALE 1990	TOTAL FEMALE 2000	BLACK (PERCENT) MALE 1990	BLACK (PERCENT) MALE 2000	BLACK (PERCENT) FEMALE 1990	BLACK (PERCENT) FEMALE 2000	HISPANIC/LATINO (PERCENT) MALE 1990	HISPANIC/LATINO (PERCENT) MALE 2000	HISPANIC/LATINO (PERCENT) FEMALE 1990	HISPANIC/LATINO (PERCENT) FEMALE 2000
Construction traders workers	560	967	0	48	62.7 (351)	27.3 (264)	0 (7)	14.6 (33)	0.06 (550)	56.9	0 (33)	68.8
Other construction workers and helpers	99	211	6	12	43.4 (43)	39.8 (84)	100 (6)	0	0	46.4 (98)	0	0
Building and grounds cleaning, and maintenance occupations[3]	1347	2217	1270	1391	89.2 (1202)	46.7 (1035)	86.1 (1093)	66.2 (921)	0	32.2 (714)	0	26.6 (359)
Food preparation and serving related occupations:	1517	2123	1766	1934	66.3 (1006)	47.9 (1016)	52.3 (950)	52 (1006)	0.04 (59)	21.6 (459)	.02 (44)	10.3 (200)
Cooks and food preparation workers	1006	976	621	500	70.7 (712)	56.2 (526)	81.6 (507)	62.8 (314)	0.01 (13)	22.3 (209)	0.03 (19)	22 (110)
Waiters and waitresses	183	272	733	614	22.4 (41)	11.4 (31)	24.3 (178)	31.4 (193)	25.1 (46)	15.4 (42)	0.03 (25)	0.07 (45)
Food and beverage serving workers, except waiters and waitresses	31	255	101	388	71 (22)	38.8 (99)	70.3 (71)	62.1 (241)	0	16.1 (41)	0	0.07 (26)
Other food preparation and serving workers, including supervisors	297	660	311	432	77.8 (231)	54.5 (360)	62.4 (194)	59.7 (258)	0	25.3 (167)	0	.04 (19)

1. Data for 1990 was retrieved from the 1990 Equal Employment Opportunity File (http://censtats.census.gov/eeo/eeo.shtml), a sample from the civilian labor force data collected in the 1990 Census. Data for 2000 was retrieved from Summary File 4 (SF 4) – Sample Data, Table Pct. 86, Sex by Occupation for the Employed Civilian Population Sixteen Years and Over.

2. Data from Summary File 4 (SF 4) – Sample Data, Pct. 86, Sex by Occupation for the Employed Civilian Population Sixteen Years and Over. Data for 1990 includes all construction trade workers except carpenters; electricians; painters; plumbers; and construction laborers.

3. Data for 1990 includes supervisors, building and cleaning; maids and housemen; janitors and cleaners; elevator operators; pest control.

Source: Paula D. McClain, et al., "Black Americans and Latino Immigrants in a Southern City: Friendly Neighbors or Economic Competitors?" typescript, Duke University, 2005.

Probing further on the issue in the April 2006 survey, 63.7 percent of respondents felt there were too many immigrants in the state, with less than a quarter (22.3 percent) believing the number of immigrants was about right. Going even deeper into attitudes, slightly more than two-fifths (44.2 percent) felt that Latino immigration into North Carolina has been bad for the state, with a majority (52.9 percent) feeling that Latino immigrants are a burden on the state's markets for jobs and housing and on the health care system.[39]

Given the recent nature of the data, the Center for Public Polling at Elon University would not release the above data broken down by race. Thus, in order to get a sense of how black North Carolinians feel about Latino immigration, data gathered from Durham in 2003 are examined. These data provide not only a view of black Americans' attitudes toward Latino immigration, but how they might differ from those of white Durham residents at the time. Results presented in Table 2.2 show that almost a third (30.87 percent) of blacks were concerned "a great deal" about the rapid growth of the Latino population, compared with less than one-fifth (17.20 percent) of whites who feel the same way. When the categories of concerned "a great deal" and concerned "somewhat" are combined, 61.07 percent of blacks were concerned with the rapid growth of the Latino population compared with 41.4 percent of whites in Durham. This represents a shift from the 1996 data when whites were more concerned about immigration than were blacks.

Opened ended responses from the survey provide an illustration of feelings of concern on the part of some blacks in Durham with the increasing Latino immigration:

> Latinos seem to get all the benefits, and it seems like they are taking all of the good benefits from low-income blacks. They seem to come and go in and out of the country and not pay taxes. They seem to be getting too much.

> Latino immigrants take away our jobs, and we have to learn their language, because they are too lazy to learn ours; employers have to learn Spanish just to communicate.

> There are some blacks that want to work and some who don't. But there are blacks who have been moved from jobs that they have worked for many years, all because the employer won't pay fairly. There seems to be some preferential treatment toward Latinos (assistance, and other services).

Table 2.2. Concern about Rapid Latino Population Growth, by Race, 2003

How much does rapid Latino population growth concern respondents?	Percentage of Respondents (Number) Race		
	Blacks	Whites	Totals
Not at all	28.86 (43)	36.94 (58)	33.01 (101)
A little	10.07 (15)	21.66 (34)	16.01 (49)
Somewhat	30.20 (45)	24.20 (38)	27.12 (83)
A great deal	30.87 (46)	17.20 (27)	23.86 (73)
Totals	100 (149)	100 (157)	100 (306)

Pearson Chi-Square (3) = 14.9317   Pr = 0.002

Source: Durham Survey of Intergroup Relations, Durham Pilot Study: St. Benedict the Black meets the Virgin of Guadalupe, Ford Foundation Grant #1025-1445, Duke University, 2003.

An interview with an elected official in Durham suggests the type of feedback elected officials receive from black constituents about Latino immigration:

I mean, comments that I hear "Oh, why don't you do something about those Mexicans?" We're talking about Hispanic/Latino, but generally they describe all of them as Mexicans, which is very unfortunate because they're not all Mexicans. "Can't you pass a law to send them on back to where they came from? Most of them here are illegal. Taking our resources. Not paying for it." And these are black folks in the . . . discussing relationships with Hispanic/Latinos. I think it's unfortunate, but that's the way it is.[40]

In 2003, it appeared that blacks were more concerned with Latino immigration than were whites, but, based on the general survey data reported earlier, this might not be the case anymore. Clearly, it appears that Latino immigration into North Carolina has become a major public policy issue for native North Carolinians, both blacks and whites.

While it is not possible to draw a direct linkage between the actual job competition situation and public opinion attitudes, it is clear that a substantial portion of North Carolina residents *perceive* Latino immigrants as taking jobs from North Carolinians, burdening the public services system and educational system, in the state illegally, and generally bad for the state. Some of this perception might indeed be grounded in some of the facts presented in the media about the effects of immigration, but clearly not all of the facts. In a February and March 2006 series of articles on the effects of immigration in the *News and Observer*, the state's largest daily newspaper, the articles on health care stated that undocumented immigrants cost the state $52.8 million in Medicaid costs.[41] In the article on jobs, the tax contribution to the state generated by Latino immigrants was by estimated at $756 million, but the costs in education, corrections, and health care was estimated at $817 million, for a net cost to the state of $61 million. This translated into the budget equivalent of $102 per Latino resident.[42] If the public read the articles or heard news reports on the series, it is possible that their perceptions were either confirmed or formed.

STATE OF NORTH CAROLINA RESPONSES

As mentioned earlier, elected officials pay attention to public opinion, and legislative behavior related to Latino immigration might differ substantially from that of the executive branch of state government. In fact, an interview with an individual who works in the executive branch implied as much:

> The state has responded at different levels, at different speeds. More specifically, the response differs between the executive and legislative branches. The response, in terms of formulation and passage of legislation, to Latinos in the legislature has been a lot more combative. Some have wanted to help the Latino community; others have wanted to restrict benefits to the group. The response at the executive has been more about helping Latinos navigate the system.[43]

This is not to say that at times the executive and legislative branches might not take similar approaches to various aspects of Latino immigration, but the legislative branch might be more pressured by constituent opinion than are state agencies. Therefore, its response might be geared more toward restriction rather than to accommodations. This section will review selected, but clearly not all, responses of the state of North Carolina to the increasing Latino immigrant population in the state. The first part examines some of the executive branch's responses, and the second part reviews the North Carolina General Assembly responses. In some instances the executive branch requires approval from the legislative branch to act, and in those instances, the discussions might overlap.

EXECUTIVE BRANCH RESPONSES

Governor's Office of Hispanic/Latino Affairs. In June 1998, Governor James B. Hunt, Jr., issued an executive order creating the state Office of Hispanic/Latino Affairs, the Advisory Council on Hispanic/ Latino Affairs, and the position of director of Hispanic/Latino Affairs.[44] This initiative was the result of several years of Latino and non-Latino advocacy groups, who originally worked with Latino farmworkers, raising the issue with state officials and Governor Hunt.[45] The purpose of the office was to coordinate and develop state and local programs to meet the needs of North Carolina's Latino residents. H. Nolo Martinez, a faculty member at North Carolina State University, was appointed the first director of the Office of Hispanic/Latino Affairs.[46] The office answers requests for information about social services, immigration laws, the census, economic development, and other issues. The director of the office also met with Latino groups throughout the state to discuss race relations, health and agriculture issues, and other concerns.[47]

The Advisory Council on Hispanic/Latino Affairs was created to bring attention to issues affecting the Latino population in North Carolina. The fifteen voting members of the council were drawn from Latino advocacy groups and individuals of Latino descent from around the state. The council has four major duties: "to advise the governor on matters concerning the Hispanic community; to establish a forum for the Hispanic community; to work on issues of race, ethnicity, and human relations; and to see that Hispanics are represented in all facets of government."[48] (Interestingly, in the 2004 Report to the Governor, the duties of the advisory council had been reduced to three with the directive to work on issues of race, ethnicity, and human relations dropped from its charge.) In a 1999 interview, Martinez said that the newly formed council, which consists of twenty-five members (fifteen voting and ten ex-officio), identified sixty issues important to Latinos that they categorized into eight areas: education; human relations; health and human services; workers' rights; immigration, licensing, and documentation; economic development; political representation; and crime control and public safety.[49]

In 2004, Governor Michael Easley appointed Axel Lluch as the second director of the Governor's Office of Latino/Hispanic Affairs. Given the advisory nature of the council and the scope of the office to provide information on Latino needs, it is difficult to evaluate the effectiveness of the council and the office. Yet, its very existence has created opportunities to discuss and raise issues that might not have been raised otherwise.

In an interview, Axel Lluch suggested as much: "The initial response of the Governor's Office to Latino immigrants was to raise awareness of Latinos. Next, state agencies began to pro-actively hire Latino liaisons, or at least bilingual staff, for example, the Attorney General's Office, the highway patrol, and other agencies."[50]

In its 2004 annual report, the latest report available, it appears that the primary function of the office still is to "answer requests statewide for information about social services, immigration laws, the census, economic development, and other issues."[51] Nevertheless, the report indicates a very active office and advisory council.

The council divided itself into committees—education, motor vehicles, economic development—and made recommendations in a number of areas. Among those recommendations made in 2004 was the call to standardize the admission policy for the North Carolina Community College System so that all community colleges would admit undocumented nonimmigrant applicants to curriculum and continuing education programs. At the moment, each community college has the discretion to "implement admissions policies that permit the enrollment of undocumented nonimmigrant applicants."[52] The council also recommended, apparently in reaction to the passage of a policy by the University of North Carolina System,[53] that the University of North Carolina System and the North Carolina Community College System change their policies that deny instate tuition rates to undocumented aliens.[54] The council has no authority to require these changes or to implement these recommendations on their own. Some of their recommendations require state agencies to act and others require the state legislature to change or pass legislation.

Drivers' licenses. In February 2004, the Department of Motor Vehicles (DMV) reduced the types of items it would accept as proof of identification in order to obtain a North Carolina driver's license. North Carolina was one of the states that the Immigration and Naturalization Service had criticized for making it easy for undocumented immigrants to obtain drivers' licenses.[55] This change was made under a program, *Operation Stop Fraud*, to strengthen the integrity of the North Carolina driver's license. This change in policy was done internal to the executive branch of government and not done by a legislative statute.

While a causal link cannot be drawn, one of the events that might have pushed North Carolina to make this change was the appointment, by Mexican President Vicente Fox, of Juan Hernandez as director of the Office of Mexicans Abroad. Hernandez began to meet with United States governors encouraging them to follow North Carolina's position at the time of accepting Individual Taxpayer Identification Number (ITIN), Mexican drivers' licenses, Mexican military identification cards, or voter registration cards from other countries as documentation for a North Carolina driver's license. The backlash from this approach may have pushed the state of North Carolina to reduce the number and type of identifications it would accept to obtain a North Carolina driver's license in 2004. Legislative action in July 2006 that became effective August 28, 2006, removed the use of an ITIN as a substitute for a Social Security number to obtain a driver's license. Now anyone applying for or renewing a driver's license must show proof of a valid Social Security number or a valid visa. Additionally, legislation currently pending in the legislature will make it even more difficult for Latino immigrants to obtain North Carolina drivers' licenses.

The pending bills, H1451 in the state house and S419 in the state senate, would severely restrict the ability of immigrants, especially undocumented immigrants, to obtain a North Carolina driver's license. If the House bill passes, the DMV would be prohibited from issuing "an identification card, learners permit, or driver's license to an applicant who fails to provide proof that the applicant's presence in the United States is authorized under federal law."[56] Moreover, any license issued to a noncitizen would automatically expire when the individual's presence in the United States is no longer authorized by federal law.[57] In addition, the senate bill would require the DMV to verify legal residency through Homeland Security's Systematic Alien Verification for Entitlements automated system.[58] Originally the bills would have eliminated the use of ITINs as a substitute for a Social Security number to obtain a driver's license, but this provision was included in legislation passed at the end of the 2005–06 legislative session. During the 2004–05 legislative session, both chambers passed bills concerning restrictions on the issuance of drivers' licenses, but the house and senate could not agree on consensus language. Given the public opinion climate in North Carolina and the past passage of similar bills, the odds are that they will achieve a consensus during the 2006–07 legislative sessions, and the state will move closer to and ahead of the 2008 date for compliance with the requirements of the federal Real ID Act.

Health. In 1993, the Office of Minority Health recognized that language issues were a barrier to access to health care for the large numbers of farmworkers in the state. The office also recognized that while translating health information into Spanish was necessary, many of the farmworkers lacked the reading skills necessary to utilize these documents. Thus, it was necessary to train bilingual providers and interpreters, in addition to translating documents into Spanish.[59] In 1995, the Office of Minority Health, North Carolina Primary Care Association, the then-named Department of Environment, Health and Natural Resources, and the then-named Department of Human Resources joined together in a collaborative effort to create the North Carolina Training for Health Care Interpreters program. The program trained interpreters and health care providers throughout the state. Also, in 1997, the Department of Health and Human Services published the first edition of the manual, "Developing, Translating and Reviewing Spanish Materials: Recommended Standards for State and Local Agencies," to provide public agencies with guidance on developing Spanish materials. The guide has been updated regularly and is now used as the guide for all North Carolina state and local governments for the translation and development of Spanish language materials.[60]

The need for cultural diversity training for health care providers was also recognized, and in 1999, the Office of Minority Health developed and established a training program, Nosotros: Latino Culture and Public Health and Human Services. This program was geared to presenting health care providers with information concerning Latino culture, and was offered through county health departments. The North Carolina Training for Health Care Interpreters and Nosotros were merged into the North Carolina Area Health Education Centers (AHEC) Spanish Language and Cultural Training Initiative, which is a now program of the Office of Minority Health and Health Disparities of the Department of Health and Human Services.[61]

Also, in 1998, the Latino Initiative was created at the Center for International Understanding at the University of North Carolina, Chapel Hill. The Latino Health Coalition, which grew out of the Latino Initiative and is currently active, "provides North Carolina health leaders with resources and information to create practical, insightful solutions that incorporate a better understanding of Latino/Hispanic cultures into healthcare delivery."[62] This program has teams of health care professionals and policymakers around the state who participate in yearly programs. In addition, it has taken groups of doctors, hospital administrators, and higher education and public health professionals to Mexico so they can gain a better understanding of the cultural and medical landscape of the native communities from which most of North Carolina's Mexican immigrants come.

North Carolina has also created four federally funded and state-funded migrant health clinics in Henderson, Sampson, Duplin, and Nash counties to meet the needs of migrant farmworkers. Individuals must pay a copayment to receive medical care. If a migrant farmworker does not live near one of these clinics, the state created the Migrant Health Fee-for-Service Program, which will reimburse private physicians, dentists, optometrists, and ambulatory care services at hospitals at the Medicaid rate for health care.[63] Clearly, the North Carolina Department of Health and Human Services[64] has been proactive in its support of services for Latino immigrants, but the costs associated with these programs have become a source of contention and debate among politicians and the general public.

In 2004, the cost to the state of North Carolina for health services provided to all Latinos, both legal and illegal, was $299 million. This figure includes hospital's uncompensated care—costs not paid by the patient or insurance companies—as well as costs covered by Medicaid. The state's Medicaid costs alone in 2005 stood at $52.8 million.[65] In 2004, the state had to change the eligibility requirements for participation in pharmacy care and hospital and ambulance use in the Migrant Health Fee-for-Service Program in order to be able to continue to operate on a year-round basis.[66] Local health care facilities are beginning to feel the strain. Duplin County, which as noted has the highest proportion of Latino residents (18.3 percent) of any county in the state, is a prime example. Duplin General Hospital lost $2 million in 2003 from providing health care services to Latinos, and lost another $2.3 million in 2004. It expected to lose a similar amount in 2005.[67] In a recent interview, the hospital's executive director indicated that if the losses continued, he would have to trim staff and cutback services—"We can go on like this for a few more years, but at some point you run out of cash, and that's when the problems really start."[68]

Day laborers. Despite the significant number of Latino immigrants in the state of North Carolina, issues related to day laborers have not surfaced as a problem. Axel Lluch indicated his surprise that this had not become an issue in the state: "Actually, I have not heard anything [about day laborers]. There may have been controversies in some communities, but they haven't filtered up to the public attention."[69] Lluch's position was supported by Ricardo Velasquez, president of the Hispanic Democrats of North Carolina, who said that he "hasn't heard of any controversies."[70]

As this section was being written, the issue of day laborers did arise. In early May 2006, in the town of Fallbrook, North Carolina, a group of residents put up a six-foot chain link fence around a vacant lot in the downtown area that was being used by Latino migrant workers looking for work. The site had been the target of illegal-immigration opponents several weeks earlier.[71] Whether this is an isolated incident or the beginning of day laborers becoming an issue only time will tell. Nevertheless, if it is becoming an issue, it will take some time before the state becomes involved in the issue.

Education. While the state appeared to be cognizant of the increasing Latino population in the area of health care, it seems to have been slow recognizing the increasing Latino population in the North Carolina public school systems. The North Carolina Department of Public Instruction might have been aware, but the North Carolina General Assembly was resistant to appropriating money for instructing Limited English Proficient (LEP) children. In 1998, the general assembly provided $5 million for English as Second Language (ESL) programs after refusing to provide funds for four years. By 2003, the figure had risen to $28.5 million. Yet, it still represented only $540 per student per year at the time.[72] As of October 1, 2005, there were 83,627 LEP students in North Carolina public schools.[73] The North Carolina General Assembly appropriated $45 million for 2005–06 for ESL programs, and the estimate is that it will cost North Carolina $61.8 million to teach LEP Latino students in 2005–06.[74]

One major problem is that North Carolina has a shortage of licensed and certified ESL teachers in the state. In 2002, there were only 900 ESL teachers in the state, and a recent estimate suggests that the number now stands at only 1,000.[75] The federal No Child Left Behind Act requires that teachers be certified in their area of specialization, and the lack of ESL licensure programs at North Carolina universities has contributed to the shortage. In April 2005, there were only twelve ESL licensure programs in the entire state.[76] In April 2006, North Carolina Central University trustees approved an ESL licensure programs, the first historically black university or college in the state to do so.[77] Other universities might have added this program this spring, but it is not known how many, if any, at this point. Many school districts have addressed the shortage in ESL licensed teachers by recruiting teachers from Spanish speaking countries through the Visiting International Faculty program.[78]

Over the past twenty years, Latino enrollment in North Carolina public schools has increased by 2,614 percent, while the overall enrollment grew by only 24 percent.[79] Between 2000 and 2004, Latino enrollment accounted for 57 percent of the total enrollment growth in North

Carolina public schools.[80] It has been estimated that of the $6 billion allotted to K–12 education in 2004, $477 million went to education of Latino students, and $210 million of that amount went to educating children of undocumented Latino immigrants.[81] The costs associated with educating the children of undocumented immigrants have become an issue among a certain portion of the North Carolina public. Ron Woodward, director of a group called N.C. Listen, a group that advocates greater restrictions on immigration, commented in a recent newspaper article, "We're overwhelmed in North Carolina trying to pay for the people who are supposed to be here. Why are we having to spend money on people who are here illegally?"[82] Others, however, feel that it is in the state's interest to spend money on educating these children because it will pay off in the future in higher earnings for this population and less state resources spent on jails and other public services if these children were not provided educational opportunities. Nevertheless, the debate over spending on the education of children of undocumented immigrants is raging and will most likely continue at a heated and increased level.

NORTH CAROLINA GENERAL ASSEMBLY RESPONSES

The reaction of the North Carolina General Assembly to increased Latino immigration into the state has been mixed. As previously discussed, for four years the legislature refused to appropriate any funds for ESL programs and then, when it finally did appropriate money in 1998, it provided only $5 million. After that point, the general assembly began to put in place legislation that could be classified as beneficial to Latino immigrants, yet, the past couple of legislative sessions have seen a shift in attitude about immigration and a shift in the focus of proposed legislation from beneficial to punitive or anti-immigration. In some ways, this shift in attitude reflects the North Carolina public's increasingly negative attitudes toward Latino immigrants and immigration. But, in some ways, the tone taken by some of North Carolina's congressional representatives might be influencing the behavior of state legislators as well. It is highly possible that public opinion is also influencing the behavior of congressional representatives, so that congressional and state assembly activities are moving in concert. But, it is also just as likely that it could be the other way around. Whatever the causal direction, North Carolina is seeing an increase of anti-immigrant rhetoric and behavior on the part of some of the congressional representatives and some of the general assembly members.

In the 2001 general assembly legislative session, several pieces of legislation were passed and signed into law that can be viewed as positive outcomes for Latino immigrants. In the area of education, the general assembly (Session Law 2001-424) added monies to the State Department of Public Instruction's Closing the Achievement Gap Program so that it could include, among other things, culturally diverse objectives and activities as part of its curriculum revisions, and so that schools would be required to hire teachers and instructional support personnel who speak the language of non-English speaking students when there is a substantial population of those students in a school. The bill in the house had 51 cosponsors and ten cosponsors in the senate. During that same session, the general assembly passed legislation (Session Law 2001-244) requiring, among other things, that if English is the second language of the parent or guardian of a student that has been suspended or expelled from school that written notice had to be given in the parent or guardian's first language.[83]

Also in that session, the general assembly passed a bill (Session Law 2001-450) that would prevent notary publics from advertising in ways that would mislead Latinos into believing that they had legal powers. Given that "Notario Público" in Spanish means attorney in some Latin American countries, the concern was that Latinos could be taken advantage of by notaries. The penalty for violation of the law is revocation of the notary's commission. Another passed bill (Session Law 2001-288) required all instructions to voters for ballots be printed in both English and Spanish in every county or municipality where the Latino population exceeds 6 percent.[84] This is significant, because only twenty-two of North Carolina's one hundred counties are covered by the Voting Rights Act of 1965 and would be required to do this under federal voting rights law.

By the 2003 legislative session, few pieces of legislation concerned with Latino and Latino immigrant issues were passed. Bills were introduced to revise the funding formula for LEP students, extending in-state tuition status to noncitizen students who graduated from a U.S. high school and met their states' residency requirements, and providing funds for interpreter services in local health departments; several other bills were introduced but were not acted upon. The general assembly did, however, pass legislation (Session Law 2003-136) outlining clear and fair standards for charging late fees so that landlords did not take advantage of tenants' language barriers. It also passed a bill that allows a Fair Housing Enforcement organization to file a complaint on behalf of a person who thinks he or she has been a victim of housing discrimination.[85]

The environment around the issue of Latino immigration had changed markedly by the end of the 2004–05 sessions and the beginning of the 2005–06 legislative sessions. Several of North Carolina's Republican congressional representatives became active in the national immigration debate. Representative Sue Myrick (R) of Charlotte has been successful in getting an undocumented immigration amendment added to the recently passed legislation, Border Protection, Antiterrorism, and Illegal Immigration Control Act of 2005 (HR 4437), by the U. S. House of Representatives. Myrick's amendment, named for a person who was killed by an undocumented alien drunk driver in North Carolina, states that any undocumented alien convicted of driving while intoxicated (DWI) will face automatic deportation. It also requires information on undocumented alien drunk drivers to be placed into the National Criminal Information Center. The amendment also gives specially trained state and local law enforcement officers the authority to detain drunk drivers in the country illegally to ensure that they will make their court dates and to transport undocumented aliens into federal custody for the purposes of deportation. Myrick's catch phrase when the amendment was passed was "You drink. You drive. You're illegal. You're deported. Period."[86] Myrick's pushing for tighter controls on undocumented immigrants is partly responsible for the state legislature's eliminating the use of ITIN's to obtain a driver's license at the end of the 2005–06 legislative session.

Myrick is currently pushing for an immigration court to be placed in North Carolina. Presently, North Carolina's undocumented immigration cases are heard in the immigration court in Atlanta. So far, the Department of Justice has denied her request. But other Republican members of the North Carolina congressional delegation—Patrick McHenry of Cherryville, Virginia Foxx of Banner Elk, Walter Jones of Farmville, and Charles Taylor of Brevard—are joining her in the effort to have an immigration court placed in North Carolina. Taylor chairs a House Appropriations subcommittee and has vowed to find the money for the court.[87] Myrick is a favorite of the North Carolina-based anti-immigrant group, Americans for Legal Immigration (ALI-PAC) that has ties to the Minutemen, the Federation for American Immigration Reform, and other vigilante groups.[88] One of the individuals interviewed identified this group as being in the forefront of actively advocating restrictions on undocumented immigration in North Carolina.[89]

This changed environment was reflected in the reactions to a bill introduced in the house (House Bill 1183) aimed at offering in-state university tuition to undocumented immigrants. On April 12, 2005,

Representative Paul Luebke (D) of Durham introduced the bill that would let high school graduates who are not legal residents pay lower, in-state tuition if they attended a North Carolina school for a least four straight years. Students would be required to apply for citizenship and meet the college's academic standards to qualify. The bill had bipartisan support and the support of Jim Hunt, the former Democratic governor. But as soon as it was introduced, the backlash was swift and strong. ALI-PAC was in the forefront of the reaction and national conservative talk radio picked up the issue. Luebke is quoted as saying—"I've been told to leave the state, I've been told to move to Mexico. . . ."[90] Cosponsors of the bill began to remove their names and Governor Mike Easley suggested the bill would run afoul of federal law. Andrea Bazan-Mason, then-executive director of El Pueblo at the time, said she was surprised by the backlash—"I didn't expect the rhetoric to get so ugly."[91] William Gheen, president of ALI-PAC, indicated that the negative backlash should send a signal to politicians, and his message to undocumented immigrants: "The illegal aliens in North Carolina—it would be best for them to make other plans."[92]

The 2004–05 and 2005–06 legislative session saw the introduction of several bills that could be classified as anti-Latino and/or anti-immigration. Representative Cary Allred (R) of Alamance introduced a bill (H1362) to "authorize state and local law enforcement officers to enforce the federal immigration laws to the extent authorized by federal law."[93] Senator Hugh Webster (R) of Alamance introduced a bill in the senate (S976) with a corresponding bill in the house (H1018) called the Taxpayer and Citizen Protection Act. It would require proof of citizenship to vote and proof of legal resident status or citizenship to receive "certain public benefits"; would require state agencies to cooperate with local governments and the Department of Homeland Security to develop a system for verifying lawful presence in the United States; and contains a lengthy section requiring the state to declare "that illegal immigration is causing economic hardship and lawlessness in this State and that illegal immigration is encouraged by public agencies within this State that provide public benefits without verifying immigration status."[94] Another bill introduced in the house (H1495) by Representative John Rhodes (R) of Mecklenburg, would create a resolution "urging Congress to enact legislation to designate English as the official language of the United States." None of these bills were voted out of committee in time to be acted on during this legislative session.[95] Nevertheless, the assumption is that these bills will be reintroduced and some or all of them will pass.

While not aimed specifically at Latino immigrants, one bill that did pass and was signed into law, S814, places limits on population density and could be used against Latino immigrants in the area of housing. One section of the bill gives local governments the ability to use zoning regulations "to avoid undue concentration of population."[96] This bill could be used to pursue overcrowding in Latino households.

At the same time as these negative pieces of legislation were being pushed, other legislation geared toward helping Latino immigrants was also introduced. Two bills of particular note were introduced during the session. One, H1461, introduced by Representative Martha Alexander (D) of Mecklenburg, called for a Legislative Research Commission to study the issue of trafficking of persons. The charge to the commission would be to identify state activities in trafficking prevention activities, identify programs and services that would help victims of human trafficking, and make recommendations to develop a coordinated system of support and assistance to victims of trafficking.[97] This bill was not acted upon.

The second bill, H767, introduced by Julia Howard (D) of Davie and Iredell, was intended to strengthen and enforce the Migrant Housing Act to ensure safe and healthy migrant farmworker housing. This bill would require heating equipment, mattresses, access to emergency services, and access to telephones for emergency situations, among other things. This bill was passed in the house and is in committee in the senate. This bill will most likely be passed during the next legislative session. The Migrant Housing Act is the only piece of legislation that focused on Latino immigrant housing, although S814 could be used against nonmigrant Latinos.

Other governmental responses: Mecklenburg County. While most counties have not responded independently of the state on issues related to Latino immigration, actions taken by Mecklenburg County deserves special note. In February 2006, Representative Sue Myrick, Mecklenburg County Sheriff Jim Pendergraph, and an official from the U. S. Immigration and Customs Enforcement (ICE) held a news conference to announce the start of a new program in which ICE would train ten Mecklenburg County deputies to screen for immigration violations. These deputies would have the authority to detain undocumented immigrants and turn them over to ICE for removal from the country.[98] Mecklenburg is the first North Carolina county to participate in this program. At the news conference, Myrick said, "This new program changes how North Carolina responds to illegal aliens. . . . My hope is that every county in North Carolina sees what we

are doing here and applies to set up a similar program with ICE."[99] It is
rumored that Alamance County will soon participate in the program, but
that could not be verified at this time.[100]

EMERGING ISSUES

Two issues associated with Latino immigration into North Carolina are
beginning to emerge as issues of concern—drunk driving and gang activity. Representative Sue Myrick's successful amendment (concerning Latinos and drunk driving) to the U. S. House of Representatives' recently
passed immigration enforcement bill developed, in part, from a series of
high profile deaths of North Carolina citizens caused by Latino drunk
drivers, most of whom were undocumented.[101] Similar accidents that have
resulted in the deaths of North Carolina citizens in Durham, Mecklenburg, Columbus, Brunswick, and other counties have pushed the issue to
the forefront. In 1997, Latinos were 5 percent of those arrested for DWI
in North Carolina. By 2004, Latinos represented 19 percent of those arrested for DWI in the state.[102] In 2003 in Durham City, 56 percent of those
stopped on suspicion of DWI were Latino, and 29 percent of all alcohol-
related crashes in Durham City involved Latino males.[103] In Mecklenburg
County, for example, in 2004 Latinos were 8 percent of the population,
but were 25 percent of the DWI arrests.[104] The district attorney of Mecklenburg County indicated that drunk driving by Latino immigrants poses
a danger to other motorists: "Any drunk driver is a danger. But here are
folks who may not have drivers' licenses, may not have insurance, and are
very much at risk of being involved in a crash causing injury or death."[105]

On the other side of the equation, research indicates that 25 percent of all Latino deaths in North Carolina are caused by vehicle col-
lisions. For male drivers under age twenty-five involved in crashes,
alcohol was involved twice as frequently among Latino drivers as
non-Latino drivers. In addition, Latino youths fifteen to twenty years
old are twice as likely as non-Latinos to engage in high risk drinking and
driving behavior.[106] This problem has not been lost on Latino advocacy organizations and leaders around the state. Andrea Bazan-Manson,
then executive director of El Pueblo in Durham, was quoted as saying
that newcomers from Mexico and other Latin American countries are
not prepared for or familiar with the more stringent laws in the United
States prohibiting drinking and driving.[107]

In June 2006, El Pueblo partnered with the Governor's Highway
Safety Program and the State Highway Patrol on a multi-pronged

campaign to address the high rates of drunken driving among Latinos. The effort will target three areas—the Triangle area (Raleigh, Durham, Chapel Hill), the Triad area (Greensboro, High Point, Winston Salem) and Charlotte. In the Triangle, the highway patrol will focus on increased enforcement of DWI laws with more traffic checkpoints targeting drunken drivers, while El Pueblo and the Governor's Highway Safety Program will design and promote an ad campaign aimed at educating Latinos about the dangers of drinking and driving. The campaign's slogan is: "Manejar Borracho? No Seas Tonto Muchacho! ("Drive Drunk? Don't Be a Fool, Man!"). The campaign will involve distribution of pamphlets and a series of television, radio and print ads in the Latino media on how drunk driving can affect families. Efforts in the Triad will include only the education component, and El Pueblo will only monitor DWI statistics in the Charlotte area.[108] Clearly, this issue is being taken seriously by not only state agencies and law enforcement, but by Latino advocacy groups as well.

The other problem that might become a serious social and political issue related to Latino immigration is gang activity. A recent report by the North Carolina Governor's Crime Commission presented some disturbing figures about Latino gang activity in the state. The study found that between 1999 and 2004, the greatest rate of growth in North Carolina's youth gang population occurred within the Latino communities. In 1999, Latino gangs comprised only 6.5 percent of the recognized 332 identified gangs. By 2004, Latino gangs accounted for 22.5 percent of the recognized 387 gangs.[109] The majority of the members are from Mexico and El Salvador with Honduras and Nicaragua being the next most common countries of origin. An estimated 65.7 percent of the Latino gang members were illegally in the country.[110] The gangs are both local and national in character with Surenos (Sur-13) and Mara Salvatrucha (MS-13) among the national gangs present in North Carolina. Gangs are located in thirty different counties, stretching from as far west as Henderson and Polk counties to the easternmost counties of Beaufort and Craven. Sur-13 is present in twenty-three counties and MS-13 exists in eighteen.[111] The greatest number of gangs were reported in Wake County (eleven), Durham County (nine), and Rowan County (nine).[112] At present, law enforcement is aware of the increases in gang activity, but the issue of Latino gangs has not been actively discussed by the general public and politicians. Given the rate at which Latino gang activity is increasing, it is only a matter of time before it becomes a public issue. Other issues might arise, but these are the two that are on the threshold of breaking into the policy arena and on the public's radar.

Conclusion

The story of the response of the State of North Carolina to Latino immigration is a mixed one. Early on, the executive branch began to respond in ways that would assist Latinos in navigating the state bureaucracy and helping them access health care and other state programs. As time passed and Latino immigration continued to increase, the response has turned more negative as North Carolina citizens have become more concerned about Latino immigration and state legislators appear to be responding to that concern. Some aspects of this negative response are also probably driven by the anti-immigration posture of some of the North Carolina congressional delegation. Whatever the causal relationships, the environment for and attitude toward Latino immigration in the State of North Carolina has turned more hostile. Yet, despite the more hostile climate, the North Carolina General Assembly seems just as slow reacting negatively to Latino immigrants as it was to react positively early on. This reluctance to act might suggest that there may be room for Latino advocacy groups to prevail on state legislators to forestall the punitive legislation.

Yet, in the broader context, Latino immigration into North Carolina will continue well into the foreseeable future. There are few signs that it will let up. The present tensions among various segments of the North Carolina population, particularly the increasing negative feelings of black Americans toward Latino immigrants, suggest that the debate over Latino immigration is likely to continue to be an issue in North Carolina politics. Only time will tell if the anti-Latino immigrant group of state elected officials gains more traction. But one thing is clear— North Carolina cannot continue with a piecemeal approach to the issues facing Latino immigrants. This is a tough situation for state policymakers to find themselves because they will have to balance the needs of a population that by and large cannot vote against the desires of North Carolinians who can and do vote. This delicate balancing act will not be easy to achieve, and politics being what they are, the default will be to take the punitive approach. Will North Carolina become another Georgia, which has instituted some of the most restrictive and anti-immigration policies in the nation? We should know in the next couple of legislative sessions.

CHAPTER 3

STATE AND LOCAL IMMIGRATION POLICY IN IOWA

Mark A. Grey

NEW IMMIGRANTS IN OLD IOWA

The vast majority of Iowans are the descendants of European immigrants who settled the state in the late nineteenth and early twentieth centuries. With the exception of some small Native American groups, the Iowa territory was largely devoid of population. With white settlement and the state's active encouragement of mass immigration in the 1870s, Iowa's population grew quickly.[1] In those days, a young state needed people, and immigration from places such as Holland, Norway, and Denmark provided them.

More than one hundred years later, Iowa needs people once again, and immigrants are filling the void. Only this time, the newcomers are not from Bohemia and Sweden, they are from Mexico, Africa, and the Balkans. To complicate things, established-resident Iowans—who still cite their immigrant heritage with some pride[2]—are not sure what to do with the new Iowans. The result is a state in transition. One that is not quite sure it is ready to make the new immigration work despite every indication that today's immigrants are crucial to the state's long-term social and economic well being.

In many respects, Iowa is a "new destination" state for immigrants, particularly Latinos.[3] Prior to 1990, Iowa's Hispanic/Latino[4] population was comparatively small. But with major influxes of these immigrants that began in the 1990s, Latinos are now the state's largest minority group. Their presence has stirred controversy among policymakers and diverse responses among native Iowans. This mixed response is born of uncertainty, fear, misinformation, and disinformation. The challenges are social and economic, but they are also political.

This chapter addresses some of the main challenges and opportunities for Iowa associated with rapid growth in the state's immigrant and refugee populations, with a primary focus on policy responses and practices at the state and local level. Iowans pride themselves on being sensible people who work through their problems in a sort of quiet, withdrawn manner. But the realities associated with the state's rapidly growing immigrant population test Iowans in new and particularly challenging ways. As this chapter will show, state and local level policy responses have emerged from this debate with mixed results. Iowa presents an important case study for how state governments deal with the new immigration. Although Iowa is a long way from becoming a majority-minority state like Texas or California, how the state has responded to the new immigration holds important lessons for the impending reality of a majority-minority United States.

The first part of this chapter will describe the demographic trends under way in Iowa, define the phenomenon of "rapid ethnic diversification" and its implications, and provide some historic background to contemporary immigration in Iowa. Before launching into a discussion of specific areas of policy and practice such as public schooling, higher education, health care, and law enforcement, it will be helpful to describe the political context within which these issues have been debated in response to the state's rapidly growing immigrant population. The rise and demise of the governor's immigration initiative in 2000–02 makes Iowa unique in that it was the only state that initiated a program to recruit and integrate immigrant workers and their families. In many respects, the policies and practices described herein emerged from the wreckage of the state's failed immigration program.

After setting the demographic and political context for immigration policy in Iowa, the chapter will address the challenges and opportunities of the new immigration in Iowa's public schools, higher education, health care, drivers' licenses and identification cards, state and local law enforcement, employment practices, day labor, and housing. The chapter will conclude with some discussion of immigration issues in the 2006 Iowa legislature and a look toward the future of immigration policy in Iowa.

DEMOGRAPHIC TRENDS IN IOWA

In many Iowa communities, immigrant newcomers are making up for the rapid loss of the state's working-age Anglo population. There are four demographic trends at work: a rapidly aging Anglo population and workforce, declining birth rates, out migration of young Anglos, and the rapid influxes of immigrants and refugees.

In the 2000 census, 17.8 percent of all Iowans were age 60 or older and 14.9 percent were over age 65. Current projections indicate that over 20 percent of Iowans will be over age 65 by 2020. If these projections hold, Iowa will have 537,000 residents over age 65 in 2020. The median age among Anglos continues to rise as well. In 2000, it was 37.9 years. (The 2000 median age for Hispanics was 22.6 years.) Based on current projections, the median age among whites will be 38.3 years in 2010 and 40.1 years in 2020. At the other end of the age spectrum, only 4 percent of Anglos were age 9 or below in 2000. (Twenty-five percent of Hispanics were age 9 or younger in 2000.)

The aging of Iowa's white population also reflects declining birth rates. In 1990, the state's average live birth rate was 14.2 per 1,000. In 2000, it was 13.1, and in 2004, it was 13 live births per 1,000.[5] Another milestone was crossed in 2002. In that year, fifty of Iowa's ninety-nine counties experienced more deaths than births.[6] In many of these counties, the difference between births and deaths was not very large, but this was yet one more indicator of Iowa's population decline, particularly in rural areas.

The loss of young Anglos is another serious problem in Iowa. Nearly half of the state's high school and college graduates leave the state. Iowa is next to last among states in terms of retaining its youth. Only North Dakota lost a higher percentage of people ages 25–39 between 1995 and 2000. More recent census figures indicate Iowa is among the top ten states in terms of losing population, with more than 35,000 people leaving the state between 2000 and 2004. Most of these out-migrants were people in their twenties, members of the so-called baby-boom echo generation born in the 1970s and early 1980s.

THE IMMIGRANT INFLUX

Despite the loss of young people and Iowa's rapidly aging population, the state's total population has remained relatively stable due to large influxes of immigrants. Much to the relief of employers, community

leaders, and policymakers who experienced a significant loss of population in the 1980s (–4.7 percent), Iowa's population grew somewhat (by
5.4 percent) between 1990 and 2000. However, it is important to note
that two-thirds of that growth was due to immigration. This trend has
continued. Between 2000 and 2004, 77 percent of the state's total population growth was due to the Latino influx.

Iowa's Hispanic/Latino population grew by 153 percent in the
1990s. The census counted 82,473 non-white Hispanics in 2000, although this figure is probably low due to the reluctance of the undocumented to complete census forms. The census count made Latinos
Iowa's largest minority population, outnumbering African Americans by
20,000. The census estimate for Hispanics in 2004 was 104,119, growing by more than 21,000 since 2000. However, even this census estimate
is probably low, and a more accurate estimate is that Latinos in Iowa
number about 125,000.

Dramatic growth in the Latino population has been concentrated in about thirty communities. Seven Iowa counties experienced ten-
fold or more increases in their Hispanic populations between 1990 and
2000. The majority of the rapid-growth communities host meatpacking plants. For example, Storm Lake and Denison experienced 1,500
percent and 1,412 percent increases, respectively, in their Hispanic populations. Smaller percentage growth rates—although numerically significant—were also experienced in larger communities such as Des Moines
and Sioux City.[7]

Non-Latino immigrant groups have arrived as well, although in
much smaller numbers. Balkan refugees, mostly Muslim Bosnians, started arriving in significant numbers in 1994. Today they may number
more than 10,000. The Southeast Asian refugees who arrived in significant numbers in the 1970s and 1980s arrived in smaller numbers in the
1990s. Starting about 1995, Iowa also started receiving African refugees,
mostly from the Sudan. The Iowa Bureau of Refugee Services reported the settlement of 7,322 refugees between 1998 and 2005. However,
this figure does not include secondary migrants who arrived from other
states in which they were initially settled.[8]

RAPID ETHNIC DIVERSIFICATION

The Iowa communities that have experienced dramatic growth in immigrant populations undergo a process called "rapid ethnic diversification."[9] This process involves the dramatic transformation of

communities, workplaces, and schools from predominately white and English speaking to multiethnic, multinational, and multilingual in a few years time. Indeed, in many Iowa communities, the bulk of immigrants arrived in a five- to six-year period. In addition to the social and economic shock experienced with these rapid influxes, there are two other implications. The vast majority of rural Iowans are white descendants of European settlers, but the new Iowans come mostly from non-European and developing regions, and they are not white. Although Iowa communities have been linked to the global marketplace for decades through the export of agricultural and manufacturing products, today even the smallest Iowa town has become transnational or "postnational" in nature.[10] They are now integrated into a global labor market in which Iowans no longer compete with each other for jobs but with people from literally around the world.

Rapid ethnic diversification presents a number of challenges. The social fabric of the community is disrupted.[11] Outright hostility or violence is quite rare, but there are other tensions including mistrust on the part of established residents and newcomers alike. Crime rates sometimes go up, but this does not reflect the presence of immigrants *per se*, but rather the transience associated with high turnover rates in meat-packing plants.[12] Housing is sometimes a challenge, particularly when newcomer population growth outstrips the housing stock. Schools find themselves with students who do not speak English and in some cases arrive with several different languages and nationalities.

THE HISTORIC CONTEXT FOR THE NEW IMMIGRATION

Iowa has a history of welcoming refugees. Indeed, the nation's first state bureau dedicated to the resettlement of refugees was formed in Iowa. In the chaos throughout Southeast Asia after the fall of Saigon in 1975, hundreds of Tai Dam (or Black Tai) refugees fled Laos and entered Thailand. An appeal to some thirty U.S. governors was made to rescue the Tai Dam refugees. Only Iowa Governor Robert Ray responded to this appeal and to a personal request from President Gerald Ford. Governor Ray formed the Governor's Task Force for Indochinese Resettlement and within two months this task force accepted responsibility for resettling more than 1,200 Tai Dam in a contract agreement with the U.S. Department of State. The first planeload of Tai Dam arrived in Des Moines in November 1975. Sponsors and employers for these new Iowans stepped forward by the score in response to a mass media appeal.[13]

The mission of the Governor's Task Force was expanded to serve all refugees in 1976. Although the effort was due to wind down in 1977, the refugee situation in Southeast Asia worsened with mass migration out of Cambodia under Pol Pot and the exodus of "boat people" from Vietnam. Renamed the Iowa Refugee Service Center in 1977, the state's refugee program followed Governor Ray's commitment to resettle even more refugees. In 1979, Governor Ray was so moved by the plight of Vietnamese boat people that he personally committed Iowa to receive 1,500 more refugees from Southeast Asia.

It was perhaps foretelling that the governor's initiative to bring more refugees to Iowa met with growing resistance by 1979. In September of that year, the *Des Moines Register* printed a poll in which 51 percent of Iowans were against resettling more refugees in the state. Despite this growing public concern about his expanded effort, Governor Ray kept his commitment.[14] Public sentiment against a governor's program to bring immigrants to Iowa was experienced again two decades later, but unlike Governor Ray, the future governor gave in.

The Refugee Service Center was eventually renamed the Iowa Bureau of Refugee Services and placed in the Iowa Department of Human Services. Since its inception in 1975, the bureau has resettled 26,000 refugees in Iowa. The origins of these refugees have changed through time. For example, Lao refugees started arriving in 1980. In 1987, Iowa received refugees from Eastern Europe. Bosnians started arriving in 1993, and Sudanese started arriving in 1995.[15]

In some cases, the acceptance of refugees in Iowa paved the way for more recent immigrants. Some refugee groups seem to be more readily accepted than others. For example, Bosnians, who are white, have been more readily accepted than black Somalis and Sudanese. Despite periodic reluctance to accept more refugees, Iowans for the most part distinguish refugees from immigrants. They may not always be able to cite the technical or legal distinction, but they often recognize differences between the refugees who have fled some life threatening situation and immigrants who come here for economic reasons. The refugees were invited—at least to the United States—but the economic migrants invited themselves.

MAKING IOWA THE "ELLIS ISLAND OF THE MIDWEST"

After he took office in 1998, Governor Tom Vilsack appointed the Strategic Planning Council to help him establish a vision for Iowa in the year 2010. This council was bipartisan and comprised thirty-seven prominent people including policymakers, university presidents, and mayors. The council—which became known as the 2010 Commission or the 2010 Council—held a series of town hall meetings around the state, conducted research, and developed a vision for Iowa's future. Their report—issued in the summer of 2000—was titled *Iowa 2010: The New Face of Iowa*. It addressed many of the issues one might expect in such a report, including a focus on quality schools, economic development, and the environment. First and foremost, the report focused on the state's looming population and workforce shortage. The commission estimated that by 2010, Iowa would need 310,000 new workers to assure the state's social and economic health.[16] This estimate in itself was not too controversial, but how the commission suggested finding these new workers was. They suggested a three-pronged approach: encourage Iowans who left the state to "come home," convince young Iowans to stay, and—most important—attract and accommodate more immigrants and refugees.

Among their bold recommendations to grow the state's immigrant population were calls to obtain from the then-named Immigration and Naturalization Service (INS) a designation for Iowa as an "immigration enterprise zone," with immigrant admission targets that were not constrained by federal quotas; to request INS assistance in the prompt processing of immigrants relocating to Iowa; and to establish regional Diversity Welcome Centers to assist new residents with overcoming legal and cultural obstacles in relocating to Iowa.

Initially, Governor Vilsack embraced these recommendations, and in the fall of 2000, he announced a bold initiative to recruit and integrate immigrants. Indeed, to help make the case, his office raised the projected number of needed workers by 2010 to 563,000. His immigration initiative included the establishment of two New Iowans Centers in Muscatine and Sioux City, creation of an immigration task force that brought together members of several state bureaucracies, and the selection of three "pilot" communities to serve as models for other Iowa communities in accommodating immigrants. The New Iowans Centers were established to help newcomers find jobs and housing, translate job applications, and interpret for job interviews. The centers were also charged with training employers to accommodate newcomer workers.

The charge of the pilot communities was to develop model services to welcome and accommodate immigrant and refugee newcomers that could be used by other Iowa communities as they, too, recruited and accepted immigrant workers and their families. The three pilot communities chosen were Marshalltown, Mason City, and Fort Dodge.[17] They each received $50,000 to conduct needs assessments and plan immigration programs. Another significant development was the establishment of the New Iowans Program at the University of Northern Iowa, although this center was established independent of the governor's initiative and without state funding.[18]

This was an exciting, heady time. Immigration advocates found themselves with a new legitimacy that can only come with the high-profile endorsement of a governor and the resources of a state government with a fresh mandate. Nongovernmental organizations such as the American Friends Service Committee and Catholic Charities stepped up their immigration programs. Immigration advocates no longer had to work in relative obscurity—they became part of a bold drive to save Iowa.

Of course, Iowa also garnered a great deal of national and international media attention for its immigration initiative. Most of the reporting acknowledged the state's shrinking population, but it often also played on stereotypes about Iowa. The *New York Times* opened one piece with "No one would call Iowa a melting pot." Yet, the Iowa effort was recognized as "something no other state has done."[19] International coverage gave Iowa an (premature) image as a welcoming state, and the governor's office and some members of the 2010 Council were flooded with e-mails, letters, and resumes from people around the world seeking jobs and new lives in Iowa.

The massive media coverage led to praise for Iowa's bold leadership and innovation, but it also made Iowa the focal point for anti-immigration activities. National anti-immigration groups targeted Iowa.[20] The Federation for American Immigration Reform (FAIR) and Project USA both spent considerable sums on television and print advertisements against the Iowa immigration initiative. Some of these groups also organized and trained local activists to fight the state immigration plan. These were generally small-scale efforts, but "talking points" generated by FAIR and other organizations made their way into public hearings and the press. These outside groups also organized petitions in the three pilot communities to withdraw those towns from the state immigration program.

Even without outside agitation and propaganda, Governor Vilsack's immigration initiative set off great controversy among Iowans. Within weeks of announcing the initiative, public opinion turned against it. A *Des Moines Register* poll in September 2000 reported that 59 percent of Iowans believed immigrants "do jobs that might otherwise go unfilled" and 32 percent believed immigrants "take jobs from Americans." Yet,

58 percent of Iowans disapproved of the state's plan to encourage immigration to the state.[21]

Other surveys found similarly mixed feelings. In one that offered five different strategies to grow Iowa's workforce, immigration ranked last. Nearly 61 percent of respondents approved of recruiting immigrants, but they preferred other approaches such as retaining young people and encouraging Iowans living in other states to return. In this same survey, 76 percent said immigrants "take jobs Iowans don't want," and 68.8 percent said immigration actually "improves the quality of life."[22]

The September 2000 *Des Moines Register* poll that showed responses against the governor's immigration plan was just the beginning. The handwriting was on the wall and it was just a matter of time before the governor's initial enthusiasm to create the new Ellis Island of the Midwest died a painful death.

Some aspects of the plan were implemented. The New Iowans Centers were established under Iowa Workforce Development[23] in Muscatine and Sioux City, and the pilot community projects proceeded in Marshalltown and Mason City, although in decidedly different ways. Marshalltown formed an active and diverse planning team led by the chamber of commerce. A comprehensive community needs assessment was completed as well as a preliminary plan of action.[24] In many respects, Marshalltown was already a model or "pilot" community for integrating immigrants,[25] and the governor's pilot community initiative gave pro-immigration activities in Marshalltown an infusion of cash and new political currency.

The Mason City pilot community task force had a similarly enthusiastic start, but interest faded as the politics became more difficult and many community leaders were unwilling to plan for potentially unfunded immigration programs. Opposition also grew to the plan, and unlike in Marshalltown, the mayor and other key leaders in Mason City had nothing to do with it, leaving the bulk of work to a dedicated mayor pro tem. Project USA built a "truthmobile" out of a trailer towed by a pickup truck. It read, "In your 20s? Immigration will double the U.S. population in your lifetime." The truthmobile showed up in parking lots outside immigration meetings, including a workshop I conducted. The purveyors of the truthmobile even inserted it into a Mason City parade without an invitation. Under the guidance of Project USA, one Mason City resident read a lengthy statement to the city council insisting that the governor wanted to "turn Iowa into another California."

A needs assessment was produced in Mason City, but there was very little follow through.[26] The issue engaged the entire community, and in many respects, Mason City became the media poster child for the immigration debate across Iowa. One particularly important point was a televised town hall meeting on immigration for which the local television station gave up two hours of primetime without commercials. Two-hundred people attended.

For all intents and purposes, the third pilot community project, Fort Dodge, never even got started. Unlike in Marshalltown and Mason City, a broad based steering committee was never formed, and a comprehensive needs assessment or plan was never produced. The Fort Dodge "assessment" was limited to a review of workforce data from secondary sources.[27] There were a few reasons for this, including a lack of interest and commitment among community and economic leaders and precious few activists in the community willing to take on the planning process. One local leader explained the reasons Fort Dodge turned down the governor's offer, "We were adamant that we were not going to divide this community."[28] In any case, even the most willing activists could not have made Fort Dodge a model community without elected officials, not only for their leadership but to access the funding provided by the state government. Indeed, two years after Marshalltown and Mason City used up their $50,000, the majority Fort Dodge's funds remained in their account.

THE POLITICAL BACKLASH

The Vilsack immigration initiative was a policy initiative in the sense that his administration promoted it, he ordered state functionaries to work on the project, and he directed funding to the New Iowans Centers and pilot communities. However, no formal policy was created to authorize the effort with the exception of the New Iowans Centers, and even that came after the fact. Indeed, the effort got under way months after the state legislature adjourned in 2000 (it convenes annually) and a few months before it reconvened in January 2001. The proposal to get some kind of special dispensation from the federal government to make Iowa an "immigrant enterprise zone" was a nonstarter and no serious appeals were made to federal immigration officials or the U.S. Department of State. A special dispensation for an individual state to set its own immigration policies and quotas was highly unlikely anyway.

Ironically, the first real policy to emerge from this situation was a bill in the Iowa legislature—introduced by a representative of Fort Dodge—to assure that the governor could no longer choose communities for pilot projects without their consent, regardless of funding. As one state legislator framed it, it was "this top-down, government-knows-best idea that created this problem in the first place."[29] The bill was signed into law by the governor. It stated,

> During any project, pilot project, or similar initiative undertaken by the governor or the executive branch which includes the designation of a model community in the state, the approval of all of the following entities must be obtained by a simple majority vote prior to the granting of an official model community designation and prior to any state financial support being disbursed to any person under the project, pilot project, or similar initiative:
>
> a. The city council of any city included in a proposed model community.
>
> b. The county board of supervisors of a county included in a proposed model community.
>
> c. Each school board of a school district serving students in a proposed model community.

Things got worse for the immigration plan. In the spring and summer of 2001, the economy slowed down and unemployment rates and layoffs grew. These facts took on a whole new importance in light of the raging debate about immigration in Iowa. Union opposition grew, and the AFL-CIO threatened to pull its support for the Democratic governor in the next election if he did not back off the immigration plan. As the president of the Iowa AFL-CIO said at that time, "Right now I couldn't get one union member to knock on doors for Tom Vilsack." Indeed, the governor was openly accused of working for the "low wage labor lobby." The governor's own rhetoric—and that of this staff—changed from recruiting "immigrants" to recruiting "skilled immigrants." This was a response to complaints by Iowans that most immigrants in the state were poorly educated Latinos who did not speak English and who held low-wage jobs in meatpacking plants that required no skills. The governor admitted as much, telling the *Washington Post* the meatpacking industry "has become the poster child for immigration problems, with some justification."[30]

By August 2001, Governor Vilsack insisted that the model immigration communities were "not required to actively recruit foreign workers but are merely intended to be 'welcoming' to immigrants."[31] The next

month, he and his staff backtracked even further, insisted that the goal of
the three pilot immigration communities was not to bring immigrants to
Iowa. Rather, "the goal was to establish a dialogue" in these communities.

If things were not bad enough, the terrorist attacks on September
11, 2001, made matters even worse. The anti-immigrant groups were
able to successfully link immigration in Iowa with fears about terrorism
and homeland security.

THE RE-ELECTION IMPERATIVE

By the winter of 2001–02, the governor's re-election bid in the fall of
2002 was in serious danger because of the unpopularity of this immigration initiative. A skilled politician with an eye toward running for president, Vilsack knew the immigration plan had to go. He talked about it
only when pressed by the media. Slowly but surely the state operatives—
who had worked on the project with so much enthusiasm the previous
year—stopped attending community meetings. The pilot communities
program was allowed to die a quiet death. Immigrants were no longer
a formal part of the state's short- or long-term economic development
plans, and with the exception of the New Iowans Centers, which ultimately survived and expanded with federal funding, state immigration
initiatives were scaled back. The New Iowans Program at the University of Northern Iowa continued and grew its staff and services, but without state funding.

The governor and legislature bowed to public and political opposition to immigration. Their most important policy decision was
making English the state's official language by passing the Iowa English Language Reaffirmation Act of 2002. This bill enjoyed an 86 percent approval rating among Iowans. Despite appeals from immigrants
and their advocates—and members of his own 2010 Commission—
the governor signed the bill with no fanfare, no ceremony, and no
press late on a Friday afternoon. He also won re-election the following November.

The Iowa English Language Reaffirmation Act is policy only in the
sense that it made English the state's official language. But in all other
respects, it does not really qualify as policy. The law "encourages assimilation of Iowans into Iowa's rich culture" and notes that the "common
thread binding individuals of differing backgrounds together has been
the English language."[32] It continues:

In order to encourage every citizen of this state to become more proficient in the English language, thereby facilitating participation in the economic, political, and cultural activities of this state and of the United States, the English language is hereby declared to be the official language of the state of Iowa.

Except as otherwise provided for . . . the English language shall be the language of government in Iowa. All official documents, regulations, orders, transactions, proceedings, programs, meetings, publications, or actions taken or issued, which are conducted or regulated by, or on behalf of, or representing the state and all of its political subdivisions shall be in the English language.

The exceptions are numerous. They include:

The teaching of languages.

Requirements under the federal Individuals with Disabilities Education Act.

Actions, documents, or policies necessary for trade, tourism, or commerce.

Actions or documents that protect the public health and safety.

Actions or documents that facilitate activities pertaining to compiling any census of populations.

Actions or documents that protect the rights of victims of crimes or criminal defendants.

Use of proper names, terms of art, or phrases from languages other than English.

Any language usage required by or necessary to secure the rights guaranteed by the Constitution and laws of the United States of America or the Constitution of the State of Iowa.

Any oral or written communications, examinations, or publications produced or utilized by a driver's license station, provided public safety is not jeopardized.

In addition, the law is not to be "construed to do any of the following":

Prohibit an individual member of the general assembly or officer of state government, while performing official business, from communicating through any medium with another person in a language other than English, if that member or officer deems it necessary or desirable to do so.

Limit the preservation or use of Native American languages, as defined in the federal Native American Languages Act of 1992.
Disparage any language other than English or discourage any person
from learning or using a language other than English.

The list of exceptions is longer than the bill itself and the legislators
exempted themselves. But what may be the most ironic point about this
law is that even if one can figure out a way to violate it, there is no penalty clause.

Passing this law was purely a symbolic nod to political pressure but
even symbols have their meaning. It was the final nail in the coffin for
the Vilsack immigration initiative. Yes, it helped Vilsack get re-elected in
2002, but he may continue to pay the political price otherwise. His sig-
nature on the law continues to dog his aspirations for national office. Indeed, it may have been one reason he was not chosen as a running mate
for John Kerry in the 2004 presidential campaign. It could cost Vilsack
votes in heavily Hispanic states in the 2008 presidential primaries.

The Vilsack immigration program was all about the future, but its
demise emerged from Iowans' responses to rapid growth in the state's
Latino population in the past. Yet, the firestorm surrounding the Vilsack
initiative set the tone for discussion and debate about the meaning of the
immigrant influx in the 1990s and the emergence of all subsequent immigration policy.

IMMIGRATION AND PUBLIC EDUCATION

Reflecting the general population, school enrollments in Iowa have been
overwhelmingly white. There were pockets of African American students in Waterloo and Des Moines and even small pockets of Hispanic
students in Muscatine and West Liberty. Growth in Southeast Asian refugee populations brought growing numbers of English Language Learners (ELL)[33] to Iowa schools beginning in the 1970s. However, these
enrollments paled in comparison to the ELL enrollments in the 1990s
and beyond.

The Iowa Code defines an ELL student as follows:[34]

a student's language background is in a language other than English, and
the student's proficiency in English is such that the probability of the student's academic success in an English-only classroom is below that of an
academically successful peer with an English language background.

Iowa school districts that enroll ELL students benefit from federal pass-through dollars as part of the No Child Left Behind (NCLB) Act, which are distributed by the Iowa Department of Education.[35] In 2005–06, roughly $100 was available per student in districts that have experienced an increase of 5 percent or more over the last two years or the number of students is greater than fifty. By state code, school districts may also "weight" their ELL students by 22 percent when applying for state funding allocations for "excess costs of instruction of limited English proficient students."[36] Students qualify for this weighting, and the additional funding that results, for three years. After three years, students are still counted as ELL, but are not eligible for the weighted count and additional funding.

During the 1990–91 school year, 108 school districts reported a total enrollment of 3,725 ELL students. Ten years later, during the 2000–01 school year, 126 districts enrolled 12,055 ELL students, 224 percent growth from 1990–2001.This growth continued, and in 2003–04, Iowa enrolled 15,810 ELL students. It is significant, however, that in 2003–04, only 4,650 (29 percent) of these ELL students were "weighted."[37] This means that school districts were left to service these students with no additional funding from the state or federal government.

The dramatic growth in Iowa's ELL enrollments parallels growth in the number of five- to seventeen-year olds who, according to the census, speak another language and do not speak English "very well." Between 1990 and 2000, the number of people ages five through seventeen grew by only 3.5 percent, but the number of these young people who spoke English less than "very well" grew by 84.8 percent.

Rapid growth in ELL enrollments was concentrated in meatpacking towns. Marshalltown is one good example. In 1990–2001, the Marshalltown school district reported only twelve ELL students, and none of them spoke Spanish. In 2000–01, there were 707. Accordingly, the number of ELL staff grew from one in 1990 to twenty-five in 2000. The number of ELL students in Storm Lake schools grew from 120 (mostly Lao refugees) in 1990–2001 to 778 (mostly Latino) in 2000–01. Indeed, in 2000–01, ELL students made up 41 percent of Storm Lake's total enrollment and that percentage has continued to grow. Indeed, Storm Lake is now a "majority-minority" school district with ELL and non-ELL minority students.

Rapid growth of ELL populations presents a number of challenges to school districts. In addition to growth in the number of these students who require special instruction, levels of English proficiency and previous educational attainment can vary wildly. In addition, schools in meatpacking towns often experience high rates of enrollment turn-over that also disrupts the educational process. This enrollment turn-over reflects employee turnover in the meatpacking plants.[38] Although Spanish is the primary language among Iowa's ELL students (72.9 per-cent in 2003–04), thirty-two other languages are spoken. Some districts have more than ten different languages presenting even more education-al challenges.

Formal policy responses at the state level to rapid growth in ELL enrollments have been limited. The legislature, for example, did define an ELL student, gave school districts the opportunity to "weight" these students somewhat higher for funding purposes, and defined an ESL or transitional bilingual program, but it does not mandate them. Only one two-way bilingual program was developed as result of rapid ELL growth—in Marshalltown—and that program was funded by the U.S. Department of Education. The state education department also has the discretion to certify ESL teachers. Finally, the department of education has published *Guidelines for Developing English Language Proficiency Standards in Iowa* and *Educating Iowa's English Language Learners: A Handbook for Administrators and Teachers*, as well as recommenda-tions for including ELL students in mainstream classrooms.[39]

HIGHER EDUCATION

The number of immigrants graduating from Iowa high schools grows steadily. However, there is little or no access to post-secondary educa-tion if the graduates are in the U.S. illegally because they are not eligible for state or federal financial assistance. The Development, Relief, and Education for Alien Minors (DREAM) Act[40] was introduced in the Iowa legislature three times since 2002. The DREAM Act would allow the children of undocumented immigrants to gain admission to public uni-versities and allow them access to state financial aid. (The version pro-posed at the federal level would also provide a path to citizenship.) In 2004, the Iowa DREAM Act actually passed the house of representa-tives with a wide margin, but stalled in the senate. In 2005, it stalled in committee and it was not even introduced during the 2006 session.

The state legislature has not passed the DREAM Act, nor has it passed legislation specifically prohibiting the admission of undocument-ed students in private or public colleges or denying them in-state tuition rates. This has left some room to maneuver.

Iowa has several private colleges, and some of them accept and fund undocumented students, although this is limited to schools—like Grinnell—that have deep sources of private funding. The state's three public universities do not have a written policy against admitting undocumented students and do admit some of these students. Some even qualify for in-state tuition rates based on the same criteria as established-resident students. The problem is money, and with very few exceptions, these students receive no financial aid whatsoever. Therefore, the numbers of undocumented students who are admitted to the public universities far outstrips the numbers who actually attend. Undocumented students often attend community colleges. These are less expensive than the private or public four-year schools, but funding remains a major obstacle.

The passage of the DREAM Act at the federal level would have a significant impact on the enrollment of Latino students in Iowa; their numbers would grow accordingly. Elections for state-level offices in 2006 will center on immigration, and even Democrats who supported the DREAM Act in the past swore off this bill in 2006 to avoid angering even their moderate base in a quest to take control of the Iowa State Senate. Democratic leaders have made informal promises that once they control the senate they will have sufficient power to pass immigrant-friendly legislation like the DREAM Act. This remains to be seen. A lot will also depend on who will be elected governor in 2006.

HEALTH CARE

As in all Iowa institutions, rapid growth in immigrant populations has presented a number of challenges for health care providers. There are four main issues:

1. access to adequate and appropriate health care, including health insurance;

2. diverse cultural expectations for the provider-patient encounter in clinical settings;

3. identification and health records; and

4. health conditions associated with migration and transience.

Rapid growth in Iowa's Latino population has grown the state's federally designated "Medically Underserved Populations" (MUPs). Of Iowa's ninety-nine counties, parts or all of fifty-nine were already designated as "Medically Underserved Areas" (MUAs) in 2005, due mostly to the lack of health care providers, poverty, and a shrinking and aging population in rural areas. However, medically underserved populations may be located outside MUAs and are subsets of populations that have difficulty accessing primary health care due to low incomes and/or cultural and language issues. This is certainly the case for many immigrant newcomers who experience income, cultural, and language barriers to health care. Indeed, of Iowa's five MUP counties, four are directly associated with large meatpacking plants or other large agribusinesses, including Marshall County, Wapello County, Webster County, and Buena Vista County.

Some communities with large immigrant populations already had federally funded community health clinics. In Waterloo, for example, the People's Community Health Clinic became the primary care provider for thousands of Latino and Bosnian newcomers. Based on the success of these clinics, other communities applied for and received federal community health clinic funds. Two examples are Marshalltown and Storm Lake, both with MUPs. Their clienteles are overwhelming Latino, with some Sudanese and Anglos. These clinics charge for services, although on a sliding scale.

These clinics have made every effort to recruit bilingual staff. Community health centers are developed under the Iowa/Nebraska Primary Care Association (IA/NEPCA). Unlike the Iowa Department of Public Health, which has a public health focus on prevention, health promotion, education, and health policy, the IA/NEPCA develops the capacity for clinical primary care for underserved populations, including immigrants.

For those working in the larger meatpacking plants such as Tyson, health insurance is available after three months on the job. However, accepting and paying for this coverage is optional. Most immigrants with families seem to accept this coverage, but some do not. There are two primary reasons for this. One is that workers who are trying to earn as much money as possible do not want the premiums to come out of their paychecks. Two, the concept and practice of private health insurance is simply unknown to the majority of newcomers because it did not exist in their home countries. In addition, most newcomers are from countries that had national health systems with free or low cost primary health care for every citizen regardless of income. Private health care is also widely available in Mexico at a reasonable cost.

Many established residents find the U.S. health care "system" confusing because the United States does not have a system per se. For newcomers, who are already struggling with the language and life in a new culture and society, learning to navigate the hodgepodge of private and public health services—and the complexities of private health insurance—is overwhelming. This is reflected in the low percentage of newcomers (37.3 percent) who have established primary care relations. Indeed, in one survey of immigrants in Iowa, the percentage of Latino males who regularly visited a doctor was only 23.2 percent.[41]

The Iowa Department of Public Health (IDPH) recognizes the cultural and other barriers to health care experienced by immigrants, but the state's "Office of Multicultural Health" has a staff of one. This staff person is energetic and good at forming alliances in the state with agencies addressing health disparities, but funding remains limited. While no IDPH programs target specific immigrant groups, they do try and incorporate immigrant groups into existing programs. Much of their literature has been translated into Spanish, and their Web site has a Spanish information page.

The Iowa Department of Human Services has a free or low-cost health care program for low-income children, called Hawk-I. It is for children who otherwise have no private insurance and who do not qualify for Medicaid. This program has been around for years, but some adjustments have been made to accommodate Latinos. All Hawk-I printed and Web-based materials have been translated into Spanish, and children no longer have to be citizens. They may qualify if they can somehow prove they have been permanent residents in the United States for five years. Most important, children can qualify for the program regardless of their parents' immigration status.

Other statewide efforts to address health disparities among minorities and immigrants are under way. For example, the primary mission of the Proteus project is to assist migrant farmworkers, but many of their services for seasonal farmworkers who reside in the state year-round are provided to low-income immigrants who work in hog confinements, sweet corn processing, egg production, and general farmwork. Proteus provides three health clinics in Iowa for these workers. Most important, these health services are provided regardless of legal status.

In 2003, the National Institutes of Health funded the Iowa Project EXPORT Center of Excellence on Health Disparities at the University of Northern Iowa.[42] This center, in league with the Iowa Center for Immigrant Leadership and Integration, has produced numerous publications and training opportunities to familiarize Iowa's overwhelmingly

Anglo health care providers with methods to address the unique health care needs of immigrants and refugees. Among these publications was *A Health Provider's Pocket Guide to Working with Immigrant, Refugee and Minority Populations in Iowa.*[43]

There also have been innovative local responses to the immigrant health dilemma. Free clinics sprang up in several communities in the mid- to late-1990s. These were generally staffed with volunteer doctors and nurses. They are difficult to sustain with volunteer staff, but a few of these remain open at least one day a week. A free clinic for Latinos opened in Des Moines with a large grant. But when its initial funding ran out, it threatened to close. Another Latino clinic was opened in Des Moines by a private physician, but it charged fees for services. The entire staff in this clinic is bilingual. All patients are expected to pay for their care, but for patients without insurance, there are generous payment plans. There is an understanding that all patients will pay at least something on a monthly basis, no matter how long it takes to pay off the bill. The result is that this clinic has a default rate of less than 5 percent, a rate any clinic would envy.

Even where special clinics were not set up, many existing health clinics and hospitals have attempted to address the challenges associated with cultural differences. The fundamental issue is that Anglo providers and Latino (and other) newcomers bring very different experiences and expectations to the clinical encounter. For example, one Latino practice that surprises many Anglo nurses and doctors is that the entire family often joins the patient in the examination room. The reason, as we explain it to providers, is that Latino families make important decisions together. This is a minor example. More serious issues concern the interplay among U.S. health care practices and expectations, the newcomer's faith, and the role of traditional or "folk" medicine (which is alive and well in Iowa).[44] One survey of immigrants in 2002 found that 28 percent of newcomers perceived "that their provider does not accept or understand their cultural beliefs and practices."[45]

One way that providers in Iowa have learned about the interplay of these factors has been to visit the home communities of Mexican migrants and to familiarize themselves with the private and public health care systems in Mexico. In this way, these Anglo Iowa providers develop a deeper understanding of the experience and expectations that Mexicans bring to their hospitals and clinics. (The Mexican doctors who host their Iowa colleagues also visit Iowa.[46]) In many cases, the providers who visited Mexico allow their experience to trickle down to their staffs through new programs and/or cultural competency training.

Of course, language is a major issue. Signage in Spanish and other languages is commonplace now. Full-time staff interpreters are also more common. However, the quality is uneven and there is growing demand for training for interpreters and for Anglo staff in how to use interpreters effectively.

Undocumented immigrants often use multiple names and identities. This is a major problem in hospitals and clinics because one patient may have two or three different sets of medical records. This makes diagnosis and follow-up difficult and presents a major headache for physicians, nurses, and records administrators. One possible solution to this dilemma—that emerged from a study tour to Mexico—is to issue photo identification cards for patients that will use one name and match that name and face with one set of records. The patient may choose any name they like, but they may only use that one name and identification card when requesting services. This approach is still in the experimental stage.

Finally, there are serious problems in terms of the health issues and diseases associated with migration and transience. Immigrants in Iowa sometimes arrive with acute infectious diseases such as hepatitis and sexually transmitted diseases. However, one infectious disease that has been over-diagnosed among Mexican newcomers is tuberculosis (TB). All Mexican children are inoculated for tuberculosis in infancy. When they are tested in Iowa schools and clinics, they often test positive—much to the alarm of health officials—but these positive results reflect the resistance to TB associated with their childhood vaccinations.

Chronic diseases have become a serious problem, particularly Type II diabetes. This disease is endemic and under-screened. Indeed, there is growing evidence that more Latinos are contracting diabetes as a result of the acculturation stress associated with arriving in new communities in Iowa and changes in their diets (and less physical activity) in the United States and Mexico. Indeed, many Iowa providers no longer refer to Type II diabetes as "adult onset" because a growing number of Latino adolescents are contracting the disease as a result of diet changes.

Some clinics have initiated diabetes screening and tracking programs, but these meet with mixed results with continued migration between Mexico and the United States. Cultural and language differences work with geography in this case, and Anglo providers must become aware of such facts as the term "diabetes" does not readily translate into Mexican Spanish. Instead, *azúcar* (sugar) in the blood makes more sense to most Mexican patients. It is difficult to diagnose and treat a disease when providers and patients do not share the same terms even when literally interpreted.

Drivers' Licenses and Identification

Iowa issues drivers' licenses and non-driver identification cards. The non-driver identification cards are used to register to vote, show proof of age to enter bars, and so on. Immigrants sometimes use them to open bank accounts, for example. For both the driver's license and identification card, applicants must provide proof of their identity and residency. The ways applicants can prove their identity is quite inclusive and does not require a photo. Photo identification is preferred, but not necessary. Ironically, applicants may present a Canadian identification card, social insurance card, or birth certificate, but Mexican government identification and birth certificates are not permitted.

New regulations for "foreign nationals" took effect in 2002 to obtain a driver's license or identification card. All applicants are asked about their citizenship. Non-U.S. citizens are required to show evidence of their immigration status. Those with temporary status may only have a driver's license for the term of their status, not to exceed two years. (It can be renewed.) Immigrants with permanent residency status receive the same license or identification card as citizens.

The 2002 law requiring proof of citizenship or immigration status was a reaction to the immigrant influx in Iowa. At play here was the confluence of key events including the demise of the Vilsack immigration initiative, growing concern about the use of fake forms of identification, and the highly publicized issuance of the *matrícula consular* by the Mexican Consulate in several Iowa communities. The *matrícula consular* (consular registration) is a photo identification card issued by Mexican consulates. Its official purpose is to demonstrate that the bearer is a Mexican national living outside of Mexico. Applicants for this card must produce a Mexican birth certificate, some other form of Mexican identification such as a voting registration card, and proof that they live in the United States such as a utility bill. (When the Mexican consulate issues these cards in Iowa communities, the demand is so great that applicants often stand in line for several hours.)

The media and some policymakers portrayed the *matrícula consular* as a backdoor way for people—who otherwise could not qualify for legitimate identification because of their undocumented status—to get identification that they could use to open bank accounts, and so on. Policymakers chose to not regulate private services, such as banks, and forbid them from accepting the *matrícula consular*. Instead, they chose to limit access to drivers' licenses and state-issued identification cards to citizens and authorized immigrants.

Reaction to this policy was mixed. Some law enforcement officials objected to the new policy because it meant many undocumented people would not get drivers' licenses but would drive anyway, illegally and without the mandatory liability insurance. Those who applauded the policy were convinced that illegal immigrants could no longer use drivers' licenses to establish a legitimate identity despite their illegal status. Of course, what these proponents of the policy failed to take into account was the ready availability of forged immigration documents that could be used to gain a driver's license anyway. Drivers' licenses and non-driver identification cards are still used by unauthorized aliens to establish identities and access services. The policymakers just added one more small step in the process.

A bill in the Iowa legislature to grant drivers' licenses to undocumented immigrants failed in 2005 and was not introduced in 2006.

LAW ENFORCEMENT

The irony of the driver's license policy requiring proof of immigration status is indicative of the position in which law enforcement officials in Iowa find themselves. On one hand, they are sworn to uphold the law, and they find themselves with hundreds of new residents who are in the country without documentation. On the other hand, the vast majority of those unauthorized to be in the United States are law-abiding, hard-working, family-oriented people whose worse transgression is usually parking cars on the lawn. Most police chiefs do not want to enforce immigration law. They may be philosophically inclined to do so, but they do not want to use the resources or personnel. Indeed, they would also find themselves in the awkward position of determining who is in the country legitimately and who is not. Many police chiefs and sheriffs who have apprehended undocumented people found out the U.S. Immigration and Customs Enforcement (ICE) staff in Iowa is limited and overworked. They generally will not travel to small towns and pick up undocumented aliens unless they have committed a crime and/or there is a warrant for their arrest. Enforcing immigration law could also pit police chiefs against local employers.

Some police chiefs in Iowa have attempted to steer a middle course. For example, Latinos pulled over for minor traffic offenses would be asked for their license, but not proof of their immigration status. As one police chief said after visiting Mexico, "It is not illegal to be illegal." However, if the person has committed a crime and/or they are wanted for some other crime, they will be arrested and face criminal and immigration charges. The dilemma for police chiefs who take this course is that criminal elements from Mexico and elsewhere hide among otherwise law-abiding immigrants making it difficult to distinguish among them. The worst cases of this problem have involved Mexican drug cartels trafficking methamphetamine, and violent gangs.

Compounding this situation is the reluctance of the undocumented to approach the police, either to inform on illegal activities or as victims of crimes. Most police chiefs encourage all immigrants to report crimes, but language and immigration issues often prevent this. Those police departments that have been fortunate to recruit Spanish-speaking officers seem to receive more information from immigrants, and they enjoy better relations with the Latino community. However, recruiting Spanish-speaking officers is a challenge, and several departments have tried to do so for years without success. To address this problem, the Storm Lake police chief hired two community service officers, one each from the Lao and Latino communities. They wear uniforms but do not carry firearms. Their job is to develop positive relations between the police and newcomers. This initiative is a model for other communities in the state and nation.

Another model that emerged from the police in Iowa is a Spanish-language video that welcomes Latinos and informs them of their basic rights and responsibilities. This video was created by the Marshalltown police chief and is titled "Welcome to Marshalltown." It is shown in churches and during the new worker orientation training in the local meatpacking plant. This video shows viewers where to get a driver's license, the need to use a child seat in the car, and so on. It also demonstrates that they do not have to bribe the police when pulled over for a traffic offense and that they should report when they are victims of a crime. It also discourages Latinos from parking their cars on the lawn, a favorite pet peeve of established residents.

State level law enforcement responses have been limited. All state patrol troopers received diversity training in 2005 with mixed results. All new trainees at the state law enforcement academy will receive short-term training on working with minorities and immigrants, provided by the Iowa Center for Immigrant Leadership and Integration. Some individual police departments also undergo diversity training that sometimes includes training on racial profiling.

IMMIGRATION POLICY AND EMPLOYMENT

Despite the symbolic nature of Iowa's official English policy, it does have real world implications. Perhaps the most important is how the Iowa English Language Reaffirmation Act of 2002 makes Iowa seem unwelcoming to immigrants, refugees, and—most important—potential workers from other countries and cultures. The state's demographic trends point to the same workforce shortage as already projected in 2000. Even cautious projections see 200,000 more jobs than workers to fill them in ten years. (In a particularly ironic twist, the *Des Moines Register* reported Governor Vilsack who "first rang the warning bell in the looming [workforce] crisis six years ago [says he] no longer believes a labor shortage is inevitable. The economy is much different, he said.")[47]

Employers cannot wait for the political process to run its course. They tried that in 2000–02 and were severely let down. Many are already engaged in recruitment efforts in the United States and abroad. They have become more public and vocal about their looming worker shortages and the need for Iowa to be a more receptive, welcoming state. Here are three examples. John Deere, the farm implement manufacturer, says 40 percent of its workers in Iowa will be eligible to retire over the next five years. Forty percent of workers at The Principal, the huge multinational financial services firm, fit within the baby boomer demographic and 18 percent are already age fifty or older.[48] The hightech firm Rockwell Collins—Iowa's second largest manufacturer—needs 7,000 new workers by 2010.[49]

Human resource directors recognize that anti-immigration policies hurt their ability to recruit international and other highly skilled workers. With its northern climate, small population, lack of large cities, and lack of natural attractions, Iowa already has a hard time competing for highly skilled and educated workers. Any high-profile indication that Iowa is not welcoming makes recruitment even more difficult. As one director of a major manufacturing firm told me, "We are not threatening to leave Iowa. But we will grow elsewhere."

When asked about the official English policy by *DiversityInc* magazine, Governor Vilsack said, "It's time to move on from this conversation because the reality is we are aggressively seeking to make Iowa the best place to live, work and raise a family."[50] Yet advocates and employers alike insist anti-immigrant policies send an offensive message. As I told the same *DiversityInc* reporter, "What the politicians fundamentally don't get is that American companies compete for labor on the international marketplace and things like making English the official language becomes known to people considering moving here."[51] This information is passed along internationally, of course, through the Internet.

Rapid growth in Iowa's immigrant populations goes hand-in-hand with the transformation of its industrial economy. The loss of high-wage manufacturing jobs in Iowa parallels the loss of these jobs in the United States. The emergence of a global economy and labor market, the movement of capital to cheaper sources of labor like Mexico and China, and downward pressure on wages all combined to make Iowa labor too expensive. As a result, plant after plant has moved out of the state and country.

While plants that manufacture goods such as tractors and car parts can be relocated to Mexico, meat plants cannot relocate because they must be close to the source of their raw material: livestock and the grains and soybeans to raise them. Until the 1980s, meatpacking jobs also paid well in Iowa, but with the demise of strong unions and production innovations, the old plants could no longer compete. The "new breed" packers opened with significantly lower wages, fewer benefits, no or weak union representation, and high rates of turnover. They also sped up production lines. All of these factors made packing jobs unattractive to native Iowans of whom there were fewer and fewer anyway. So, the new plants developed a deep dependence on immigrant and refugee workers.[52]

The availability of meatpacking jobs served as the initial attraction for most Latinos (and many refugees) to Iowa. The jobs do not require English, education, or previous job experience. It was also easy to obtain the jobs with forged papers and getting "caught" was rare.

Part of the difficulty Iowa communities are experiencing has to do with this fundamental shift away from the good old days of high-wage manufacturing jobs that mainly employed white Iowans to low-wage jobs that mainly employ immigrants and refugees, many of whom are undocumented.[53] As the old way of life disappeared, it disenfranchised the established population.[54] The demise of the Vilsack immigration program was a direct result of this resentment, which drives much of the current negative feeling about immigration today. Perhaps the final nail is this coffin has now been hammered in by the closure of the Maytag manufacturing plant in Newton, Iowa, and the loss of 4,500 well-paid jobs held almost exclusively by white Iowans.

Day Labor

Day labor has not become a major issue in Iowa. Pockets of day laborers remain quite small, intermittent, and scattered across the state. There have been no policy initiatives to curtail or regulate day labor at the state or local level.

Housing

Housing is often a critical challenge in communities that experience rapid growth in immigrant populations. There are challenges associated with the lack of low- and moderate-income housing, and immigrants and established residents sometimes have contrasting cultural expectations for how to use housing.

Dramatic population loss in the 1980s, particularly in rural communities, kept private developers from building new housing. This was particularly the case for low- and moderate-income housing. Very little has been built in rural areas, and most of that was built with federal subsidies. The lack of new housing stock in many communities means that rapidly growing numbers of immigrant newcomers often have a hard time finding adequate housing. In some cases, this has forced newcomers to locate in surrounding small towns as far as an hour's drive to work.[55]

In some communities that experience rapid growth in immigrant populations, large mobile home communities have been built. This has not been the case in Iowa. In many communities, the opposite has happened. In Postville and Marshalltown, for example, mobile home parks were demolished after they were inhabited by Latinos. The motivation to eliminate these parks was mixed, although anecdotal evidence abounds that neighbors and/or park owners no longer wanted newcomers in their neighborhoods. There has also been considerable resistance to building new mobile home parks in several counties.

Some of the resistance to building new housing has resulted from contrasting ideas about how to use housing. Established residents often have different ideas from newcomers about what is a "family" or a "household," who and how many should live under the same roof. Because extended families are relatively rare among Anglos, adult children and grandchildren are expected to start their own households. But Latinos and other immigrants may consider a "family" to be much larger and flexible, with the inclusion of uncles, aunts, cousins, and others.[56] Because they have larger families, and because housing is often expensive, newcomers tend to have more people living in one house or apartment than Anglos. There is also evidence from meatpacking towns that two related families may actually share one house with adults taking turns in the beds.[57] These families share the cost of housing in ways that may not "make sense" to Anglos, but makes sense to the newcomers.

The number of Hispanic-occupied houses in Iowa has grown quickly. In 1990, there were only 8,925 Hispanic-occupied units and 3,762 (42 percent) were owner occupied. In 2000, there were 20,362 Hispanic-occupied units of which 50 percent were owner occupied. Home ownership among Hispanics in Iowa (46.6 percent) is somewhat higher than the nation (45.6 percent). Yet, Hispanics are one and one-half times as likely as Anglo owners to be "cost-burdened," that is, more than 30 percent of their household income is spent on housing.[58]

Predatory lending is a problem in Latino communities. It takes two forms. One is the sale of homes on contract. Under the terms of these contracts, which are often not translated into Spanish, the buyers make payments, but they do not accumulate principal as with a mortgage. Legal ownership is not transferred to the new owner until the last scheduled payment is made, which may take many years. If a payment is missed, the contract will often allow the seller to cancel the contract, repossess the house, and keep the sum of payments previously made. Many Latinos do no know the difference between a mortgage—for which they may be unqualified—and a contract sale and assume they are the same thing, with terrible consequences.

Predatory lending may also involve high interest rates. These loans may take the form of a loan or contract sale. In either case, if the newcomer/buyer has no, or a very poor, credit record, or if they are undocumented, interest rates well above legitimate market rates may be charged, and the newcomer has little or no legal recourse.

State-level responses have been limited. The Iowa Finance Authority (IFA) is a quasi-governmental agency that promotes home ownership. IFA has translated some of its materials into Spanish, and it hired a Spanish-speaking staff member from Mexico. This staff member works with numerous social service and housing programs in the state to promote two programs that facilitate home ownership for first-time buyers: La Programma Firsthome and La Programma Firsthome Plus. Firsthome works with lenders to secure low-interest mortgages, and Firsthome Plus provides assistance with down payments.[59] Some banks have also initiated programs to sell mortgages to Iowa's growing

Latino population as well. The problem for IFA and private lenders is that relatively few Latinos currently qualify for mortgages. This market will grow with time, of course, and with potential immigration reform at the federal level. However, the undocumented are very unlikely to have sufficient income, credit records, and job security to qualify for loans.

OTHER STATE POLICIES

The lack of legislative action during the 2005 session did not keep the legislature from convening an interim study committee on new Iowans. The charge of this bipartisan committee was to "review the impact of the growing population of immigrants, migrant workers, and refugees who are relocating to the state to live and work."[60] They held four public hearing in different towns, including Storm Lake and Des Moines. Topics raised during the testimony included the usual suspects: drivers' licenses for the undocumented, public safety and police issues, workplace issues, access to health care, and education for children and adults, including access to higher education. Many speakers also urged the legislators to encourage immigration reform at the federal level. These hearings included several undocumented immigrants who stepped forward to testify. Written testimony was also accepted.

A final meeting of the committee was held November 21, 2005, to distill the oral and written testimony and develop "consensus recommendations" for possible legislative action. These recommendations were:[61]

▲ A state law prohibiting human trafficking should be adopted.

▲ Incentives should be used to attract bilingual public safety officers and medical personnel.

▲ Increase funding for preschool, after school, and adult ESL education and recommend increasing K–12 ESL funding from three to five years.

▲ The committee encourages those involved to continue making progress in establishing interpreter registration standards.

▲ Encourage the governor to develop a task force that would include state agencies, private industry, and commerce that would

make a recommendation to the general assembly on how to address the public safety problems created by the lack of a comprehensive identification system and racial profiling.

▲   Encourage the U.S. Congress to reform federal immigration policy.

▲   The general assembly should continue to monitor the efforts to
    streamline the process whereby eligible legal immigrants can ob-
    tain a comparable professional license in Iowa.

▲   Direct the Department of Education and the Board of Education-
    al Examiners to develop a proposal for alternative licensure for
    bilingual persons interested in providing language instruction.

▲   Encourage local communities to develop a mentoring program
    for all young persons, including new Iowans.

▲   While understanding the legal issues involved, the general as-
    sembly should invest in the education of young Iowans educat-
    ed in this state and consider passage of the Iowa version of the
    DREAM Act.

It was encouraging that the legislature convened a study committee on immigration issues. The public hearings were well attended, and
many newcomers—including some undocumented immigrants—had
their first opportunity to speak directly to policymakers. Many of their
recommendations could lead to sound policy. However, the looming reality of an upcoming session during an election year led the study committee to take no risks, make no specific commitments, and offer vague
"consensus recommendations" without forming actual legislation.[62]

Because of—or in spite of—the limited outcomes of the interim
study committee on new Iowans, there was considerable legislative activity in 2006. A bill to repeal the official English law never left committee,[63] but the official English law was amended. With the encouragement
of the Iowa Newspaper Association and the Iowa League of Cities, the
legislature amended the law to provide that "All notices, proceedings, and
other matter whatsoever, required by law or ordinance to be published
in a newspaper, shall be published only in the English language and in
newspapers published primarily in the English language."[64] Under the old
law, newspapers had to be published "wholly" in the English language

to qualify to print public notices. With more ads and news stories in Spanish, the Iowa Newspaper Association convinced the legislature to change the term "wholly" to "primarily." The bill passed both chambers unanimously.

One bill that did emerge from the study committee addressed human trafficking.[65] This bill started out with a human trafficking focus per se, addressing such problems as commercial sexual activity, debt bondage, and forced labor. It related to immigration in terms of the recruitment, transportation, and exploitation of immigrants for the sex trade, debt bondage in restaurants, "involuntary servitude," and exploitation of undocumented workers. The bill made engaging in human trafficking a felony. It also provided for training law enforcement officials on the topic and a victim compensation fund.

Left as it was, the human trafficking bill addressed a small but growing problem in Iowa. It was also politically safe. Who would vote against a law prohibiting the trafficking of human beings? The bill seemed to be on its way to easy passage. Then election year politics kicked in. In February 2006, Democratic leaders chose to insert new language in the bill that criminalized hiring unauthorized aliens, created and funded a new special prosecutor in the state attorney general's office to enforce the law, established penalties and fines for violating the law, and prohibited employer retribution against employees who blew the whistle on illegal hiring.[66] Of course, the bill mirrored federal law, but as one legislator told the press, "state authorities could do a better job."[67]

Including this anti-immigrant language in an otherwise politically safe human trafficking bill was a deeply cynical step by Democratic leaders to protect themselves against Republican attacks on the immigration issue in an election year. Of course, the leadership denied this publicly, but admitted privately that it was a preemptive strike in the coming war of words about immigration. Democrats made more preemptive strikes of this kind. A resolution in the house "supporting efforts to promote comprehensive immigration reforms that encourage legal immigration, deter unauthorized immigration, promote economic growth, and ensure secure borders" was introduced by fourteen Democrats but no Republicans.[68] The full house never voted on the resolution, but those who introduced it could say they did during their re-election campaigns in 2006.

The anti-immigrant language inserted into the human trafficking bill was withdrawn only to be inserted again a few weeks later. Ultimately, the human trafficking bill passed without the anti-immigration language and the governor signed the bill in April 2006.[69] Despite the fact that the anti-immigrant language was ultimately pulled, it still served its purpose: the Democrats could correctly assert that they, too, could introduce get-tough immigration bills. One more bill that both parties could claim as their own, but never got out of committee, was a bill that made using a motor vehicle to transport "illegal nonresident aliens" a felony.[70]

POLICY UNDER THE RADAR

There is another level of policy that often goes unnoticed by the media and general public. This is the level of administrative law, the series of rules that govern the actions and practices of state agencies. Here are two examples.

The New Iowans Centers were created during the Vilsack immigration initiative. The original two remain open, and six others have opened, although with minimal staff. State funding for the centers is actually quite limited. Most operations and the expansion to eight centers in 2005 were funded by federal migrant worker funds and the U.S. Department of Labor. Regardless of the funding source, the rules that govern the centers are part of the Iowa Administrative Code. They are restricted to serving immigrants defined as "a person who enters the country with the expectation of legally residing in the United States of America rather than returning to the person's country of origin."[71]

The Iowa Department of Human Rights has a Division of Latino Affairs. With growth in the state's Latino population, this office has grown. The division traditionally maintained the state's list of interpreters for the courts, police, and health care providers. However in 2004, concerns about the quality of interpretation led the division to try and establish minimal standards for Spanish-English interpreters. (The state court system had already initiated its own system to minimally train and register interpreters.) However well intentioned were the efforts of the division staff, this policy initiative met with stiff resistance and proved far more complicated than presumed. At issue were the minimum qualifications to be included on the state's official list. Although quality training has become available in Iowa on a limited basis, the number of fluent English and Spanish speakers who could be trained as interpreters turned out to be fewer than assumed. Indeed, some people who had been acting as interpreters in the courts dropped out of training sponsored by the Iowa Center for Immigrant Leadership and Integration on the first day realizing that their language skills were not up to snuff. Presumably these dropouts also declined to interpret in the courts again, although it was already too late for the clients who already suffered from the poor skills of their supposed interpreters.

There were also serious concerns about certifying interpreters. At issue was who had the authority to grant certification, who was liable for the malpractice of certified interpreters, and whether anyone who already had a job and family obligations could sacrifice the time and expense to undergo the required extensive training.

Public hearings were held by the Division of Latino Affairs about interpretation standards. Interpreters and educational agencies jockeyed to make sure they were kept in the policy loop. The final result of these deliberations was a new administrative code that now carries the weight of law. In brief, the law requires minimum training and language skills to qualify for the state's official list of interpreters.[72] Generalists must pass a language exam and complete 150 contact training hours.[73] Specialists in settings such as health care and social services are required to complete an additional eighty contact training hours.[74] Both generalists and specialists are required to complete thirty contact hours of continuing education each year.

These regulations became effective in June 2006. The catch, of course, is that one does not have to be on the Latino Affairs list in order to work as an interpreter. The code states that "persons who provide interpretation services in Iowa may represent themselves as qualified interpreters only if they are currently in the statewide roster of qualified interpreters." Despite this language in the code, the division itself admitted that inclusion on the roster is "voluntary," but "it is hoped that interpreters who make it onto the statewide roster . . . will be given preference in contracting and hiring."[75] What remains to be seen is how people actually do end up on the roster. At this point, there do not seem to be sufficient training programs to provide eighty to 150 hours of training or a sufficient number of fluently bilingual people to make these training programs economically viable.

CONCLUSION

Policy at the state level does not always dictate practice at the ground level. As illustrated in this chapter, there are many efforts across the state to make the new immigration work in communities, institutions, schools, workplaces, and health care settings. These efforts take place regardless or in spite of state policy and high-profile debates about immigration in the media. Many community leaders have recognized that they cannot wait for state policymakers and therefore must fend for themselves in making the new Iowa work.[76]

CHAPTER 4

GEORGIA'S RESPONSE TO NEW IMMIGRATION

Stephanie A. Bohon[1]

INTRODUCTION

On April 17, 2006, Governor Sonny Perdue signed the Georgia Security and Immigration Compliance Act (SB529), the most sweeping immigration reform bill ever passed by any state. Focusing on unauthorized immigration, the bill encompasses issues pertaining to public employment, law enforcement, emergency assistance, tax withholding, education, and health care. The final form of the bill represents a compromise between forces in the state clamoring for decisive action against what they perceive to be a rising tide of unauthorized immigration and business forces heavily reliant upon immigrant workers urging caution in any response that makes Georgia appear hostile to newcomers. Overall, SB529 marks the culmination and refinement of various legislation introduced into the Georgia House and Senate over the past ten years, as Georgia's lawmakers grapple with unprecedented demographic changes, including the new flow of immigrants into the state.

GEORGIA'S CHANGING POPULATION

An examination of policy responses to immigration in Georgia is complicated by the rapid population changes that occurred in the 1990s, including massive in-migration from other states and a shifting and growing minority population. The recent influx of immigrants

to Georgia contributed to and coincided with a number of other significant demographic changes in the state, including an increase in the total
population by more than two million people, which resulted in an overall population increase between 1990 and 2004 of almost one-third. At
the same time, the Latino population in the state increased 429 percent
and in-migration of African Americans accelerated sharply. As a result of
these changes, Georgia currently has the seventh smallest non-Hispanic
white population (as a percent of the total) in the nation.[2]

Because of these changes, it is difficult to disentangle which policy
responses are prompted solely by immigration and which are reactions
to challenges posed by the shifting population dynamics. In a state historically unfamiliar with a large Latino and Asian presence, all members
of these ethno-racial groups are too often identified as immigrants. In
the case of Latinos, they are often viewed suspiciously as unauthorized
immigrants, regardless of their actual legal status. Additionally, all newcomers put strains on health care, education, and social service systems,
but immigrants (especially those who are unauthorized) are often identified as the source of the strain.

Senate Bill 529 illustrates how these issues have become mixed. It
purportedly targets "persons in this state who are not lawfully present
in the United States,"[3] yet the pressure to enact parts of this legislation
came from growing demands on social services posed not merely by an
estimated 250,000 unauthorized immigrants, but also by the nearly two
million authorized newcomers who entered the state in the past ten years.
While a quarter of these two million new residents are immigrants, almost a million of Georgia's newest citizens are U.S. natives hailing from
neighboring states in the South. Because many of these native newcomers are disadvantaged racial minorities, the funding pressure for state entitlement programs has increased recently, while the declining economic
fortunes of the state have limited resources to provide these funds.

Setting these demographic changes aside, some of the pressure to
pass SB529 and related legislation can be traced to the very real need for
lawmakers to respond to increasing immigration to the state. In 1990,
fewer than 3 percent of all Georgia residents were immigrants, compared
to 10 percent nationally. During the 1990s, however, immigrants began
to settle in new destinations in the Southeast. In ten years, the immigrant
population in Georgia has more than doubled, often in places that had
no infrastructure for coping with non-English speakers. Language is not
the only barrier. For some immigrants, Georgia is a secondary destination, chosen after living for some time in California, New York, or Texas; for most, however, the new Georgia gateway is their first home in

the United States, and it is in Georgia where these newcomers will make their political, social, cultural, psychological, and economic adjustments to life in the United States. Unlike in traditional gateway states, these newest immigrants do not have a pool of second- and third-generation coethnic neighbors to aid in their transition.

The shifting immigration flows, from places already poised to absorb immigrants to places that are not, have forced lawmakers in new destinations such as Georgia to confront many new challenges. These challenges involve balancing three fundamentally different sets of policies governing legal admission, humanitarian relief, and unauthorized entry while meeting statewide social, economic, cultural, moral, and public safety goals. In a new gateway state such as Georgia, policymakers with little previous experience to draw upon must confront these challenges in order to integrate smoothly immigrant populations whose needs may differ considerably from those who settle in traditional destinations.

WHAT CAN WE LEARN?

The pressure to respond to immigration is felt at many levels within Georgia. Most obviously, state officials elected to the general assembly can introduce legislation in the house or senate; if approved, it is presented to the governor's office for signing. The governor's office may also shape immigration policy by encouraging or discouraging legislative efforts and by appointing officials who have significant influence in structuring immigrant-related policies for the agencies that they head. Policy is also created by the courts through the interpretation of existing laws in ways that may have a significant impact on immigrants. County and municipal governments as well as state and local agencies also create policies within their jurisdictions as they adjust to the demands of immigrant clients and constituents. The resultant policies are often quite different from county to county and city to city, with some localities working to make life easier for newcomers, while others seek to minimize potential disruptions by banning practices viewed as foreign. Examples of the former are policies to provide services to speakers of various foreign languages. Examples of the latter are English-only sign ordinances.

The primary purposes of this chapter is as follows:

1.   to offer a brief history of immigration to Georgia and to profile Georgia's growing immigrant population;

2. to present an overview of policy approaches attempted and en-
    acted at both the state and local levels aimed at addressing the
    challenges of new immigration;

3. to examine the needs of Georgia's immigrants with regard to
    housing, health care, transportation, law enforcement, and em-
    ployment and to discuss the effectiveness of new policies in ad-
    dressing these needs; and

4. to explore the response of native Georgians to immigrants and
    immigration-related policies.

In this chapter, immigrant-related policies from all sources will be
detailed, although greatest attention will be paid to state-level policies
originating with the general assembly. There is special attention throughout this chapter to bills and resolutions introduced in the general assembly in the 2005 and 2006 sessions, because more immigrant-related
legislation was introduced in those years than in the entirety of the period from 1995 to 2004. Also, much of the legislation proposed in the
1995 to 2004 sessions was refined and reintroduced in 2005 and 2006.
Because of its landmark status, the Georgia Security and Immigration
Compliance Act also will be discussed at length in several sections of
this chapter.

This chapter is intended to aid decisionmakers in formulating new
policies that effectively address the issues faced by the new immigrant
population and to inform readers about the many responses that are occurring statewide. There is also hope that the policy successes and fail-
ures in Georgia will serve as a guide to other states and local areas facing
the challenges and opportunities posed by a new immigrant influx.

IMMIGRANTS IN GEORGIA

Between 1995 and 2000, slightly more than 200,000 immigrants entered the state of Georgia, resulting in a 233 percent increase in the immigrant population. This flow represents part of a larger trend in the
shifting of the immigration streams away from the "big six" traditional
immigrant receiving states—California, Florida, Texas, New York, Illinois, and New Jersey—and into emerging gateway states in the Midwest
and Southeast. By 2004, there were an estimated nearly 725,000 immigrants living in Georgia, up from fewer than 175,000 in 1990.[4]

FIGURE 4.1. IMMIGRANTS BY REGION OF ORIGIN, 2004

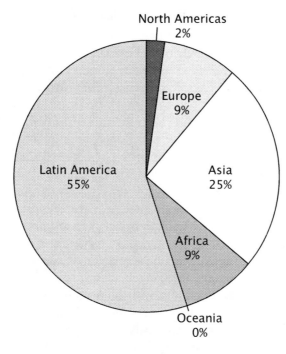

Source: U.S. Census Bureau, Census 2000, Summary File 3.

Two factors are striking about immigration to Georgia. The first is the geographical dispersion of the foreign-born population. While immigrants tend to cluster in a single (usually urban) area within a state, in Georgia, twenty-five counties saw their immigrant populations increase by at least 50 percent in the 1990s. Granted, metropolitan Atlanta is home to the largest portion of Georgia's new immigrants, but there are a sizeable number living in the rural areas of South Georgia, as well.

The other noticeable feature of Georgia's immigrant population is its diversity (see Figure 4.1). Currently, immigrants from almost every country are present in the state. In DeKalb County alone, there are immigrants from at least ninety-five countries. Some of this diversity can be accounted for by the fact that a sizeable portion of the immigrants settling in Georgia have selected the state as a secondary migration destination.[5] That is, immigrants are coming to Georgia after first settling in other locations. Another reason for the diversity is that Georgia—especially metropolitan Atlanta—has become a prime resettlement location for refugees.

Among Georgia's foreign-born population, Latin Americans are the most prominent, with slightly more than half of all immigrants coming from that region, especially Mexico. This is true nationally; in fact, the distribution of immigrants in Georgia by country of origin largely mirrors that of the United States as a whole. One noticeable exception is Africa. African immigrants, who comprise 9 percent of Georgia's immigrants, are only 3 percent of all immigrants to the United States. This discrepancy can be accounted for by refugee resettlement as well as the fact that Atlanta became a highly desirable residential location for black movers (foreign and domestic) in the 1990s.

Many of Georgia's immigrants are recent arrivals. According to the 2004 American Community Survey, about a third of all Georgia's immigrants arrived in the United States between 2000 and 2004. Because of their short history in this country, citizenship rates and English language fluency tend to be low. Only a quarter of Georgia's immigrants are U.S. citizens. Additionally, nearly 63 percent of all immigrants report not speaking English very well. Overall, 11 percent of Georgia's population over the age of five speaks a language at home other than English, and more than half a million Georgians speak Spanish at home.[6]

The policy challenges posed by immigrants across the nation are exacerbated when they settle in emerging immigrant gateway states. Over time, traditional gateways have developed organizations, services, and advocacy infrastructures geared toward serving the immigrant population. Emerging gateways lack these structural advantages. Additionally, immigrants in emerging gateways lack an available pool of longer-term immigrants and U.S.-born coethnic residents who can help in the immigrant adjustment process.[7] In short, immigrants to new gateways rely more heavily on the ability of the state to respond quickly to the demographic changes that their presence requires, yet the quick response is impeded by a lack of policy experience to draw upon.

NATIVE REACTIONS

Rapid population changes—particularly those that result in a shift in the racial composition of the population—often lend themselves to both real and perceived new social problems. Those problems associated with population growth, such as overcrowding, are easily attributed to immigrants because they are easily differentiated from natives by their accent, customs, and often phenotype. In Georgia, a state traditionally inhabited by white and black residents, immigrants from Latin America and Asia are particularly noticeable. Consequently, they are scapegoats for the frustrations of the larger society. The history of other U.S. states and that of other nations shows that immigrants are often blamed for societal troubles such as crowding, rising unemployment, and strains on social services, despite the fact that immigration has been shown to bring more benefits than harm.[8]

In a statewide poll conducted of Georgians in 2001, more than a quarter of state residents equated rising crime rates with immigration, and almost three-quarters asserted that immigrants get too much assistance from the government. State residents also expressed resentment about the speaking of Spanish in public places and the strain that immigrants were perceived to be putting on education and health care systems. Prominent among their concerns is a growing unease surrounding the impact of recent arrivals who are unauthorized entrants to the United States. Seventy percent of Georgians contacted in the 2001 Peach State Poll believe that the majority of immigrants entering Georgia are undocumented aliens, although there is no reliable data to support this claim.[9]

Certainly, as Georgia's immigrant population has grown, the state has seen a rapid increase in the percent of the population that is unauthorized,[10] and it is estimated that close to 40 percent of immigrants in Georgia are undocumented.[11] On the other hand, the total number of unauthorized immigrants in the state is estimated to be about 250,000, a mere 2.6 percent of the state's total population.[12] Nationally, 65 percent of all unauthorized immigrants are thought to be living in just six states, and Georgia is not one of them,[13] although some of the rhetorical claims suggest otherwise. According to one state legislator, "All of a sudden, I've got 10 million [unauthorized immigrants in the United States], and in Georgia we have an abundance of that 10 million."[14] Far from an "abundance," Georgia has a small fraction of the country's unauthorized immigrant population.

Of course, many native Georgians, including the legislator quoted above, are welcoming to immigrants and perceive them as crucial to many of the state's primary industries, such as agriculture, poultry, and textiles. According to one farmer, "Round here folks say that Mexicans are all right. They talk like they're hard workin' and say it looks like the big farmers can't hardly get along without them."[15] These sentiments are also reflected by an immigration lawyer who remarked, "Immigrants are key to the Georgia economy. Hispanics keep the poultry industry running in Gainesville and the carpet industry productive in Dalton."[16] This view was seconded by a poultry factory supervisor who opined, "If there weren't Hispanic [immigrant] workers, nobody in America would be eating chicken."[17]

Many native Georgians also recognize that their own ancestry hails from abroad, and that much of our country is built on immigration. For those who have forgotten, there has been plenty of organized movement within the immigrant community to remind them. In a 2002 demonstration to protest the forced evacuation of a largely immigrant-dominated trailer park in Athens, Georgia, one small child held a sign reminding those passing by that "We're all from somewhere else."

IMMIGRATION POLICY IN GEORGIA: AN OVERVIEW

While the bulk of new immigrants arrived in Georgia in the 1990s, policy responses to immigration has lagged behind. As a general rule, municipal and county governments and state organizations were able to react more quickly than the state government. Smaller area governments and institutions had new policies in place as early as the late 1990s; most state-level policies have only been considered seriously since 2000. This lag is not surprising, since the challenges posed by immigrants vary across the state, and local attitudes about immigrants vary widely as well. As State Representative John Lunsford points out, "It's an extremely complicated issue. What would solve a problem in Catoosa County, Georgia, would devastate a farmer in Valdosta. OK? You can't use the same litmus test statewide. It just won't work."[18]

An additional obstacle faced by the state legislature is reconciling any new state policies with existing laws at both the state and federal level. Senator Mitch Seabaugh underscores this point:

> You have this labyrinth of state law and federal law that you have to go through to make sure that whatever we do at the state level does not conflict with federal law, and we found that to be a very difficult track to navigate. And that has been probably the biggest obstacle: to make sure that whatever it is that we do at the state level does not violate federal law, so that we don't have it turned over on a technicality. We want to be able to deal with the matter, put something in place that deals with the situation, and move on to new challenges rather than keep revisiting the same thing over and over.[19]

As federal government policies have changed with regard to immigration, states have also had to react appropriately, which has made it difficult for the state legislature to develop its own comprehensive approach to serving immigrant populations. One example is the federal No Child Left Behind Act, which, according to one second language learning consultant, "intensified the state policy" with regard to organizing the English to Speakers of Other Languages (ESOL) curriculum. States had to change their ESOL policies to be in compliance with the No Child Left Behind Act.[20]

THE GEORGIA GENERAL ASSEMBLY

Numerous legislative proposals regarding immigration have been introduced by state lawmakers in the last few years. With very few exceptions, this legislation has been aimed at limiting immigration—particularly unauthorized immigration—in some ways. Since 1995, only a handful of bills have been proposed for the sole purpose of promoting immigrant adjustment or regulating cultural practices that the U.S.-born may find unacceptable. One notable exception was House Bill 10, passed in 2005, that made female genital mutilation a felony under the state statutes for assault and battery. Other bills that met with less success included a proposal to provide drivers' licenses to nonresident immigrants and another that would protect unlicensed providers of complementary and alternative heath care practices commonly used by immigrants.

Although authorized immigrants in Georgia far outnumber the unauthorized, almost all of the immigrant-related bills introduced in the Georgia General Assembly in 2005 and 2006 related to unauthorized immigration in some way. Most of these bills were not passed. Examples of failed legislation are House Bill 911, the Georgia Taxpayer and Citizen Protection Act; Senate Bill 653, the Georgia Homeland Protection Act; Senate Bill 336, the Georgia Fair Employment Act; and Senate Bill 640, the Georgia Workers Security Act. These bills would have required that immigrants provide proof of citizenship to register to vote and to apply for any public assistance, without exceptions. Immigrants would have had to provide valid proof of legal residency in order to work, enroll in school, obtain a driver's license, or acquire a permit to carry a handgun. Some of the proposed legislation would have made it a misdemeanor to provide false or fraudulent documents for the purpose of work and imposed a minimum fine of $12,800 on employers who hired unauthorized workers. More stringent legislation would have required all licensing agencies to deny driving, hunting, fishing, business, and other licenses to employers who violated the 1986 Immigration Reform and Control Act. Other proposed legislation would have required the state's electronic voter databases be verified against those compiled by the Social Security Administration, Homeland Security, and the Department of Justice and created an immigrant enforcement position within the state Office of Homeland Security. A final piece of proposed legislation would have allowed deportation as an acceptable excuse for failing to appear in court for immigrants who have been arrested but are out on bond.

Some of this failed legislation was later incorporated in Senate Bill 529, the Georgia Security and Immigration Compliance Act. Included in this were the requirements that contractors and subcontractors on public works jobs ensure that all of their workers have legal authorization to work, as verified using the federal Basic Pilot Program,[21] and a provision that encourages local law enforcement officers to become trained and deputized under the Department of Homeland Security.

Several legislators argue that the pressure to act on unauthorized immigration comes from increased financial pressure to fund existing programs in a post-1990s economic downturn. According to Representative John Meadows:

> We've had slow economic times back in around 2000, and more and more services are being cut or looked at a lot closer. And then we've had so many more people using those services, particularly the health care end of it, and I think it just got out of [hand]. . . . You know, when you have an increase in people and an increase in usage all of a sudden it [unauthorized immigration] is an issue.[22]

His comments were echoed by his colleague John Lunsford who notes, "When it [an expense] gets to be five, six, or ten percent of your wages, then all of a sudden you realize you've got an issue there."[23]

Other legislators noted that their decision to act was based on a perception that the federal government was not effective in regulating unauthorized immigration. According to Senator Mitch Seabaugh, "There's been a lot of waiting for the federal government to lead on this issue because of their responsibility to 'secure the borders.' But because of their inaction, our constituents also expect us at the state level to do all that we can do in order to address the issue."[24] Representative Pedro Marin concurs, "Immigration reform is a federal issue, but nonetheless, it's touched everyone's life every day. Concerns are, you know, we are bombarded by these folks. They don't understand where they're coming from."[25] Other legislators recognize that the federal government has provided programs for states to utilize in addressing the problem of unauthorized immigration, but policies must be in place to tap into these programs. According to John Lunsford, who chairs the House Immigration Reform Caucus, "The federal government is giving us the tools to deal with it because they can't deal with it. They're not dealing with it."[26]

In recent years, the general assembly has also adopted a number of resolutions related to immigration. Among these are "a resolution recognizing the great value of continued immigration into the State of Georgia."[27] This follows a 2005 resolution extending the state's gratitude to the U.S. Border Patrol for their efforts to curb unauthorized immigration.[28] Other resolutions cite responses to immigration by local agencies as grounds for granting special recognition to some individuals and organizations. For example, the Clarkston, Georgia Health Collaborative was recognized by the state senate for "advocating for the involvement of refugee owned businesses in plans to transform downtown Clarkston, developing multilingual resource guides that locate businesses and health related resources in the Clarkston areas, and coordinating town hall type meetings such as meetings between immigrants, refugees, and law enforcement officials."[29] In another example, the senate recognized Community Health Centers Day, citing service to immigrants as one of the valuable services provided by these facilities.[30] Finally, a resolution calling for the U.S. Congress and the president to pass comprehensive immigration reform was pre-filed but not adopted.[31]

THE GOVERNOR

The governor's office, under the leadership of Sonny Perdue, has taken a more generalized approach to dealing with immigration than the general assembly. It is difficult to gauge the sentiment of Governor Perdue or his predecessor, Governor Roy Barnes, with regard to immigration. While the governor has signed the Georgia Security and Immigration Compliance Act, at least one member of the general assembly reported that the governor had initially indicated that such legislation was unnecessary.[32]

Relatively soon after his election in 2002, Governor Perdue created the Latino and Asian-American Commissions for a New Georgia. These commissions are charged with consulting with the governor and working on his behalf with U.S.-born Asians and Latinos, as well as immigrants. The fact is, however, that immigrant Latinos and Asians in Georgia far outnumber the U.S.-born. Consequently, most of the commissions' work is with the immigrant community.

The commissions have not been without controversy. Initially, the governor was criticized for failing to appoint a Mexican immigrant to the commission on Latinos. While all of the original commission members were Latino—most of them immigrants—vocal critics argued that the appointments signaled the governor's lack of understanding regarding the volume and impact of Mexican immigration.

Recently, six Latino commission members resigned in protest after Governor Perdue signed the Georgia Security and Immigration Compliance Act (SB529). According to press accounts, some members viewed the new law as anti-immigrant, but most of those who resigned were simply angry that the governor had not consulted with them about the legislation. They also complained that the commission had been given no "real work" to do. In his resignation letter, former commissioner Alex Salgueiro wrote, "As a dedicated Republican and a citizen of Georgia, I do not feel it is a good use of my valuable time to serve on a sham commission."[33] In addition to the upheaval with the Latino commission, the chair of the Asian-American commission, Josephine Tan, has recently been criticized for her silence on the passage of SB529. According to an editorial in the *Athens Banner-Herald,* Tan's silence underscores the notion that SB529 "has become a Latino witch hunt" from which Asians have been spared.[34]

LOCAL GOVERNMENTS AND STATE ORGANIZATIONS

As previously noted, county and municipal governments and state organizations have responded more quickly to the growing immigrant population, and their approach has been much broader. However, local area policies are also so divergent that it is now possible to identify places that are hostile to immigrants and those that are welcoming. For example, some locales have enacted stringent "English only" sign ordinances and dusted off old bordello laws that limit the number of people who can live in a house. These areas are also beginning to enforce old loitering statutes in order to curb day labor.

In other places, county and city officials have created policies to encourage the successful integration of newcomers and to ensure that their rights are protected. In Columbus, county commissioners took steps in the late 1990s to ensure that the local police force informed the appropriate embassies if foreign nationals were arrested for crimes. In some towns, municipal governments have erected day labor centers to protect immigrant workers from unscrupulous employers and to create a place to hold English language classes. In Dalton, local school officials worked with the University of Georgia to recruit native Spanish-speaking aides for the classrooms.

State agencies have also responded. Agents with the Cooperative Extension Service have created a number of programs across the state to help immigrants to navigate Georgia laws, purchase homes, and learn culturally appropriate child care techniques. Many state agencies working with housing, employment, and family services began work in the 1990s to get vital documents translated into foreign languages and to hire interpreters. Local area schools have also hired immigrant paraprofessionals and expanded their ESOL and migrant education programs. Additionally, many state organizations, such as the Georgia Municipal Association and the Georgia Association of Defense Lawyers, have made an effort to bring in immigration experts to brief members of their organization on the unmet needs of immigrants.

HOUSING

Upon immigrating, an important first step is securing shelter. For all newcomers, the choice of housing is limited by availability and affordability. For immigrants, housing choices are also limited by access to information. Those whose English skills are limited (usually the most recent arrivals) often do not have the skills to navigate the entire available housing market.

Some landlords have seen the arrival of new immigrants as an opportunity. They capitalize on the potential new market by advertising rentals in Spanish, Vietnamese, and other languages. Most landlords focus their advertising on a single immigrant group. As a consequence, many housing complexes are highly segregated by nationality or panethnicity. For example, landlords who advertise their rentals in Korean attract Korean immigrants.

Some of the more unscrupulous landlords exploit the newest immigrants. Decrepit trailer parks and apartment building that have largely been eschewed by even the poorest of the native population are now the home to immigrants. Many immigrants are unaware of the standards for rental housing required under the law. Others who complain about conditions are illegally evicted. One social services worker described the situation:

> [Immigrants] keep their homes the best they can, but the services might be lacking because the landlords do not fix them. I visited a home that had no hot water during the winter. . . . People just come from other countries and do not know. Landlords take months to fix something, and when they do, they fix them the cheap way. Apartments and homes in general are rented out dirty. People have to clean them themselves when they move in. A lot of the homes do not have a central heater or air condition, and the families have to buy one when they move in. Their babies are getting sick more. They get colds or dehydration.[35]

Those who purchase their own homes avoid these problems, but that is not easy for the newest immigrants. Language and financial resources are obvious problems. Another barrier to home ownership is becoming educated about the process of buying and selling a house. For example, because banks in some foreign countries are unstable, immigrants from these places also fear the banks in Georgia. They are surprised, then, when realtors refuse a cash down-payment on a new home and urge them to bank their money first.[36]

As with landlords, some realtors have also taken advantage of immigrants. Reports of housing fraud abound. Abuses include bait-and-switch techniques where immigrants think they have purchased their dream home only to find that they have purchased a house they have never seen. In other cases, immigrant home buyers have been swindled out of earnest money due to their lack of understanding of the process.

Many of these abuses can be curbed by creating more effective policies to protect immigrants, but little has been done, to date. In fact, it is more common for local areas to enact or enforce policies that hinder immigrants in resettlement. Some have restricted advertising in foreign languages. Others are creating ordinances to restrict the number of people who can live in a home. This primarily affects immigrants who tend to live in more crowded conditions than what is normative in the United States. In fact, among Latino immigrants, the situation of overcrowding is so common that in Georgia there is now a Spanish phrase for it, *camas calientes* (hot beds). The phrase describes housing where so many people share living quarters that the beds never have a chance to get cold.

Immigrants live in *camas calientes* not by choice, but because it is often the only economically feasible option. Policies that outlaw overcrowding often result in leaving immigrants in even more dilapidated housing conditions, as they search for the next most viable housing option. [37]

PEOPLE OF HOPE

Confronted with an immigrant housing crisis, the policy response is often inaction. One of the most notorious examples of this occurred in Athens. In 2001, the owner of the Garden Springs trailer park sold the property to a Florida-based developer who planned to build luxury apartments on the property. In order to begin building, trailer park residents—about 500 impoverished immigrants and African Americans—had to vacate the premises.

The problem with leaving Garden Springs was that the original landlord had previously sold the trailers on the site to the tenants, collecting both the revenue from the sales and continuing rent on the land. In most cases, the trailers were not up to code, so the new homeowners were forced to put thousands of their own dollars into renovations after completing the purchase; which they did. With the transfer of the Garden Springs property to a new owner, however, Garden Springs residents found themselves in a situation where they owned their homes, but they did not own the land that the homes sat on. The new owners wanted them out, but, because several of these trailers were manufactured prior to 1976, they could not be moved without violating local ordinances.

The situation at Garden Springs spurred many Athens residents to action. Organizations such as the Athens Grow Green Coalition rallied behind the mostly immigrant residents. They asked the county commissioners to void the sale of the property—a sale that would not be allowed under the ordinances in many other states, including Florida.[38] When the county commissioners refused, many local organizations, including several area churches, put pressure on the county government to give the residents a variance so that they could move their trailers. The council denied this request, as well. In a final effort, after several well attended rallies and protests, hundreds of residents attended a county commission meeting to convince policymakers to impose a building ban while the county studied the need for luxury housing. It was hoped that such a move would give Garden Springs residents more time to prepare for their upcoming evictions. The majority of the commission voted down this request, as well.

Some members of the commission argued that Garden Springs' residents could simply avail themselves of various low cost housing around town. Their arguments ignored the complex living arrangements that poor immigrants often make in order to negotiate day to day living. Communities such as Garden Springs often have complicated informal arrangements for sharing transportation, child care, and other tasks. Breaking up a neighborhood breaks up these important ties and reduces ways for immigrants to meet their needs effectively. Recognizing this, churches, corporations, and foundations banded together to create the People of Hope, Inc. The organization was created to purchase and build a new, communally owned housing development for the evicted residents of Garden Springs. The effort remains ongoing.

EDUCATION

The largest cost of immigration is education. Providing English to Speakers of Other Languages (ESOL) and migrant education are costly, and the expenses are often felt at the local level, while immigrant tax revenues are largely collected at the state and national level. Additionally, immigrant children can drive up school attrition rates and lower standardized test scores. Despite these difficulties, there is considerable evidence that policymakers in Georgia have made immigrant education a priority.

Many school districts with large immigrant populations have created newcomer centers. These centers provide a first point of access for immigrant families whose children are entering Georgia schools. These programs enroll students, assess their language skills, and help students and parents understand the expectations of the school system. School districts with newcomer centers usually make an effort to hire staff members who are native speakers of the languages used by the predominant immigrant groups. In some school districts, this has meant finding education professionals conversant in dozens of languages.

According to Cheryl Wienges, an ESOL consultant to the Gainesville City schools, the State of Georgia has been at the forefront of providing resources for second language learners. Nonetheless, school districts have not always availed themselves of the resources available to fund ESOL programs. According to Wienges:

> [The state] funded this program really early on, really well. . . . At one time someone said that it was the best in sixteen southern states. I

tend to believe that, because of what I heard from other states and all. I think it was not perfect by any long stretch, but a pretty good program. . . . I don't necessarily think the school systems have taken advantage of what the state has funded.[39]

ESOL ENDORSEMENT

Wienges' assertions have been documented elsewhere.[40] Because of new regulations under No Child Left Behind, schools are now required to offer ESOL to students who need it. Prior to that, some Georgia schools were not providing adequate ESOL curriculum to all of their second language speakers. In some South Georgia schools, for example, ESOL was exclusively offered through the migrant education curriculum. As immigrant families became permanent residents, their children became ineligible for migrant education and lost access to ESOL courses.

The root of the problem is the inability to find enough ESOL certified teachers or to encourage teachers to become ESOL certified. Geography contributes to this problem. Kennesaw State University is the primary provider of ESOL endorsement, but its location in the north of the state makes it fairly inaccessible to South Georgia teachers six hours away. Additionally, while there is a fairly large pool of elementary and middle school teachers with ESOL endorsements, there remains a shortage of high school content teachers, such as economics teachers, who meet this requirement. The result is that places like Dalton, Gainesville, and Atlanta have an abundance of some types of ESOL teachers and not enough of others, while South Georgia schools still struggle to fill needed positions in all areas. Wienges maintains:

> It was much harder to get certified teachers at the high school. . . . and in elementary school [in Gainesville], we had lots of teachers that were ESOL certified that were not teaching ESOL. . . . It always was much more problematic in the rest of Georgia than in the metro Atlanta and just outside the circle to get an endorsement.[41]

In response to this problem, in January 2006, the state ESOL coordinator began offering an on-line course for ESOL certification. It is hoped that this move will reduce some of the geographic disparities in ESOL offerings and allow more high school teachers to earn their endorsements.

THE HOPE SCHOLARSHIP AND THE "BIG LIE"

Asian and African immigrant students face language barriers in the classroom that can be ameliorated through the ESOL curriculum. This is true of Latino immigrants, as well, but the influx of Latino students has also driven down the state's already low attrition rate. Nationally, Latinos have the lowest high school and college completion rate and lowest college enrollment rate of any major ethno-racial group. In Georgia, where 60 percent of Latinos are immigrants, Latino drop-out rates are the highest in the nation.[42]

Two interrelated factors contribute to this problem: poverty and legal status. Georgia led the nation in the 1990s with the creation of the HOPE scholarship. Under this program, residents of Georgia who graduate from high school with a "B" average receive free college tuition and a stipend for books if they attend a state college or university. Teachers often use the promise of a HOPE scholarship as a motivator for secondary students to do well in school. However, students who are unauthorized immigrants are not eligible for HOPE scholarships as they are not technically state residents.[43] Because many of these students are also poor and do not qualify for federal financial aid, they find that their college aspirations are blocked. The frustration is so widespread that Latino immigrant students have a name for it: "The Big Lie." They believe that teachers are duplicitous in encouraging them to do well in school in order to achieve goals that are unattainable. One recent high school graduate noted:

> We provide education from kindergarten on to nondocumented [students]. Education should continue, because we are selling them false hope. You cannot ask someone to have good grades and do better if you cannot do it at the end of the road.[44]

Representative John Lunsford disagrees with this perspective. He contends:

> When you think of college education, you kind of think of a college class—or I do—as like a plane flight, you know. It has a certain number of seats in that flight. And when the seats are full, the plane's leaving the gate. And if those seats are taken up by people who are illegally here within our state, [instead of] someone that is legally here who may not score quite as high. . . . A legal citizen of our state, they may not get one of those seats, and I think they should have first priority.[45]

His sentiments are shared by other members of the house. In February 2005, the house read (but did not adopt) a resolution calling for a constitutional amendment that would prohibit unauthorized immigrants from receiving state-funded education at the primary, secondary, and post-secondary level in all states.[46]

In the senate, Chip Rogers and his colleagues introduced a bill to bar unauthorized students from enrolling in the state's university system.[47] In response, Senator Sam Zamarripa and his colleagues prefiled the Georgia Higher Education Protection Act. This bill put the establishment of residency strictly under the authority of the university system.[48] Ultimately, Rogers' bill was withdrawn in favor of SB529, which Rogers also coauthored. It is worth noting that SB529—which restricts unauthorized immigrants' access to state services—excludes post-secondary education from the restriction. Additionally, since SB529 only applies to adults, primary and secondary education is not affected.

HEALTH CARE

The cost of providing health care to immigrants is relatively minimal, since immigrants tend to be healthier than native populations. Additionally, as immigrants use less medical care than natives, they substantially subsidize the health care costs of the U.S.-born.[49] This is especially true in Georgia, where most of the immigrant population is not old enough to require chronic care. When immigrants do need health care, however, they face several obstacles. First, many immigrants, especially farmworkers, lack insurance. Second, many health care facilities and 911 services lack adequate bi-lingual staff to correctly interpret health problems for those who have limited English proficiency. Third, immigrants are often the target of fraudulent health care providers. Finally, many immigrants lack transportation to places where health care is offered.

Across Georgia, public health facilities and private organizations have reached out to the immigrant community in order to alleviate some of these obstacles. In Dalton, Georgia, immigrant carpet mill workers are given release time from work to serve as interpreters at local hospitals. In South Georgia, public health officials and private organization have set up mobile clinics to reach farmworkers who do not have private transportation. In Atlanta, Venus Gínes has founded *Dia de la Mujer Latina* (Day of the Latina Women), a health fair that provides free mammograms to immigrant women. The program has been so successful it has been expanded to twelve states, Mexico, Puerto Rico, and the Dominican Republic.

One of the policy concerns with providing health care to immigrants is that those who cannot afford it are provided indigent care by the counties. Because taxes usually are not collected at the county level in Georgia, the costs of health care are absorbed at a level of government that does not benefit from immigrant tax dollars. Additionally, there is a concern among policymakers that providing indigent health care to immigrants who are undocumented saps limited resources away from other health care programs. Representative John Lunsford notes, "We have disabled kids, kids with autism, kids who are so mentally disabled that their parents can't leave them alone . . . and we're struggling to pay the medical bills and get care for these kids."[50] According to Lunsford and other legislators, the state is currently unable to provide an adequate level of care to state residents because of the drain that unauthorized immigrants put on the system.

Many state residents concur with this assessment. Representative John Meadows relates a conversation he had with the resident of a nursing home:

> The lady says, you know, "Every dollar you spend on an illegal is a dollar not spent on those of us that have paid our way, who deserve the care and treatment that has been promised to us." And I said, "You know, you're right." And that's when I decided that, you know, we've got to do something different.[51]

In response to these concerns, some members of the house proposed House Bill 1238, the Illegal Immigrant Fee Act. The proposed legislation imposes a 5 percent wire transfer fee on people sending money to foreign countries who cannot show proof of legal authorization to work in the United States. Revenues for the fees were intended to supplement indigent health care costs. Ultimately, the bill passed the house, and the senate voted to incorporate the measure into SB529. Representative Lunsford and Senator Rogers, who carried SB529 in the legislature, successfully argued against the incorporation. According to Rogers:

> We were somewhat concerned about the legality of that [the wire transfer fee]. And I'll tell you the main reason why I was concerned about it was because we were using the standard of employing a person for verifying their status at the wire transfer fee center. And the reality is that someone could be legally in the United States but not be legally eligible to work, and therefore we would be penalizing

them, prohibiting them from sending money without this additional tax, even though they were legally present, because the standard we were applying was one from the I-9, which is the standard for hiring someone.[52]

Lunsford goes on to describe the concern that the surcharge was a "punitive situation. And we weren't trying to be punitive. We were trying to be progressive."[53]

While Senate Bill 529 does not include the wire transfer fee, it does restrict the access of adult unauthorized immigrants to many state provided health services, and it requires that employers assess a 6 percent withholding on wages reported on 1099 forms. Some legislators hope that some of the revenue from this withholding will be used for indigent health care, although state law does not allow this to be specified. When the final form of SB529 was signed by Governor Perdue, the restrictions on indigent health care for unauthorized adult immigrants exempted emergency medical care, prenatal care, immunizations, and tests for transmittable diseases.

DRIVERS' LICENSES

One of the most contentious immigrant-related issues addressed by the state legislature in recent years has been related to driver licensing. In 2003, Representative Pedro Marin and his colleagues coauthored House Bill 578, the Economic Development and Public Safety Act. Following California and several other states, the bill would have made it easier for immigrants living in Georgia—both authorized and unauthorized—to obtain a driver's license. The license would be different from a regular Georgia driver's license in that it required an annual renewal, and drivers could use their permits only to drive to school, work, church, and the doctor's office. Justification for the bill centered on public safety. Proponents of the bill argued that immigrants without legal access to drivers' licenses drove anyway, even if they did not know the rules of the road. Additionally, since state law prohibits the sale of auto insurance to nonlicensed drivers, making drivers' licenses more accessible would reduce the number of uninsured drivers on the road.

Although not an immigrant, Marin gave himself as an example of the obstacles that immigrants can face in attempting to obtain a driver's license:

When I moved from Puerto Rico, I'd been driving for many years. . . . I never read the [Motor Vehicle] book or anything. Just went to get my exam. And I failed. I failed. Why? Because where I come from in Puerto Rico we don't have school buses or we don't have railroad tracks. We don't have railroads. So, on those types of questions I failed. So I had to go back to the book. So I put myself in the position that we need to teach the rules of the road to these [immigrant] folks.[54]

HB578 provoked a firestorm in the press and among Georgia residents who worried that giving drivers' licenses to unauthorized immigrants would give them access to restricted practices, such as gun purchases. The bill failed by a vote of 64 to 105. Marin then asked for and was granted a reconsideration, which passed; however, the bill was not reintroduced. According to Marin, "What happened was that the year after that, it was an election year. It was just a hot topic that nobody wanted to touch."[55]

Ultimately, on May 5, 2005, Governor Purdue signed House Bill 501.[56] The bill requires that only legal residents of the state of Georgia be allowed drivers' licenses. This makes acquiring a Georgia driver's license impossible for unauthorized immigrants, although they can still obtain licenses in several neighboring states. It also makes it difficult for authorized immigrants who cannot show proof of local residency to obtain a license. For example, an immigrant woman without a job who has no electric bill or rental document in her name because she shares an apartment with four or five male relatives will find it difficult to become licensed.[57] Additionally, House Bill 501 provides that immigrants who lose their legal immigrant status while in Georgia will immediately have their drivers' licenses suspended.

Recent actions by the federal government may make House Bill 501 superfluous. At the time of this writing, President Bush is expected to sign a military spending bill that would include provisions for the U.S. Department of Homeland Security to approve all state issued identification cards, including drivers' licenses. This provision of the act, called Real-ID, would effectively remove states' abilities to offer drivers' licenses to immigrants who cannot provide federally acceptable identification. Marin argues that Real-ID ties states' hands in what he sees as a public safety issue; nonetheless, he is hopeful that the federal government will provide other means of licensing access to immigrants. He notes:

After Washington passed the Real ID act, this [state consideration on driver's licensing] is no use. But still, you know, we have to have it, and hopefully with Senate in Congress and the House going to conference committee in the future putting some immigration reform package together, hopefully we will get some type of area where these folks can be provided with drivers' licenses.[58]

LEGAL ISSUES

The recent volume of immigration has created an opportunity for the proliferation of certain crimes as well as considerable policy debate regarding the best ways to deal with immigrants who commit crimes. While law enforcement agencies do not report crimes by the country of origin of the perpetrator or victim, interviews with law enforcement officials suggest a link between immigrants and eight particular types of crime: (1) driving under the influence of alcohol, (2) prostitution, (3) driving without a valid driver's license and/or insurance, (4) domestic violence, (5) gang activities, (6) consumer fraud, (7) home invasions, and (8) the purchase and sale of fraudulent documents.[59] In some instances, such as driving under the influence of alcohol, immigrants are reported to be likely to commit crimes. In other instances, such as home invasions and consumer fraud, immigrants are likely to be victims of crime. In a third set of instances, the presence of immigrants allows for the creation of or an increase in types of crimes.

Among some immigrant communities, the considerable likelihood of immigrants to be young and male lends itself to behaviors that are less likely to occur among populations that are older or have a larger female presence. Heavy drinking is particularly common in neighborhoods with many immigrant men. Such behavior contributes to the tendency for these men to be arrested for driving under the influence of alcohol (DUI). Additionally, when a large number of single immigrant men live in a concentrated area, they attract prostitutes. In a 2002 study of Latino immigrant men, respondents noted that many of the prostitutes were U.S.-born white and black women; the prostitutes themselves were rarely Latino immigrants.[60]

Among other immigrant communities, however, prostitution is more common. In fact, the trafficking of immigrants for the purposes of prostitution is a growing concern among lawmakers. According to Representative John Lunsford, "We heard report after report of people who were brought here for that [sexual slavery] purpose."[61] The testimony of these witnesses prompted Lunsford and his colleagues to add a section to SB529 that makes it a felony to smuggle or otherwise bring immigrants into the state for the purposes of sexual or labor servitude. The minimum sentence for trafficking under the new law is one to twenty years for those convicted of trafficking in adults and ten to twenty years for those convicted of trafficking minors. The law also applies to intermediaries who act on behalf of traffickers. According to Lunsford, this provision is important because, "we didn't need to create a new slave class in America."[62]

In addition to sexual and labor slavery, the influx of unauthorized immigrants has lent itself to a thriving black market business in the sale and distribution of fraudulent documents including passports, drivers' licenses, Social Security cards, and work authorization ("green") cards. The proliferation of these documents makes some lawmakers reluctant to crack down on employers who hire unauthorized workers. Senator Mitch Seabaugh asks:

> If they [employers] go through and obtain the documentation but the documentation is not any good, then to what degree does an employer have to go to make sure that the documentation is valid? And if it's not valid, how are they able to be fairly treated in that situation instead of just being set up for failure because of the proliferation of paperwork that's out there that looks good? It looks like it's valid, but it's not . . . and how do you do it in a way that doesn't stifle business from a standpoint of overly burdensome to the administration of paperwork and yet be able to hold them accountable if they're hiring illegals?[63]

Certainly, the issue of forged and fraudulent documents has fueled much of the debate over how to restrict the hiring of unauthorized workers.

The commission of crimes by immigrants has also created debate over the best ways for local law enforcement to deal with immigrants who commit such crimes. According to Seabaugh, his constituents are deeply concerned that immigrants who commit crimes are merely deported without punitive action such as jail time or fines.[64] Another legislator, Representative Ron Forster, argues that immigrants who commit crimes should be deported rather than requiring the state to incur the cost of incarceration.[65] Representative John Meadows also favors deportation over incarceration, but he also sees the limitations to such a policy:

How do I deport them? Who's going to come get them? Does that mean I put two deputies in a car and drive them across Alabama, Mississippi, Louisiana, and Texas and deposit them on the other side of the border? And then the story I've heard is that they can beat you back [to Georgia].[66]

UNAUTHORIZED IMMIGRATION

The mere presence of unauthorized immigrants creates a legal issue. A concern of many policymakers and a frustration of some state residents is that local law enforcement has had little jurisdiction over immigration enforcement. Prior to the passage of SB529, state and local police were unable to question immigrants about their legal status. Under the new law, however, state and local law enforcement are required to ascertain the nationality and verify the lawful admission status of anyone charged with a felony or DUI. Additionally, SB529 permits peace officers to participate in federal training programs through Homeland Security that deputize local law enforcement as federal immigration officers for the purposes of immigration and customs law compliance.

One of the concerns that prompted these law enforcement sections of SB529 was that unauthorized immigrants who committed crimes such as DUI were receiving preferential treatment in the justice system by failing to provide their legal identity. Because Georgia law provides tougher sanctions for repeat DUI offenders, the concern was that unauthorized immigrants arrested for a crime were posting a cash bond. Because they could not be tracked, if they were subsequently arrested on the same charge, they would continue to be treated as first-time offenders. SB529 makes it more difficult for this situation to occur.

IMMIGRANTS AS CRIME VICTIMS

Of course, while some immigrants have committed crimes, others are crime victims. Georgia is already seeing an increase in consumer fraud targeted toward immigrants. Insurance scams are prominent among these crimes. One example is the sale of "prenatal care packages" to pregnant immigrant women. At a cost of about $300, women purchase these packages assuming that they are health insurance coverage for the delivery of their child. Instead, they are merely a scam targeting the immigrant community. The sale of supposed "international drivers' licenses" is another common fraud.

Immigrants who come from countries where banking practices are less secure than those in the United States also find themselves victims of crime. Fearing the security of local banks or, in the case of unauthorized immigrants, worrying that banks might require more information than they care to provide, too many immigrants keep their money in their homes or on their persons. As a consequence, Georgia has seen an increase in home invasions and muggings perpetrated by thieves who often target their victims on known paydays.

Representative Pedro Marin is currently working with the Gwinnett County Policy Department on a program that distributes brochures to the local immigrant community. Called "Don't Be a Victim," these brochures educate immigrants on using banks, avoiding home invasions, and reducing their likelihood of becoming a target for muggers. The idea for creating the brochure came from the crime investigation unit. So far, they have distributed 10,000 copies, and they plan to print and distribute many more.

Efforts such as these are important. In one particularly notorious case known as the "Night of Blood," five people were arrested after an invasion of four mobile home parks in rural Tift County and neighboring Colquitt County in October 2005. The invasions, presumably for the purpose of robbery, resulted in the death of six Mexican immigrants and injuries to five more. Most were shot or bludgeoned with baseball bats. The mayor of Tifton showed his concern by flying the Mexican and American flags at half-mast, a move that was criticized by some local community members and praised by others. In response to the Night of Blood, one wealthy member of the local community threatened to end his association with local banks unless they proposed new policies that would encourage immigrants to bank their money. In response, some local banks have agreed to accept the *matrícula consular*—an identification card issued by the Mexican government—as proper identification to open a bank account.

IMMIGRATION CASE LAW

Of course, not all state policies are enacted by the general assembly. A body of policy, called case law, is also created within the judicial system. Case laws are policies enacted by the judiciary through interpretation of the existing laws. In matters of immigration, a particularly important case law was created by the Georgia Supreme Court in *Smith v. The State*.[67]

In May 2001, a defense team in Hall County argued that the capital murder indictment of their client be overturned because the composition of the jury pool violated the Sixth Amendment guarantee to the right of a jury of peers. By law, judiciaries must create a master jury list (that is, a list of people who could potentially be called for jury duty) whose composition is proportionally representative of cognizable groups of adults in the relevant jurisdiction. For example, if a county's adult population is 50 percent male, then the master jury list must also be close to 50 percent male. In Georgia in 2000, the cognizable groups were *male, female, white, African American,* and *other,* and people registering to vote (the list from which the jury pool was selected) were asked to identify themselves by these gender and race categories.

The defense team in the Hall County case argued that Latinos and Hispanics, who comprised more than 17 percent of Hall County's adult population (African Americans comprised only 6.8 percent), should be considered a cognizable group. They also argued that the representation of Hispanics and Latinos on the master jury list was unconstitutional because they comprised only an estimated 2.6 percent of that list. In order to meet the Sixth Amendment standard, the defense argued, the master jury list must be close to 17 percent Hispanic or Latino.

In October 2002, the Georgia Supreme Court upheld a lower court's decision that Latinos and Hispanics are a cognizable group for the purpose of jury selection. However, the court also ruled that only those Hispanics and Latinos who were jury eligible by virtue of U.S. citizenship should be included when calculating their proportional representation. In short, since native-born and naturalized immigrant Latinos or Hispanics comprised only 3 percent of Hall County's Hispanic or Latino population, their 2.6 percent representation on the master jury list was constitutional.

Only one justice dissented on the *Smith* decision. Justice Bentham argued that Latinos and Hispanics should be a cognizable group, but to exclude noncitizen immigrants from proportional representation "run[s] contrary to American notions of fairness, inclusiveness, and justice." Bentham argued that because Hall County is not a port of entry or a border county, it is unfair to assume that the preponderance of members of any particular ethno-racial group are noncitizens.

In practice, the decision in the *Smith* case has three important implications. First, since jury ineligible members of other cognizable groups are given proportional representation on the master jury list, the case law creates one standard for Hispanics and Latinos and another standard for all other ethno-racial groups. Second, it sets a precedent by which noncitizen Latinos and Hispanics are afforded fewer rights to representation under the law than citizens. Third, it makes it very difficult to correctly "balance" the master jury list, since noncitizen Latinos and Hispanics must now be excluded from the cognizable groups of men, women, whites, African Americans, and others. In an experiment with justices appointed to the eleventh circuit court, none were able to correctly balance the list.

EMPLOYMENT

According to Representative Pedro Marin, "Immigrants don't come here because we've got good schools. They don't come here because we've got good health services or social services. They come here for one thing alone, and that's to work."[68] High demand for workers and relatively high wages, especially in the construction industry, have served as a draw for many. Additionally, in the 1990s, many native Georgians left low-skilled jobs in poultry processing and textiles in order to take higher paying jobs or ones with better working conditions. This left vacancies in those industries that were filled by immigrants. Furthermore, the booming construction industry created work in construction auxiliary jobs such as landscaping.

While many Georgians believe that immigrants take jobs that no one else wants, an examination of immigrant employment in Georgia suggests that the jobs they have are relatively good. Table 4.1 examines the occupations and industries where most of Georgia's immigrant labor force was concentrated in 2000. This table also shows the 1999 average annual wage or salary for immigrant workers in those occupations and industries. Clearly, wages and salaries within the largest immigrant-employing industries are much higher than the $10,712 that a full-time worker can expect to gross making the current federal minimum wage. The average immigrant wages and salaries are highest in the hospital industry, but that average includes not only immigrant orderlies and secretaries employed by hospitals, but immigrant physicians as well. Wages and salaries by occupations are lower, but even the lowest paying job held by immigrants—cashier—grossed more than the federal minimum wage.

TABLE 4.1. TOP FIVE INDUSTRIES AND OCCUPATIONS EMPLOYING IMMIGRANTS AND AVERAGE ANNUAL IMMIGRANT WAGE, GEORGIA, 2000

RANK	INDUSTRY	NUMBER IN LABOR FORCE	AVERAGE WAGE
1	Construction	48,700	$18,136.63
2	Food service	26,093	$17,989.09
3	Food manufacturing	10,025	$15,399.17
4	Hospitals	9,358	$44,550.28
5	Educational services	7,520	$18,870.68

RANK	OCCUPATION	NUMBER IN LABOR FORCE	AVERAGE WAGE
1	Construction laborers	14,038	$15,676.62
2	Carpenters	10,092	$17,398.72
3	Production workers	8,196	$17,401.40
4	Cashiers	7,730	$13,245.06
5	Cooks	7,167	$14,483.49

Source: Steven Ruggles, Matthew Sobek, Trent Alexander, Catherine A. Fitch, Ronald Goeken, Patricia Kelly Hall, Miriam King, and Chad Ronnander, "Integrated Public Use Microdata Series," Version 3.0, machine-readable database, Minnesota Population Center, Minneapolis, 2004.

Most Georgians recognize that the recent influx of immigration has had a stimulating effect on the economy. In a 2001 Peach State Poll of Georgian attitudes toward immigrants, 67 percent reported that immigrants create new jobs or take jobs that no one else wants. Less than 27 percent reported the belief that immigrants take jobs from native workers.[69]

INFORMAL WORK AND DAY LABOR

While good job opportunities abound for both men and women, many immigrant women, particularly those who lack fluency in English, find that their child care responsibilities preclude them from working in the formal sector. Working in the informal sector, or black market, is one means by which many women (and some men) are able to balance both responsibilities. These workers hire themselves out as domestic workers by cleaning houses, doing laundry, or providing meals to workers for which they are paid "under the table."

Many of the men who have trouble finding work in the formal sector, either because of lack of skills or lack of work authorization, resort to day labor. Day labor refers to temporary contingency work, usually lasting one or two days, where laborers are selected because of their availability rather than their job skills. Day laborers in Georgia typically stand on a street corner or designated location each morning in hopes of being selected by a passing contractor or other potential employer. Once selected, many day laborers report not getting paid or being paid less than promised. Employers who mistreat unauthorized day laborers often threaten them with deportation in order to frighten them into submission.

The congregation of day laborers at a fixed point often creates problems for local communities. Workers on street corners or near gas stations and other places of business often swarm passing motorists who perceive their actions as threatening. Because of this, business owners report that day laborers discourage customers from patronizing their businesses. Additionally, when day laborers congregate for long hours on street corners, they also tend to commit misdemeanors such as littering and urinating on the sides of the road.

While no bills have been introduced at the state level to directly address informal work or day labor, some local governments have worked to address these issues. Some local governments have dusted off languishing loitering ordinances in order to rid the streets of day laborers, while other local governments and some private agencies have been instrumental in opening day labor centers. These centers provide a central location for day laborers to congregate that is indoors and provides bathroom facilities. Workers are queued by time of arrival, so jobs are distributed on a first-come, first-served basis, which cuts down on the competition for scarce day jobs. Additionally, both workers and employers are required to register with the center so that wage abuses are minimized. Finally, most day labor centers offer daily skills training, particularly English language classes, for workers who do not manage to secure work.

Day labor centers are not without their critics. D. A. King, lobbyist and founder of the Dustin Inman Society, argues that day labor centers are tax-payer funded efforts to encourage and support unauthorized immigration.[70] The Dustin Inman Society is a nonprofit foundation whose goals are to educate Georgians "regarding America's un-secured borders, and the resulting illegal immigration crisis."[71] Others criticize the private,

for-profit day labor centers that have proliferated in Atlanta and other
Georgia metropolitan areas for sending workers to hazardous sites without prior authorization and for imposing a series of deductions on workers' pay that results in employees receiving less than minimum wage.[72]
These charges have not been leveled at city-organized day labor centers.

UNAUTHORIZED WORKERS

Senate Bill 529 is the most comprehensive effort by the state government to curb unauthorized immigrant labor. First, SB529 requires that
all state agencies, contractors, and subcontractors participate in the federal government's Basic Pilot Program to verify work eligibility with the
Social Security Administration. Second, in order to minimize the unfair
advantage now given to employers who knowingly hire unauthorized
workers, SB529 prohibits employers from claiming as a business expense wages in excess of $600 paid to any single employee who does not
have legal work authorization. Additionally, employers who file a Form
1099 are required to withhold 6 percent state income tax on any employee who does not provide a valid taxpayer identification number. Finally, SB529 makes it a felony to engage in trafficking for the purposes
of labor servitude.

This issue of labor trafficking came to the attention of many Georgians in 2005 when Mei Lin and Shih Kai Feng were arrested and sen-
tenced on conspiracy and fraud charges in connection with business
practices at their employment agency in Chamblee. According to press
accounts, the Sin Sin Employment Agency grossed over $1.2 million by
recruiting unauthorized Latino workers for jobs in Asian restaurants in
five states. Workers were forced to live and work in crowded conditions,
endure twelve- to fourteen-hour work days, and purchase essentials such
as food, shelter, and transportation from a "company store." Employees
reported being beaten and starved. Those who were injured on the job
were fired. Unscrupulous employment agencies are so common that there
is a name for those who end up working for such organizations: *hombres de paso* (wayside men). It is hoped that SB529 will give local law enforcement more authority to investigate fraudulent employment agencies,
since it took federal officials six years to make a case against the Fengs.[73]

The use of labor recruiters has also created new problems for industry. On April 26, 2006, the U.S. Supreme Court heard arguments in a
landmark federal racketeering (RICO) case against Mohawk Industries.
U.S.-born workers at Mohawk filed a class action suit against the textile

manufacturer in 2004 alleging that the company artificially depressed workers' wages by paying a Texas company to recruit unauthorized immigrant workers. Mohawk has argued that, while they regularly use outside recruiters, they did not knowingly enter into a scheme to violate immigration laws and traffic in forged work authorization documents.[74] Although the Supreme Court is unlikely to rule on this case before July, a ruling in favor of the workers might open up several of Georgia's businesses to similar lawsuits.

Representative John Meadows is a former mayor of Calhoun, where Mohawk Industries is headquartered. While he describes himself as a "hard-liner" on the issue of immigration, he also notes that businesses are not always able to properly screen workers. That problem, according to him, is exacerbated by the use of labor recruiters:

> Who's illegal and who's not illegal? I don't know. Most of the companies that I know of do everything they can to insure that the person that they hire is legal. You know, when you fill out your I-9 form . . . you're just supposed to ask for these forms of identification, and if they're put in front of you, you're not the judge and jury sitting there. You're got to basically take what they put out there. It's when you find out that those pieces of information they have given you are wrong, you should get rid of those people. You should have them fired immediately. A lot of companies up here use staffing agencies, and they'll come to work for a trial period—a ninety day trial period or whatever before they're hired or not hired—and the staffing agency, . . . their rules are they're supposed to be presenting legal people, and I don't know how much checking they do, but I would hope that it's a little more, because the person I send you should be legal. But it doesn't happen that way. They fall through the cracks. Apparently a lot of them do.[75]

GUEST WORKERS

It is unclear what impact SB529 will have, if any, on another often-exploited immigrant group: H2B visa workers in the timber industry. The H2B visa program was established by the federal government as an immigrant guest worker program to supply nonagricultural workers. One industry that takes advantage of that program is the timber industry; they routinely engage labor contractors to provide H2B workers as tree planters. Researchers in the area explain that the work is low-paying and arduous:

Planters spend most of their time bent over, and swinging the hoedad
or dibble stick for eight to ten hours a day takes its toll on backs and
shoulders. The planters are normally paid between $.015 and $.06
per seedling, so there is not much time to relax. . . . The planters
said that it generally takes three weeks to break in a new planter so
that they can take the harsh, physical work, and begin to work fast
enough to make money.[76]

While H2B worker wages are federally regulated, unscrupulous labor contractors regularly charge so much for "finding" jobs for workers and providing lodging and food that few workers make minimum
wage. Also, by paying by the piece, rather than by the hour, contractors
can pay considerably less than what is mandated by the Department of
Labor.

For H2A workers—immigrant guest workers in the agricultural sector—conditions are much better for the workers, but they may be dis-
advantageous to the employer. Georgia growers using the H2A program
must provide transportation to and from the country of origin (usually
Mexico), provide housing that maintains mandated standards of space
and livability, and pay a federally mandated wage far above federal minimum. Since as many as 25 percent of all farmworkers are unauthorized,
growers use the H2A program because they fear that an ill-timed raid by
Immigration and Customs Enforcement might prove disastrous to time-
sensitive crop production. One large grower noted that he enrolled in
the H2A program after 700 of his employees' Social Security numbers
were returned as questionable by the Social Security Administration. At
the same time, growers contend that the federally mandated wages are
too high, and that growers who "do the right thing" by using legal H2A
workers are at a disadvantage when compared to those who knowingly
hire unauthorized workers.[77]

DIRECTIONS FOR THE FUTURE

Georgia lawmakers drew national attention with the passage of Senate
Bill 529. The process of creating and passing the bill was a long one that
came after much trial and error. The primary author of the bill, Senator Chip Rogers, described the process as "tak[ing] what we thought was
the best, workable ideas and put[ting] them into a comprehensive bill as opposed to doing this piecemeal and bill by bill by bill."[78] Legislators less favorable toward the bill characterized the process as the bringing together of

bills that were "really harsh" and working through a compromise "with the thoughtfulness and patience and leadership" of legislators sympathetic to immigrants.[79]

Throughout the process, legislators on both sides of the issue have been vilified. Senator Chip Rogers, head of the Senate Immigration Reform Caucus and arguably the state's biggest proponent of laws to curb unauthorized immigration, is quoted as saying, "They've called me a racist, they call me anti-Christian, they say I hate children, they've used every name in the book to try to intimidate me and stop me from what the people clearly want me to do."[80] Representative Pedro Marin and Senator Sam Zamarripa, who are generally viewed as pro-immigrant, are also under fire. According to Marin, "I have received hate email, hate mail. My car was vandalized once. I have a website against me."[81] In fact, Zamarripa and Marin both have "watch" Web sites sponsored by American Patrol. The sites call Zamarripa a *reconquista* and Marin an "ethnic pimp" for Mexican causes, despite the fact that he is Puerto Rican.[82]

Both sides of the issue agree that Georgia's actions represent a first step in a process that will take a lot of time and trial to get right. Senator Mitch Seabaugh describes the process thusly:

> A lot of times we can't get a lot of answers to questions until [we] at least try something, and so we'll put this [SB529] into work and we'll see where we head, and hopefully, over time, we will have one of the most effective policies of all the states. And I hope that our state will be a leader in dealing with some of these issues. And sometimes it just takes the intestinal fortitude and the persistence to go ahead and put something out there and just keep working at it until you get it right.[83]

What will be the "right" policy for the state will depend heavily on the will of the voters, an increasing number of whom are immigrants. Certainly, the history of Florida and California remind us that immigrants can be very instrumental in influencing policy and determining who will be in a position to make policy. As one Georgia lawmaker recently said, "I think they are underestimating the force that is coming into the state."[84]

CHAPTER 5

STATE AND LOCAL POLICY RESPONSES TO IMMIGRATION IN MINNESOTA[1]

Katherine Fennelly

INTRODUCTION

Minnesota is a low immigration state; only 6 percent of the population is foreign born, compared to 12 percent nationwide. Yet several factors contribute to exaggerated perceptions of the size of the immigrant population. The first is an uneven dispersal of immigrants across the state. Large concentrations of immigrants live in the Twin Cities, in particular suburbs, and in rural communities that have food processing plants that attract immigrant workers.[2] In these towns, a proliferation of languages and cultures and the rapid increase from few to many non-European origin residents feeds the perception that Minnesota is, in the words of one anti-immigrant researcher, "a new Ellis Island."[3] Furthermore, since 25 to 40 percent of immigrants in the state enter as refugees (see Figure 5.1, page 102), their national origins differ markedly from those of immigrants in other parts of the country—with higher percentages of Africans, Asians, and residents from the former Soviet countries.[4] In 2004, just under a quarter of the foreign-born population of Minnesota was composed of Latinos of any race.[5] Most of these individuals were from Mexico and Central America. Asians represent the largest foreign-born population in the state—principally Hmong, Vietnamese, Laotians, and Cambodians.[6] Africans (predominantly Somalis) represented a smaller percentage of the total foreign-born population in the 2000 census but the largest group of new immigrants

101

FIGURE 5.1. PERCENTAGE OF IMMIGRANTS WHO ARE REFUGEES, UNITED STATES AND MINNESOTA

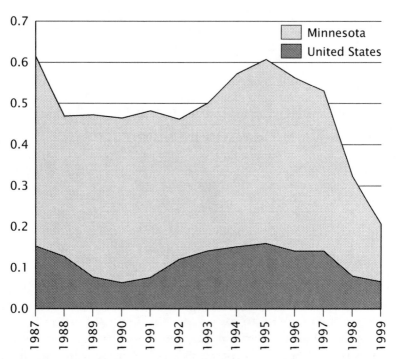

Source: Katherine Fennelly, "Latinos, Asians and Africans in the Northstar State: New Immigrant Communities in Minnesota," in *Beyond the Gateway: Immigrants in a Changing America*, Elzbieta M. Gozdziak and Susan F. Martin, ed. (Lanham, Md.: Rowman and Littlefield, 2005).

in 2004. In rural and suburban communities that have had no history of ethnic or racial diversity, the presence of new African and Asian refugees and Latino immigrants is another cause of the heightened visibility of immigration to the state.

Minnesota has a reputation for welcoming immigrants and refugees as part of its tradition of strong social programs and progressive politics. The state can boast of long and distinguished list of state councils, nonprofits, foundations, advocacy, and mutual assistance groups that serve the foreign-born. Nevertheless, some of this support appears to have eroded in recent years, as Minnesota voters have moved noticeably to the right, both in political party affiliation, and in attitudes toward immigrants. From 2003 to 2006, the state of Harold Stassen, Hubert Humphrey, Walter Mondale, and Paul Wellstone has a House of Representatives with a Republican majority. Democrats regained the majority in both houses in the November 2006 elections, but Tim Pawlenty, a conservative Republican governor who has made a punitive response to undocumented immigration a major theme of his administration, was reelected to a second term.

This chapter will describe the growing partisan divide over immigration in Minnesota and provide details on initiatives related to education, health, social service, housing, labor, and security policies. Some of the data and quotes in the chapter come from key informant interviews. Between February and April 2006, graduate students at the Hubert H. Humphrey Institute conducted thirty-four interviews with U.S.- and foreign-born policymakers familiar with issues of importance to immigrants and refugees in Minnesota. The persons interviewed included several state agency directors, managers and directors of immigrant-serving organizations, foundation program officers, and elected state and county officials. Everyone was asked how the state of Minnesota has responded to increases in the numbers of immigrants and refugees over the past ten years and what policy changes they had observed. Depending upon their areas of expertise, respondents were then asked for specific comments about changes in state policies related to health, education, housing, or public safety (see Appendix A, page 136, for survey questionnaire).

Partisan Views of Immigration Policy in Minnesota

In January 2004, at the beginning of his second term of office, Republican Governor Tim Pawlenty issued a multi-pronged proposal to "curb illegal immigration," incurring the wrath of immigrant-serving groups and many nonprofit agencies. Ironically, it was a *pro-immigrant* letter from the mayor of Worthington, Minnesota (a town with a large pork processing plant and a largely immigrant work force), that purportedly motivated Governor Pawlenty's public statements on the costs of undocumented immigration. The mayor of Worthington had written a letter to the governor requesting his help securing legal identification for undocumented immigrants in his city. According to an article in *USA Today*,[7] the mayor's letter stimulated the governor to commission a report by the Minnesota Department of Administration on the costs of undocumented immigration.[8] The resulting report, issued in December 2005, was widely criticized for relying upon data from the Center for Immigration Studies, an anti-immigrant think tank, and for employing broad estimates to tally costs, while claiming that benefits in the form of taxes paid by immigrants could not be included because the "exact dollar amount attributable to illegal immigrants is unknown."[9]

As a counterpoint, members of the Democratic Farm Labor (DFL) legislative caucus referred to an independent research report that estimated that undocumented laborers had a substantial and positive impact on the Minnesota economy.[10] They charged that the governor was "playing to racism" and using immigration as a wedge issue to gain support for his national political ambitions.[11]

Later in 2006, the Office of the Minnesota Legislative Auditor issued a more positive, if cautious report on the economic impacts of immigration, concluding that "immigration probably has positive economic impacts overall, although certain workers and levels of government might experience adverse impacts."[12] The authors referred to the shortcomings of the 2005 report, noting that "a study by the Minnesota Department of Administration estimated the additional public costs due to illegal immigrants, but did not estimate the additional tax revenues they generate."

The governor's January 2004 proposal included the following strategies:[13]

▲ Establish a ten-member Minnesota Illegal Immigration Enforcement Team that would be federally trained and authorized to question, detain, and arrest suspected undocumented immigrants.

▲ Override city ordinances in Minneapolis and St. Paul that prohibit police officers from taking action against undocumented immigrants unless they are arrested for a separate crime. (Pawlenty said the ordinances violate federal law.)

▲ Put into law a 2002 state administrative rule that prominently marks drivers' licenses of legal foreign visitors with their visa expiration dates. That proposal was a central theme of the Republican governor's 2002 election campaign, but it was blocked by the DFL-controlled senate. The Department of Public Safety under Governor Jesse Ventura implemented the license designation by administrative rule, and it continues in force.

▲ Toughen and add penalties for possession, creation, and sale of false identification. Currently, it is not a crime in Minnesota to possess a false identification unless intent to commit a crime can be proven.

- ▲ Require officers to note the citizenship and immigration status of all arrestees at booking.

- ▲ Increase felony penalties for human trafficking when minors are exploited to up to twenty years in prison. In addition, a task force would be set up to seek ways to combat human trafficking.

- ▲ Add a state fine of as much as $5,000 to a current federal penalty of $11,000 for employers who knowingly hire or recruit undocumented immigrants. In addition, state contracts would prohibit the use of undocumented immigrants to perform contracted services.

Some analysts suggest that the governor was unprepared for the pro-immigrant backlash that followed the issuance of his first set of proposals. One administration official described a rash of gubernatorial staff phone calls to agency heads asking how they could engage in damage control. Another confirmed that the governor "got in huge trouble and within weeks he was calling up agencies asking what could be done that would be 'pro' immigrant." A few weeks later, Pawlenty announced a series of proposals designed to support *legal* immigration.[14] These included:

- ▲ a tax credit of $300 per family to encourage immigrants to become citizens by offsetting the costs of English language classes and citizenship application fees;

- ▲ provision of basic "financial literacy" information on income tax credits, home ownership, and business start-up opportunities;

- ▲ pressure on the federal government to grant more visas to graduates of U.S. colleges and universities and green cards to immigrants with high-tech skills;

- ▲ establishment of "foreign investor visas" for foreign investors who invest at least $500,000 in new or existing Minnesota businesses, create at least ten new jobs, or maintain the current level of employment at a struggling business;

- ▲ establish a $3 million grant program for employers to provide English language instruction for their employees;

▲   expand the number of foreign physicians working in underserved
      areas in Minnesota; and

▲   increase immunizations for immigrants.

In 2004, former Vice President Walter Mondale was so concerned
over partisan bickering and what he has described as the loss of "civic engagement and shared vision" in Minnesota that he commissioned a
study on the topic. The authors of the final report attributed the political shift to changes in the economy, growing political polarization, and
to "increasingly racially diverse immigration into the state."[15] In spite
of this interpretation, it is unclear whether increased immigration has
led to changes in the social and economic views of Minnesota voters,
or whether conservatives have merely been given greater visibility and
political clout that has brought restrictionist views to the fore. In any
case, disagreements over immigration policies have further widened an
already large divide between Democrats and Republicans in the state.

During the 2006 legislative session, representatives in the Republican-
controlled Minnesota house put forward a number of bills incorporating items from Governor Pawlenty's proposals, but support from the
DFL/Democratic Party that controls the senate kept most of the restrictive measures from becoming law.

In response to the governor's proposals on immigration, DFL legislators in the senate sponsored their own proposals to expand English
language classes, give tax credits to businesses offering English and citizenship instruction, penalties for employers who exploit immigrants,
and the formation of a Governor's Commission on New Minnesotans.[16]

In a rare bipartisan effort, Democrats and Republicans joined forces to support the Minnesota DREAM Act, a bill that would grant in-state
tuition to undocumented students. On April 19, 2006, the bill passed the
House Ways and Means Committee by a vote of 26 to 8. It appeared poised
to pass both houses until the governor voiced his opposition and wrote a
personal letter to each member of the Higher Education Committee asking
them to remove the provision from the Higher Education Bill.[17]

POSITIVE RESPONSES TO IMMIGRATION

Not all of the local responses to increased numbers of immigrants in
Minnesota have been negative. A number of individual cities and towns
in Minnesota have taken steps to demonstrate support for foreign-born

residents. One of many examples is the institution of Spanish language instruction for police officers in Apple Valley. Other police departments use the AT&T Language Line, and some routinely call the Border Patrol to interpret, but the public safety director of Apple Valley explained that "I saw all of the Spanish-speaking officers in Worthington, and it all just kind of connected for us; it was just the right thing to do." The police chief added, "If you are going to provide good public service, you have to be willing to adapt."

A foundation officer interviewed described the variation among communities in terms of attitudes of elected and appointed officials:

> Austin, for example, has a mayor and employers and local businesses that are very supportive of new immigrants; they understand the benefits and want to help them acculturate. . . . It all depends on leadership— if you have a mayor talking about viewing the population as criminals, then people start talking about not wanting immigrants. For example, the mayor in Montgomery decided that there were too many Mexicans downtown. He decided to evict people and to tear down houses to make opportunities for potential buyers, even when the buyers did not exist.

ATTITUDES TOWARD IMMIGRANTS

Minnesotans' views on immigrants and immigration are complex and contradictory. Adults in the state demonstrate both marked approval for programs and policies supporting immigrants and refugees and considerable xenophobia. Minnesota is home to a long and distinguished list of state councils, foundations, and community development groups sponsoring projects for the foreign-born, as well as immigrant-serving organizations with international reputations, such as Minnesota Advocates for Human Rights, the Center for Victims of Torture, the American Refugee Committee, the International Institute, and the Human Rights Center at the University of Minnesota. One active advocacy group, AFFIRM (Alliance for Fair Federal Immigration Reforms in Minnesota), a coalition of forty religious, labor, and civil rights groups, is lobbying for immigration reforms that promote family reunification; protection of human, civil, and worker rights; and the creation of a pathway to citizenship.

Support for immigrant and refugee services by local foundations also has been impressive: between 1994 and 2005, forty-seven Minnesota foundations made over 340 grants supporting work with immigrants and refugees.[18] According to the Minnesota Council on Foundations, these philanthropic efforts have not required a change in focus because most of the issues faced by immigrants and refugees are the same as those often faced by low-income groups: housing, employment, education, and health care.[19]

As a result, grant makers have generally incorporated support for immigrants into a broad and growing focus on diverse populations.[20] The political clout of immigrants in Minnesota is growing, as evidenced by the election of Hmong and Latino state representatives, and in January 2002, the election of Mee Moua as the first Hmong state senator in the nation. Senator Moua's story of fleeing repression in Laos as a child, entering the country as a refugee, and later becoming an attorney and the first Hmong state senator during the 2006 legislative session captured for many the immigrant dream of success in the United States. Another example of the growing political clout of immigrants is the multi-denominational Joint Religious Legislative Coalition that galvanized a thousand clergy and constituents to convene at the state legislature to push for rights for the poor, the homeless, and undocumented immigrants.

An official in the Minnesota Department of Human Services gave a recent example of how multiple organizations in the state have come together to support new immigrants and refugees:

> We recently had to deal with the influx of 4,000 people of Hmong origin from Thailand. We were able to do that with Mutual Assistance Associations and voluntary organizations—large ones like Lutheran Social Services. They have a direct relationship with the federal government in placing refugees. They are very helpful in helping refugees have access to state programs. They help families get into MFIP (Minnesota Family Investment Program) through the various agencies. We are working with local organizations . . . and foundations that provided emergency support for groups, like the recent Hmong community, and we maximize our work through help from our congressional delegation.

In concert with media attention to anti-immigrant groups, the 2003 resettlement of 5,000 new Hmong refugees in Minnesota generated some negative backlash. State Senator Mee Moua described some of the negative comments called in to her office when the resettlement was announced: "I feel terrible for my staffers because they really take the brunt of it. We'll hear things like, 'I'm a white man, and this is my country and we don't need any more of your kind.' Or, 'Our state is burdened enough and we don't need more of your kind to take our welfare.'"

Recently, national furor over the size of the population of undocumented immigrants has reached Minnesota. The governor used demographic estimates that there may be as many as 85,000 unauthorized immigrants in Minnesota as justification for proposals to crack down on this population. His stance and parallel federal debates on undocumented immigration have polarized the public. With urging from church leaders, union officials, and Latino radio hosts, an unprecedented 35,000–40,000 Minnesotans marched in favor of immigrant rights in St. Paul in March of this year, and immigrant advocacy groups marshaled support for petitions, public statements, and visits to legislators.

The current divide in the state legislature over programs and policies for immigrants mimics the sentiments of voters in the state. In 2004, researchers from the Minnesota Community Project[21] surveyed 700 likely Minnesota voters across the state and asked them to select *two* statements that described their feelings:

Immigrants . . .

▲   take jobs nobody else wants

▲   contribute to cultural diversity

▲   are a drain on public schools

▲   are hardworking and make a valuable contribution

▲   do not assimilate

▲   get too many government handouts

The attitudes of respondents were equally divided between those who selected two positive statements from the list, and those who selected either two negative, or one positive and one negative statement (see Figure 5.2, page 110).

Further analysis of the data revealed a strong partisan split, with statistically significant differences in the attitudes of individuals who identified themselves with the DFL/Democratic Party, the Republican Party, or

Figure 5.2. Minnesotans' Attitudes toward Immigrants

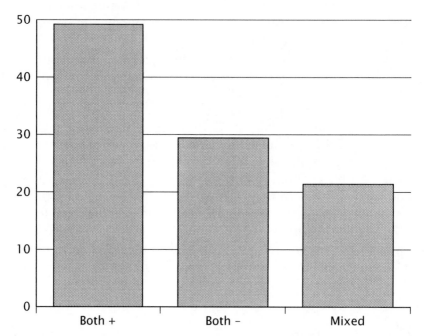

Source: Stan Greenberg, Anna Greenberg, and Julie Hootkin, "The Changing Shape of Minnesota: Reinvigorating Community and Government in the New Minnesota," Greenberg Quinlan Rosner Research, Inc., prepared for the Minnesota Community Project, December 14, 2004.

said that they were Independents (see Figure 5.3). Sixty percent of Democrats supported two positive statements about immigrants, compared with just over half of Independent voters, and only thirty-four percent of Republicans.

Policies Related to K–12 Education

At a time when enrollment of non-Hispanic white youth has been stagnant or declining in many districts, enrollment of Limited English Proficiency (LEP) students has increased dramatically (see Figure 5.4, page 112).[22] Some anti-immigrant groups point to these increases as a major economic drain on the state. Yet, school programs are funded by property taxes paid by immigrants and non-immigrants alike. Furthermore, the enrollment boosts attributed to the children of immigrants are a crucial source of state revenue for many schools.

In Minnesota (and a majority of other states), funds are allocated to schools based upon a per-pupil enrollment formula. On the one hand, this means that it is formula funds corresponding to increased enrollments of immigrant youth and the U.S.-born children of immigrants that keep many Midwestern schools from closing or consolidating. On the other hand, other than a modest amount of additional funds for students in English Language Learning (ELL) programs, the formula does not take into account additional responsibilities assumed by administrators and teachers in schools with large immigrant populations.

Immigrants traditionally have been concentrated in the metro area, and there are large differences between programs in Minneapolis/St. Paul and in other parts of the state. According to a study by the Council

FIGURE 5.3. ATTITUDES BY PARTY AFFILIATION

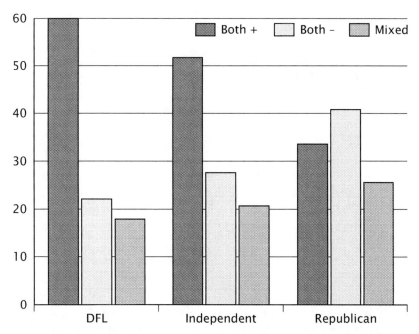

Source: Stan Greenberg, Anna Greenberg, and Julie Hootkin, "The Changing Shape of Minnesota: Reinvigorating Community and Government in the New Minnesota," Greenberg Quinlan Rosner Research, Inc., prepared for the Minnesota Community Project, December 14, 2004.

Figure 5.4. Minnesota K–12 LEP Enrollments, 1998–2004

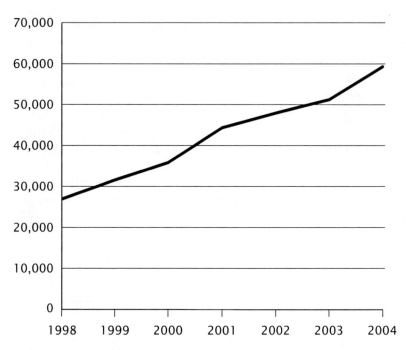

Source: "Minnesota ABE Impact Report," Adult Basic Education Office, Minnesota Department of Education, 2006.

of Great City Schools, the St. Paul School District is among the best in the nation at improving the achievement of ELL students and bringing their reading scores closer to those of native-born youth.[23] The report attributes this success to bilingual instruction programs that bring extra language teachers into subject matter classrooms, rather than removing students for ELL. In the program, ELL teachers develop models of training for mainstream teachers and work as coaches to support them.

In general, the policymakers whom we interviewed gave high marks to the ways in which Minnesota schools have responded to the needs of immigrants and refugees over the past ten years. A Somali Muslim cleric who works as an ELL teacher in a St. Paul school described accommodations made by the schools that included giving staff the necessary training for cultural and English proficiency instruction, embedding cultural studies into the curriculum, and hiring people from the community as community specialists to work in the schools. He noted that:

At least from the Somali perspective, I do feel Minnesota has been very welcoming—especially when we came in large numbers—the school system responded with overwhelming support and accommodation. One of the main factors that attracted the Somalis to Minnesota was this welcoming.

This teacher gave the St. Paul school district a *B* report card grade for its response to the educational needs of immigrant youth because of the diversity of programs and options, the acquisition of culturally specific books and materials, and strong collaboration between ELL and mainstream teachers.

The Minneapolis School District uses several different models of language instruction. In the Kindergarten Language Development Model (KDLM), students are taught in their native languages for part of the day and in English during another part. For some new students, such as Hmong children who have recently arrived from refugee camps in Thailand, there is a Transitional Language Center (TLC). Minneapolis has used this model with bilingual teachers who teach content matter to students clustered by national origin group in order to give them more support.

A foundation officer confirms that some schools have done "extraordinary work in creating a climate of respect for students who are from other faiths, traditions, and cultures," but she also laments cutbacks in funding, and gives the state only a *C*– grade on meeting the educational needs of immigrant youth:

> For one thing, we have seen major disinvestments in after school programs, which are very important in young people's identity and social support, considering that their parents are pretty much employed. You have to have consistency, you have to challenge young people, and we are not doing that with after school programs. You have success stories, but if you look at the graduation rate, we are losing ground with immigrants and refugees, just as we have with African-Americans and Native Americans.

In 2000, for the first time there were more immigrants living in Minnesota suburbs than in central cities. Like the central cities, suburban schools and neighborhoods in the suburbs are growing increasingly segregated by race/ethnicity.[24] As a result, African and Latino immigrants are being concentrated in poor, segregated schools that offer fewer resources, weaker educational preparation, and substantially lower achievement levels.

Some districts have responded well to the children of immigrants. Eden Prairie schools, for example, have sponsored intensive training to help staff learn how to serve new refugee children, and the LEAP Academy in St. Paul has an excellent program of intensive English for Hmong students. However, there are marked differences across schools, and the legislator quoted earlier gives K–12 programs "a failing grade for the state, and a C in the metro area; the results don't lie—immigrant youth have high drop-out rates."

A number of federal initiatives have had a deleterious effect on educational programs for diverse youth, as noted by a foundation officer who has worked with immigrant and refugee programs for eighteen years:

> The 1996 Welfare Reform Act put a great deal more stress on the states to get people to work in [a] hurry, sometimes bypassing or shortcutting English language programs. There has been a philosophical shift toward "work first," rather than education. (At the same time) we see a greater diversification of populations of refugees who come here—many more immigrants for whom services are very difficult to secure or pay for.

According to several policymakers, the federal No Child Left Behind Act (NCLB) and its emphasis on standardized tests is a problem for many immigrant children. Although a change in policies exempting them from testing for the first few years has helped, once they are required to be tested, both the youth and the schools feel extra pressure. One individual commented that "what makes mainstream kids struggle is increased exponentially for immigrant children who don't necessarily speak English at home." Others mentioned that teachers complain about the stress created by the large number of required tests, and the instruction time taken up "teaching to the test."

The head of a Latino organization believes that the temporary NCLB testing exemption for ELL children may actually be deleterious if it results in a reduced commitment to that population. He asks whether Minnesota schools have a commitment to help those children achieve positive learning outcomes, and notes that it took a class action suit in the 1970s (the "Latino Consent Decree") to force the St. Paul schools to pay more attention to the needs of Latino youth. The need for further improvement is dramatically evidenced by the high dropout rates among Latino students. "For every one hundred Latino youth—only nine will have completed some level of college by their mid-twenties, and the dropout rate is far beyond fifty percent." He emphasized the urgency of this problem for the state as a whole, given the increase in diverse populations, and the likelihood of losing qualified applicants for thousands of jobs that require baccalaureate degrees.

There is also a large gap between the graduation rates of non-Latino immigrants and U.S.-born students, and a need for better counseling for college admissions. The Somali ELL instructor we interviewed commented that "the parents don't have those skills, so students don't have information to navigate the forms and process to get into college. A lot of times they are on their own, and may not make good choices." Another individual added:

> Parents need help making the bridge to the school. Many cultures see their teachers/schools as assuming responsibility for education of children. Many immigrant children are from families working multiple jobs, so parents aren't around, and some families are quite impoverished. Young children are not really ready for school, because the parents/grandparents do not speak English and do not have access to bilingual preschool programs.

Other problems include a state-mandated five-year limit on ELL instruction, and policies prohibiting older immigrant students from continuing in regular high schools. The state requires that students over the age of twenty-one enter GED programs or qualify for adult basic education (ABE). They are referred to Area Learning Centers that rely upon independent learning and do not have sports or programs that help new students with limited English proficiency become socialized and integrated. Older immigrant students need more intensive instruction and assistance rather than less, and many drop out because of a lack of support and attention. The state commissioner of education describes the challenges related to educating older immigrant youth:

> One area we really grapple with is a student who comes to this country at, let's say sixteen years of age—who doesn't have more than three or four years before they're out of school—that student doesn't have enough time for all the education they need. You know, we can educate kids until they're twenty-one, but what do we do with those over-twenty-one-year-old students? We have ABE programs where it's a few hours a day or a few days a week but it's not full blown school in the same way. I think there's a real question of how to best use our ABE programs—when it's not appropriate anymore for a student to be in

high school classes—we should be able to expand ABE for those who are not done with their high school diploma yet—an expanded, more intense version of that. Because probably by that point, if students are that old, they're working and don't have as much time, we have to think about that. At that age, they're probably already more mature and don't really need a six-hour school day. There is a group of students like that who would probably benefit from some other model besides the six-hour school day.

In sum, although Minnesota has many innovative programs for immigrant youth, budget cutbacks, rapid diversification, and concentrations of low-income youth in inner city schools have led to poor outcomes for many foreign-born students. Refugee students, for example, have special needs that are not adequately recognized in many K–12 schools, such as high rates of post-traumatic stress disorder (PTSD) resulting from exposure to war and violence. First and second generation Latino youth have very alarming high school dropout rates. Ironically, Minnesota ranked seventh out of the fifty states in high school graduation rates for white students in 2000, while recording one of the lowest graduation rates in the country for Latinos (53 percent). [25]

POLICIES RELATED TO POST-SECONDARY PROGRAMS, ADULT BASIC EDUCATION, AND ENGLISH LANGUAGE PROGRAMS

Minnesota has had a very good record in the provision of high quality ABE programs, including GED and adult diplomas, ESL, workforce preparation, family literacy, basic skills enhancement, and citizenship/civics education. In fact, the state spends eight times the federal allocation for adult immigrant education. In a recent federal audit, Minnesota received five commendations for ABE programming. On the other hand, ABE funding has been frozen at a time when demand is increasing exponentially.

In 2006, both legislative houses in Minnesota addressed Governor Pawlenty's proposals to provide additional funding for English language classes for legal immigrants, although the allocation has been criticized as modest, nonrecurring funds that will not replace previous cuts in program budgets for ABE. By the end of the 2006 session, the legislature voted to provide the first inflationary increase in four years to state ABE programs. They also appropriated $1.25 million for one-time grants in 2007 and 2008 to provide additional adult literacy services to newly arrived immigrants.[26]

Figure 5.5. Minnesota Adult ESL Enrollments, 1998–2004

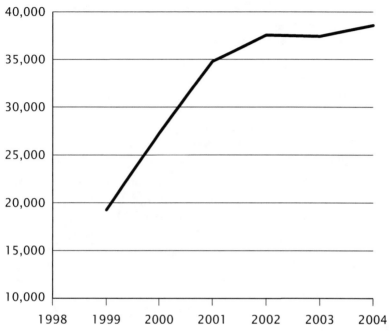

Source: "Minnesota ABE Impact Report," Adult Basic Education Office, Minnesota Department of Education, 2006.

Noncredit English language instruction is an important component of ABE that is administered by the Department of Education with federal funding. In 2005, the programs served 48,000 ESL learners, and programming in the state has increased ten-fold since 1989 (see Figure 5.5). This dramatic increase has resulted in long waiting lists. Although community colleges have been open to accommodating immigrant students for noncredit classes with Pell grant funding, they have not kept up with the demand.

The state director of ABE programs cited several exemplary programs, such as one at the International Institute of Minnesota that combines ESL, GED, and job training. Other outstanding programs include one operated through a contract with the Hmong American Partnership, and others in the suburban communities of Anoka and Robbinsdale. Assessments of the quality of these programs are based upon the results of standardized testing and comparisons with target goals that are negotiated with the federal funders. The director commented that:

Needs are increasing—there are more immigrants and refugees to serve and more high school dropouts. As we put more standards on high school students, they look for options and go to work, so they check out of the educational system just to come back later. Minnesota, like other states, has terrible graduation rates, especially for minority students, but as ABE alone we're not able to deal with this huge demand—between these dropout statistics and the increase in immigrants—it's simply overwhelming our system. You can see this in our impact report.

Recent state funding cuts in ABE programs have had a negative impact on services for immigrants seeking to learn English. In order to stem backlash from his initial speeches regarding penalties for undocumented immigrants, Governor Pawlenty announced a series of initiatives that included one-time, supplemental funding for ESL programs for immigrants and refugees. An official engaged in administering an ABE program commented that "this allows for very limited programming because it won't be there the next year, so the issue is: how do we sustain grant-driven programs like that?"

POLICIES RELATED TO HEALTH CARE, SOCIAL SERVICES, AND PUBLIC ASSISTANCE

Minnesota has been a leader in a health and social service programs for diverse populations over the years. In 2002, the state legislature passed a bill to allocate $350,000 toward the elimination of health disparities between white and minority populations, including the foreign-born. The funding was inadequate to address the large disparities, but it demonstrated recognition of the problem. In spite of these efforts, racial and ethnic groups in Minnesota face significant barriers to care and high levels of adverse health outcomes. In 2003, the Department of Human Services surveyed 4,902 enrollees in the Minnesota Health Care Program (MHCP) for low-income families. They found that "among the racial and ethnic populations included in the study, the groups most likely to be immigrants (Hispanic/Latino, Hmong and Somali) generally report the greatest number of barriers."[27]

In 2002, the commissioners of Health and Human Services called for the creation of an Immigrant Health Task Force to make recommendations regarding the health needs of the foreign-born. Among other things, the report focused on the need for education of providers, funding of interpreters, preparation of immigrant health providers, and public policy changes regarding the collection of data on the foreign-born.[28]

In Hennepin County (which includes Minneapolis), the Office of Multicultural Services runs a variety of educational programs and health services with workers who speak thirty-two different languages. A health care provider who directs an international medicine program echoes the compliments of other policymakers when she says: "I have been proud to be a part of Minnesota, taking care of refugees and immigrants over the past twenty-three years. It is my impression that Minnesota has done a pretty good job in reaching out to new arrivals . . . working with non-profit organizations to provide orientation, education, and support."

In spite of a history of progressive health and human service programs, federal cuts in benefits to immigrants have had a significant impact in Minnesota as legislators have mimicked congressional steps to restrict benefits for immigrants by insuring that individuals who are not documented do not receive any public assistance, including MFIP (Minnesota Family Investment Program), food stamps, or health care. One foundation officer commented on the politicization of immigration policy discussions in the state: "As this big debate begins this week on the immigration legislation, the tendency of so many politicians to use immigration as a wedge issue is just horrifying. They talk about the 'drain on classrooms, educations and welfare.'"

A state senator representing large numbers of immigrants describes the change:

> The state has historically done a good job in responding to immigrants and refugees coming to Minnesota, but in the last four years our state has fallen short of its obligation to meet immigrants' needs. We have systematically taken away state money that supports programs such as adult basic education, community education, English Language Learning, and other programs that directly benefit immigrants in the state.

The executive director of the Jay and Rose Phillips Family Foundation described the ways in which foundations have tried to respond to the funding shortfalls by strengthening the leadership and management practices of existing nonprofits, and their efforts to collaborate:

> Unfortunately, the increase in our immigrant populations has corresponded with a downturn in government support. We are increasing our payout, not as a way to replace federal dollars, but in recognition

that these are hard times, especially for new organizations. And hard times are when you need to invest in new thinking and in strengthening organizational effectiveness.[29]

The impetus for many of these cuts was federal welfare reform that severely curtailed the access of many foreign-born residents to needed services. In August 1996, the Personal Responsibility Work Opportunity Reconciliation Act (P.L.104-193) was signed into law, ending a sixty-year federal entitlement guaranteeing families some basic level of assistance during periods of economic hardship. The federal government permitted states to deny assistance to some immigrant groups under welfare reform, but Minnesota did not elect that option. With the denial of federal funds for cash assistance and food stamps, state funds were used to make up the difference. However, in 2003, the state legislature stripped most health coverage from undocumented immigrants. The institution of copayments for health services created another barrier for low-income immigrants, as did restrictions on the breadth of coverage of the Minnesota Care state health insurance plan.

Several components of welfare reform negatively impacted the health and well-being of foreign-born residents. Even when legal immigrants meet eligibility requirements, mandated verification of legal status has had what one policymaker calls "a chilling effect" because immigrants are worried that they might jeopardize their immigration status. Furthermore, there has been little accommodation of services to meet the needs of immigrants. The executive director of a nonprofit coalition notes that "diversionary work programs and the MFIP public assistance program offer the same services to immigrants as to residents, but are not tailored to their special needs."[30] Culturally appropriate and bilingual programs are essential.

Eligibility for benefits depends upon an individual's immigration status and date of arrival in the United States. Those who entered the country after December 1997 generally have been excluded from all benefits except emergency care. As explained by an attorney at an organization serving Latino clients,

A pregnant woman who is undocumented can only get health benefits for labor and delivery if she arrived after 1998. . . . Another example is SSI, a federal program for low-income seniors and the disabled; eligibility depends upon status and arrival time . . . the state has responded to federal budget cuts by providing some benefits, but it has also cut back benefits to immigrants . . . other state funded benefits have time limits; I don't know what will happen to those immigrants when the benefits sunset. In July of 2003 there was new legislation passed that got rid of the Emergency General Assistance Medical Care program (EGAMC). As a result, lawful permanent residents (LPRs) have no safety net coverage for emergencies. Similarly, undocumented immigrants between eighteen and sixty-four who can't meet the categorical eligibility requirements for Medical Assistance have no safety net medical coverage. Before elimination of the EGAMC program they could have gotten health care coverage for "emergencies" and for chronic health conditions, such as diabetes, heart problems, and mental health problems.

An elected official noted that after welfare reform "Minnesota tried to bridge the gap, but because it is so large and the budget is constrained, we cannot make up the federal budget cuts, and we cannot even sustain our own in-state programs that are currently in place." Others criticized the state for stringent budget cuts that disadvantaged all low-income residents. In fact, between 1996 and 2004, Minnesota was one of only nine states where the percentage of low-income children without health insurance increased by 11 percent, rather declined. An editorial in the *Minneapolis Star Tribune* attributed the increase to the "no new taxes" policies of the governor and the legislature.

By insisting that Minnesota fix its budget deficit without raising taxes, they had to make dramatic cuts in the state's health care system— chiefly Medical Assistance for poor families and Minnesota Care for the working poor—and, in so doing, they whittled away steadily at a system that had made Minnesota a national leader.[31]

The director of a legal center dealing with the needs of children added, "I don't think we've done a good job at all responding to federal budget cuts that affect low income individuals . . . the last cuts were not very good to low-income people, including refugees and immigrants." She added that "not enough attention is paid to mental health and long-term stress. This is a huge piece—especially for children."

The complexity of categories of immigration status makes questions of eligibility even more difficult. A recent study conducted by the State Legislative Auditor's Office found that over 70 percent of the health benefit determination cases contained errors, and 18 percent of these affected eligibility for benefits. These errors have serious repercussions for refugees, asylees, and permanent residents who account for 80 percent of the noncitizen recipients of Medical Assistance (MA), General Assistance Medical Care (GAMC), and Refugee Medical Assistance in fiscal year 2005. The auditors were careful to attribute the errors to the difficulty of determining whether noncitizens are eligible for public health care, rather than to deliberate error. They recommended that the Department of Human Services designate a specialist in eligibility designation, and provide updated guides and training on eligibility and how to validate immigration status and assess sponsor income. Access to health and social services varies greatly depending upon immigrant status.

Refugees are eligible for entitlement programs for eight months. After that, they may or may not be eligible to continue to receive medical assistance; if they are employed, their coverage depends upon the availability of employer-based programs.

The manager of a county cultural service program described the plight of asylees who receive no food or cash support, and individuals under federal temporary protective status (TPS) who are ineligible for benefits, and who must reapply annually to stay in the country. People with developmental delays and many elderly immigrants are ineligible for Social Security, at a time when many resources for mental health disability have dried up.

The international clinic director quoted earlier calls the cuts in health services for refugees and immigrants "part of a totally dysfunctional system of health care for citizens." She adds that the state has not responded to the health needs of immigrants, and that eligibility is so complicated that

> I don't even know how to describe how awful it is to express these miserable situations that people get into. The trends are not good. There is an increase in the uninsured population. Resources are dwindling. This has been overwhelming to the community clinics that are available. Millions of dollars absorbed by hospitals are not getting reimbursed.

The manager of a large public health program confirmed the negative impacts of budget cuts on immigrant health:

> The trend over the past decade has been a reduction in the core public health infrastructure funds that come through the Department of Health to county health agencies. Although there are funds to help new refugee arrivals, there are no funds for immigrants or for longer-term help for refugees. Furthermore, there is no system in place to

track the health needs of non-refugees. As a result, access to needed health and social services is a huge issue. Particular needs include
high-quality interpreter services, advocacy, and transportation to
medical appointments

When asked how the state has responded to federal budget cuts that
affect access to services for low-income individuals, she commented:

> We have not responded; our state governor has not taken leadership.
> Local collaborations between neighborhood-based organizations and
> health care organizations are where the leadership is coming from—
> the state departments of health and human services have been at the
> table, but more leadership has come from nonprofit and private col-
> laborations. If you are looking for positive examples of what the state
> government has done, there really are no examples.

In spite of recent cuts, some policymakers believe that health programs for immigrants in Minnesota are still better than those in many
other states. There are many excellent individuals and agencies working
in this area, but the future is not promising because, as one state official
complained, the health needs of the foreign-born are "not on the radar
screen" of state government. Of particular concern is the lack of health
insurance, especially among lower-income immigrants and the undocumented. Another program director called the state response to the needs
of immigrants "one of inactiveness." He noted that, unlike undocumented residents,

> Refugees get some assistance, but not undocumented immigrants,
> and the legislature only looks at short-term costs of care. There is
> some state funding for diverse communities, but it is insufficient, and
> cut-backs in federal programs and the lack of work-based insurance
> exacerbate the problem. Needs are particularly acute outside of the
> metropolitan area. Although community organizations do what they
> can, the needs outweigh their ability to offer services.

The need for additional trained and competent interpreters in Minnesota is acute. The Department of Human Services has made more
translated materials available as the result of a lawsuit and—unlike programs in many other states—Medical Assistance in Minnesota reimburs-
es interpreter services. However, there is little information in other
languages about benefits or choices among health plans, and lack of

bilingual staff makes many individuals reluctant to access services. The state response to this problem has been minimal, although some important documents have been translated into Spanish, Hmong, and Somali. Counties have been asked by the state to submit a "limited English plan" to make services accessible, but there has been little enforcement of the regulation.

Editors of the *Minneapolis Star Tribune* recently cited another budget cut that negatively impacts low-income immigrants—the reduction in eligibility for subsidized childcare programs. "Since 2003, Minnesota has cut just over $200 million from child-care assistance programs. Those reductions prompted eligibility changes that denied more poor families child-care help. Lawmakers also increased parent copays and froze reimbursement rates for providers—despite the fact that their costs have gone up."

In sum, the legislature has cut health care and social service eligibility for immigrants, making it difficult to qualify for Medical Assistance. Although federal cuts were the driving force behind these changes, many of the policymakers interviewed for this report directly implicated the governor in further curtailing services for immigrants.

POLICIES RELATED TO SECURITY ISSUES

Concern over national security has served as the impetus—and in some cases the guise—for a number of restrictive immigration measures in Minnesota, including color-coding immigrants' drivers' licenses and denying licenses to undocumented residents. After the inauguration of Governor Pawlenty in January 2003, his first bill before the legislature was a proposal to stamp visa expiration dates on drivers' licenses. When the legislature failed to pass the measure, Pawlenty's chief of public safety used administrative discretion to mandate the changes.[32] A Latino community organizer commented on this policy:

> We have enough support from senators and legislators, but everything gets blocked by the governor. This is getting worse after September 11th. He is denying access to Minnesota ID, and it's really hurting illegal immigrants. If they don't have it, they don't have access to many services.

A policymaker working on programming for children compared the Pawlenty response to that of previous administrations:

> When Perpich was governor, the Tiananmen Square events occurred in China. . . . Perpich made a very clear statement that the Chinese could stay in Minnesota—he was very welcoming to Chinese students—they would not have been able to go back to the country and feel safe. When the state (welcomed) Hmong resettlement—that was also a very clear statement. . . . However, more recently, with Pawlenty's statements about illegal immigration—it makes it very confusing, since many don't distinguish between legal and illegal immigrants. These statements make you feel that you are not welcome—regardless of immigrant status.

In addition to the governor and the legislature, some other state officeholders have taken controversial public positions directly or indirectly related to immigration. Just before the 2004 election, Secretary of State Mary Kiffmeyer, a Republican, was criticized for distributing flyers that suggested that voters be wary of people coming to voting precincts with "shaved heads or short hair who smell of unusual herbal/flower water or perfume . . . wear baggy clothing or appear to be whispering to themselves, as they might be 'homicide bombers.'" Some local election officials refused to distribute the posters, suggesting that they could lead to harassment of particular racial, ethnic, or religious groups.[33] On the other hand, a few years earlier, in 2001, Kiffmeyer went to the state legislature to propose that election ballots be printed in multiple languages to reduce errors on the part on voters with limited English proficiency.

Some of the anti-immigrant rhetoric in Minnesota has been exacerbated by high-profile crimes and security threats. A month before the World Trade Center attacks, Zacarias Moussaoui, the so-called twentieth hijacker, was arrested on immigration charges in the state, as a result of alerts from a flight-school instructor. A few months later, a number of Somali money-transfer services were raided and accused by the federal government of unwittingly providing a source of funding to the al Qaeda terrorist network. The *Minneapolis Star Tribune* reported that soon thereafter an audience member at a town meeting in the Minneapolis suburb of Bloomington was applauded when he questioned the loyalty of Somali immigrants.[34]

Widely reported crimes that may have increased fear of immigrants have included purported Mexican gang involvement in methamphetamine distribution in the state, and the highly publicized arrest of Alfonso Rodriguez, Jr., a Latino resident from Minnesota charged with the kidnapping, rape, and murder of North Dakota student Dru Sjodin. In neighboring Wisconsin, Chai Soua Vang, a Hmong resident of St. Paul, was convicted of murdering six deer hunters and wounding two others during a confrontation over trespassing in the Wisconsin woods. No studies are available to gauge the impact of these highly publicized stories, but fear of crime is one concern frequently cited by some anti-immigrant groups in the state.

Policies at the federal level have fueled many of the changes in the local immigration policies aimed at promoting public security. Many undocumented immigrants in Minnesota have been intimidated by a wave of anti-immigrant rhetoric and by the threat of Immigration and Customs Enforcement (ICE) raids. In Faribault, for example, the annual *Cinco de Mayo* celebration was not held this year—in part because Latino community members have been keeping a low profile. Similarly, members of a local group that has scheduled "talking circles" with foreign-born community members report that attendance has dropped off since the ICE raids. In May 2006, federal raids reached Minnesota, as ICE agents in the state began aggressively to pursue individuals with previous deportation orders. In response to reports that the agents were falsely representing themselves as police, Minneapolis mayor R. T. Rybak joined the city police chief and the city council to protest the practice, charging that it undermined the credibility of local law enforcement.[35]

On the other hand, Governor Pawlenty has been a major proponent of collaboration between local and federal officials to identify undocumented immigrants. A state official working with the governor defended his policies as a necessary response to the threat of terrorism:

> There is a perception that our borders are porous; illegal immigration, the way we deal with it is haphazard and lacks consistency. Therefore people involved with homeland security see it as problematic that people are coming and going and contraband is being smuggled in carloads across the border, figuratively I mean, and it doesn't bode well for security and for potential terrorists if that kind of coming and going can take place. Approximately a year ago we rolled out a new MN driver's license and ID card with multiple features, security features, on the card and in the card. At the time we were of the belief that this was of the most secure license in the country, but in the last twelve to fourteen months other states may have caught up with us. We were at the front end of security for licenses, and we felt that was a good way to secure the state ID card, which is a gateway document for a lot of other documents. The new ID card was an anti-fraud/anti-theft preventative measure. Certainly there is some overlap with the terrorist/homeland security areas and probably will continue to be that way.

A legal advocate for immigrants described some of the negative impact of these measures on refugees and asylees:

> The most important thing I've observed from my clients is that it's very difficult to manage the bureaucracy of identification documents, work permits, green cards. Adults who come from another state have a problem because ID from other states is not acceptable in Minnesota. Most of the asylees and refugees don't have their work documents up to date; they are not required to because they are asylees and refugees. Juveniles run into problems when they get old enough to want a driver's license. My clients talk to me about that problem a lot.

One proposal that has been particularly controversial is the banning of "sanctuary ordinances"—policies passed by the city councils of Minneapolis and St. Paul prohibiting law enforcement officers from asking residents for proof of visa status unless it is related to a criminal charge or investigation. Both the police chiefs of St. Paul and Minneapolis have spoken out in favor of sanctuary ordinances, and against the ban, on the grounds that it would erode hard-won trust in immigrant communities and make it less likely that foreign-born residents would report crimes.[36] Nevertheless, the banning of sanctuary ordinances and tougher penalties for creating and using fake identification were included in a House Omnibus Public Safety Bill that was approved by a vote of 94 to 37. Other provisions of the governor's proposals to stiffen penalties for using false identification and to deputize law enforcement officials to enforce federal immigration laws have been incorporated into the House Public Safety Bill (HF3308). No equivalent bills passed the Democratic (DFL)-controlled state senate.

In March 2006, HF3308 was introduced into the Minnesota House of Representatives. The bill included provisions based upon several of the public security proposals put forward by Governor Pawlenty in December 2005. These included the creation of a human trafficking task force, increased penalties for "labor trafficking," and for developing or using fraudulent documents. The bill also gave the commissioner of public safety the authority to enter into memoranda of understanding with federal immigration and justice officials to verify citizenship and immigration data of individuals who are arrested.

As noted earlier in this chapter, a number of immigrant rights, religious, and human rights organizations in the state, as well as the police chiefs of St. Paul and Minneapolis, made public statements against HF3308, arguing that the provisions would stigmatize immigrants and make them less likely to cooperate with law enforcement officials. Some legislators were surprised by the opposition from law enforcement agencies; their concern appears to have led to the suppression of a companion bill in the state senate.

The governor's stance and the House Public Safety Bill alienated many immigrant advocacy groups. At one hearing for HF3308, there were over twenty individuals testifying in opposition, and only one testifying in favor. In spite of this, when asked which groups have been advocating for less restrictive policies, a member of the governor's staff responded "none that I'm aware of; no one is advocating for less than what we have now. There are groups concerned about adding *more* restrictive policies, but I don't think that anyone believes we should have less than we do now." He went on to defend Governor Pawlenty's stance on immigration, saying:

> We need to do more on illegal immigration than just protect the borders and fight illegal immigration. We need to find ways to regulate immigration to make it legal for people to come here. The governor is not just enforcement and anti-theft oriented. He has a balanced approach to this. He's met with members of the immigrant community and gotten their input. He is not anti-immigrant, and I think it's important to point that out.

At the same time, a Latino law enforcement officer gave a different perspective:

> For the past four years there have been a series of bills and rules enacted by the Department of Public Safety. There has been a lot of focus on homeland security, and what disturbs the community is that the bills seem to be directed mainly at immigrants and immigrant drivers. They use homeland security to address immigrant policy. Most of the bills are targeted and focused on immigrants.

POLICIES RELATED TO RACIAL PROFILING

A 2005 research study by Hispanic Advocacy and Community Empowerment through Research (HACER) and the Council on Crime and Justice[37] found that Hispanic youth in Minnesota were overrepresented by 92 percent in apprehensions in the year 2000, although they were less likely than non-Hispanic white youth to be charged with a felony or with drug or property offenses. The authors of the report suggest that prejudgments and stereotypes play a role in these figures. They cite a probation officer in Kandiyohi County, Minnesota, who stated:

> I think there might be some prejudice on the part of the community— you know, I think a lot of the old timers, you know, tend to say "He's a Hispanic kid. He's gonna steal your car. He's gonna, you know, he's sellin' drugs. He's doin' this." I think maybe they would tend to give a white kid a little break that they wouldn't give the Hispanic kid.

In 2001, the Minnesota legislature enacted a statute calling for a study of racial profiling across the state. Sixty-five law enforcement agencies elected to participate by collecting and analyzing traffic stop data from January 1 to December 31, 2002. Analysis of the resulting 194,189 traffic stops demonstrated that Latinos (and African Americans) were much more likely than non-Hispanic whites to have their vehicles stopped and searched, but also *less likely* to be found with contraband. The authors of the report concluded that there was "a strong likelihood that racial/ethnic bias plays a role in search policies and practices in Minnesota."[38]

Students in the author's seminar on immigration and social justice analyzed reports from the racial profiling studies from the perspective of the constitutional rights of immigrants. They concluded that racial profiling constitutes "a violation of the 14th Amendment's provision for equal treatment under the law, the 4th Amendment's provision for search and seizure based on probable cause and the Civil Rights Act's prohibition of discrimination based on national origin by agencies receiving federal funds."[39] In the course of their research, they also uncovered a disturbing and apparently widespread practice in the state and the region, whereby Border Patrol agents are routinely called as "interpreters" for Latinos with limited English proficiency. In many of these cases, the individuals pulled over were not informed of the alleged traffic violation. In cases where the Border Patrol investigated Latino drivers' or passengers' immigration status and found they were undocumented, they could then revert to their roles as government agents authorized to detain them for deportation proceedings. Professional interpreters should be individuals who are impartial; the use of Border Patrol agents as interpreters who then initiate questioning beyond the scope of the alleged traffic infraction violates this standard, and is a perverse means of implementing federal guidelines mandating the use of interpreters for individuals charged with offenses. The students concluded that:

Since part of the Border Patrol's official mandate is to enforce the Immigration and Nationality Act, questioning [individuals with limited English proficiency] during routine traffic stops . . . is a clear misuse of the circumstantial overlap of the roles of local law enforcement and Border Patrol. Given the established prevalence of racial profiling for these stops in the first place, immigrants are clearly discriminated against since they are more likely to be stopped, and to have their immigration status questioned.[40]

Racial profiling is a statewide problem in Minnesota, but there has been more attention to the problem in the Twin Cities than in other parts of the state. Some of this may be due to a racial profiling law suit brought by the NAACP against the St. Paul Police Department in 2001. As a result of the suit, the St. Paul police department initiated a series of community meetings and police training sessions. One policymaker we interviewed described community–police relations in the Twin Cities as tenuous: "Law enforcement in the Twin Cities has far more to lose when it comes to racial profiling issues, as the spotlight has been on them for so long." She added that police practices regarding questioning of immigrants may not always conform to publicly stated policies.

There's an implication in the tone of casual questioning that occurs when a Latino is pulled over by the police: "Where are you from?" (answer: "St. Paul"). "No, where are you really from?" This is widespread. One way that the police department got around racial profiling is how the police would report the race of the person stopped. The line of questioning would include nationality and citizenship, but then "race" is marked as "White."

POLICIES RELATED TO LABOR FORCE ISSUES

Jobs in manufacturing, the hospitality industry, construction, food processing, and agriculture have been a strong magnet for immigrants, who constitute about 40 percent of the Latino population in Minnesota. Food processing jobs have been a particularly important lure for Mexican immigrants from rural states of the Mexican Central Plateau, who have a long history of migration to the Midwest as seasonal agricultural workers. As a result, Mexicans are now the largest foreign-born group in the state (16 percent).

Minnesota has the highest Latino labor force participation rate in the nation. For example, 70 percent of Latinos in Minnesota were employed in 1999, compared with 61 percent nationally.

Unlike some other states, Minnesota has had few sites where day laborers congregate to find daily work, perhaps because the economy is strong and full-time jobs have been available for immigrants. The weather in Minnesota may also limit the practice, since during many months of the year the temperature is too low to make outdoor day laborer solicitation feasible.

POLICIES RELATED TO HOUSING

There is a severe shortage of affordable housing in Minnesota. The state has a well-established program of emergency housing and housing finance programs, but as one official noted, it does not come close to meeting the state's needs. He attributes much of the problem to serious cuts in federal funding for housing, and asked, "Should you give a low report card grade to a state that is trying to fill a hole it did not create? I think we are doing some of our best work. The state cannot fill in all the gaps that the federal government created."

Federal cuts have affected Section 8 housing for low-income families, and as one advocate for children and family services described it,

> there are really, really long waits for that rental assistance. . . . What I observe is that the immigrant community struggles with lack of affordable housing, low incomes, low cash available, and the realities of the high cost of health care. I just read something about the significant Hmong population living at "Mary's Place." That's the first time I've learned of an immigrant population living in a homeless shelter.

In 2002 and 2003, students in a University of Minnesota graduate class on Immigrant Health Issues conducted in-depth interviews with sixty-two health and social service providers working with immigrants in the state of Minnesota. In spite of the fact that many of the providers worked with immigrants and refugees with severe health problems, the lack of affordable housing was one of the most frequently mentioned issues facing their clients.

The cost of housing is so high that many immigrants need to work eighty hours a week in order to pay the rent. Limits to the number of occupants in a unit cause also problems because it makes it difficult for low-income workers to share the rent. The coordinator of a Latino organization in the Twin Cities commented that, while there are successful housing programs for some groups, there are none for undocumented Latinos, one of the most marginalized groups. Many landlords are requiring Social Security numbers and drivers' licenses that make it difficult for Latinos to find housing. Others are exploited by unscrupulous landlords.

> Documents are written in English, not in Spanish, so they sign whatever. They need somebody to look after them. There are no advocates or mediators. They are by themselves. . . . Sometimes they lose their jobs because immigration starts following them and then they miss work and can't pay rent, and then they get evicted and then . . . no one will rent to you again.

Another immigrant advocate noted:

> There are tenant problems within buildings, and within individual units. Our organization does a lot of organizing, and we find things like unreasonable fees, unreasonable lack of improvements, and conditions that are bad. Members of the immigrant community might not be as aware of their rights, might feel intimidated about questioning landlords. There are lots and lots of problems, and lots of lies dealing with property management. . . . When people get threatened with eviction, the eviction threat goes on their record, and it ends up being a problem getting housing in the future.

Other housing problems have more to do with communication and cultural barriers than with availability. The manager of a large housing program described these barriers as huge, citing examples from Somali residents:

> Homes and housing in Somalia are different than here. They cook with a lot more oil, and there are fire and safety issues. Many landlords don't want to deal with it. A recent issue came about when inspectors came in and looked at traditional drapes and said they had to get rid of them because were creating mold. We need to do community building and help people understand what mold does. . . . Things don't translate easily. . . . Laws and housing there are different. It can be a great pleasure, but as an owner, many people don't want to have

to deal with that or with food that is greasy and sticks to the walls or with the smells. To house the Somalis next to others isn't always easy.

One group with particularly severe housing needs is Latino migrant farmworkers. In 2002, Centro Campesino published a report on migrant worker housing,[41] in which they reported severe shortages of adequate and affordable housing. Many families paid rents that were well above the standard affordability guideline of 39 percent of income allocated to housing, and 87 percent described the quality of their housing as "negative." Over a fifth reported having experienced discrimination when searching for housing.

In spite of the obstacles, there are some examples of successful housing programs for documented immigrants and refugees. One expert cited a development in Eden Prairie that has "opened their doors to Somalis," and the evolution of a large housing project by the University of Minnesota from predominantly Southeast Asian to Somali residents. Some other sites provide safe, affordable housing, but many more are needed.

CONCLUSIONS

Has the reception of immigrants cooled in Minnesota? A majority of the policymakers interviewed for this study feel that it has. In general, they concurred that, because of its strong nonprofit and philanthropic organizations, Minnesota has done a good job of responding to the changing demographics of the state, but that state funding reductions in the past five years have undercut important programs. Although there are still many examples of exemplary programs for immigrants and refugees, service providers are finding it more difficult to keep programs intact, let alone to secure support to keep up with inflationary costs and rising demand.

Public attitudes toward immigrants and support for programs benefiting them also appear to be changing, as the result of several factors. These include concerns over social spending, the rising numbers of foreign-born residents, increases in unauthorized immigration, and fears regarding national security and cultural identity. Most of these issues mimic national debates, but some observers had thought that Minnesota's "social compact" would provide a degree of immunity to anti-immigrant discourse and to the pressure to cut health and social programs. Instead, as the state experiences a population shift to conservative and highly segregated suburbs, many voters appear to have reduced their support for the state's traditionally progressive political agenda.

This defection is particularly noteworthy because of the state's pride in its historically liberal populist bent. Minnesota ranks first in the nation on voter turnout, first on six of the seven most recent evaluations of the United Way's "State of Caring Index,"[42] and second (after New Hampshire) as the "most livable state" on the 2006 Morgan Quitno index.[43] Yet social programs are expensive, and Minnesotans have joined voters in many other states protesting rising taxes. In a paper commissioned for the Minnesota Community Project, researcher John Farrell describes the end of an era of social liberalism in Minnesota, defined as activist government, high public investments, and civic participation. He notes that recent elections have reversed the traditional dominance of the Democratic (DFL) Party, which controlled the house for two-thirds of the past thirty-two years and dominated the senate for all but two of those years.[44]

Furthermore, there are cracks in Minnesota's social success story. Income inequality is increasing in the state,[45] and many of the leading social indicators mask deep disparities between the white majority and populations of color. Minnesota ranked seventh out of the fifty states in high school graduation rates for white students in 2000, while recording one of the lowest graduation rates in the country for Latinos (53 percent). When Barbara Ehrenreich tested her ability to live on a minimum wage salary in three American cities, it was Minneapolis that presented the biggest housing challenge.[46] While the state can still boast of myriad programs designed to improve the health and welfare of all residents, support for many of these programs is eroding as voters follow the national trend toward increasing conservatism and concern over social spending that contributes to rising taxes and budget deficits. To wit, over half of the savings that resulted from welfare reform in Minnesota came at the expense of benefits for immigrants.

When former Vice President Walter Mondale commissioned the Minnesota Community Survey in 2004, he was startled by the depth of anger of a number of suburban and exurban residents toward what they perceived to be the "free ride" received by immigrants in the state. In the words of a white woman in Anoka County:

> These groups are getting very large, and it seems when they come over here they are getting all the tax breaks. They get all this help. They get this, they get that . . . and those of us who have fought for this country, who have paid our taxes, who raise our children, and who live in

this country and in this state are the ones that are paying for all those people to get all those breaks and our children and our lifestyles are not increasing—they are staying stagnant. Some are still staying at poverty level because these people who are coming into Minnesota from other countries are getting what we, as Minnesotans or American citizens, ought to be having.

In the wake of welfare reform, the attacks on the World Trade Center in 2001 provided further rationale for individuals advocating for more restrictive immigration policies. As a result, views that would formerly have been called xenophobic, or even racist, have been cloaked in rhetoric regarding national security. In a state that has the largest Somali population in the United States, anti-Muslim sentiments have easily translated into anti-immigrant rhetoric.

The recent national furor over competing proposals for immigration reform has further polarized Minnesotans. The presence of 40,000 marchers supporting immigrant rights reflected strong support from nonprofits, immigrant advocacy groups, unions, and the Catholic Church. On the other hand, the constant barrage of media stories about undocumented immigrants has led many individuals to overestimate the size of this population, and to assume incorrectly that the majority of immigrants in the state are unauthorized.

The irony of the controversy over immigration policy in Minnesota is that immigrants are vital to the future of the state's economy. Over 94 percent of the population is U.S.-born, and the vast majority is of European origin. By 2020, Minnesota will have more retirees than school children, and migration will become the largest source of new workers in the state. In spite of these realities, if current trends persist, it will be partisan politics at both national and state levels, rather than economic or social justice arguments, that determine the course of future policies toward immigrants.

APPENDIX A

SURVEY FORM USED IN TELEPHONE INTERVIEWS WITH INDIVIDUALS KNOWLEDGEABLE ABOUT STATE SERVICES AND POLICIES FOR IMMIGRANTS IN MINNESOTA

Name of respondent:
Title:
Date:
Name of interviewer:

I'm calling on behalf of Professor Katherine Fennelly at the Humphrey Institute of Public Affairs. As part of a national project we are preparing a report on state and local policy responses to recent increases in immigration in Minnesota. In order to do that, we plan to speak to people like you who are knowledgeable about how Minnesota state policies affect immigrants and refugees.

I'd like to speak to you for about 30 minutes to get your thoughts on this. Please note that this is a research study and that your participation is completely voluntary.

INSERT RELEVANT PAGE ACCORDING TO THE TOPIC OF YOUR INTERVIEW

PRIMARY AND SECONDARY EDUCATION

1. How has the state of Minnesota responded to increases in the numbers of immigrants and refugees over the past ten years? What policy changes have you observed?
2. How has the state responded to increases in enrollment of children from diverse cultures in primary and secondary schools?

3. What are some specific changes in programs or funding related to primary and secondary schooling?

4. In your opinion, what are examples of successful programs and policies related to the education of immigrant children? (BE SURE TO GET NAMES AND LOCATIONS)

5. Are there important unmet needs related to immigrant children in Minnesota schools? (IF YES, GET DETAILS)

6. Has No Child Left Behind had a particular impact on immigrant youth? (IF YES, How? PROBE FOR HOW MN HAS RESPONDED)

7. (IF NOT MENTIONED): How would you describe state funding and programs for Limited English Proficiency students?

8. What "report card grade" would you give to the state of Minnesota in responding to the educational needs of immigrant youth? A, B, C, D or F.

9. Are there particular reports that we should read that describe state policies related to this topic? GET SPECIFIC INFORMATION ON HOW TO OBTAIN REPORTS

10. Are there any other comments you would like to add?

Thank you very much for your time!

ACCESS TO POST-SECONDARY EDUCATION

1. How has the state of Minnesota responded to increases in the numbers of immigrants and refugees over the past ten years? What policy changes have you observed?

2. Can you comment on issues related to financing and access to higher education on the part of immigrant youth?

3. What are the prospects for passage of the DREAM Act in Minnesota?

4. How have colleges, universities and technical schools in Minnesota responded to the educational needs of immigrant youth?

5. What are some examples of successful programs and policies? (BE SURE TO GET NAMES AND LOCATIONS)

6. Are there important unmet needs related to education for immigrant children? (IF YES, GET DETAILS)

7. What "report card grade" would you give to the state of Minnesota in responding to the post-secondary educational needs of immigrant youth? A, B, C, D or F.

8. Are there particular reports that we should read that describe state policies related to this topic? **GET SPECIFIC INFORMATION ON HOW TO OBTAIN REPORTS**

9. Is there anyone else who is very knowledgeable about the topics we have just discussed whom you suggest we contact? **IF YES:**
  a. Name
  b. Title
  c. Agency
  d. Phone number
  e. Email

10. Are there any other comments you would like to add?
  Thank you very much for your time!

HEALTH CARE

1. How has the state of Minnesota responded to increases in the numbers of immigrants and refugees over the past ten years? What policy changes have you observed?

2. How much access do immigrants in Minnesota have to needed health and social services?

3. How has the state responded to these needs?

4. What are some specific changes in programs or funding related to access to health care for immigrants in Minnesota?

5. What are examples of successful programs or policies related to access to health services for immigrants? **(BE SURE TO GET NAMES AND LOCATIONS)**

6. Aside from access, what other health related needs are faced by immigrants in Minnesota?

7. How has Minnesota responded to federal budget cuts that affect the access of low-income individuals to health care (and therefore also affect immigrants who are in low-income categories)?

8. What "report card grade" would you give to the state of Minnesota in responding to the health needs of immigrants? A, B, C, D, or F.

9. Are there particular reports that we should read that describe state policies related to this topic? **GET SPECIFIC INFORMATION ON HOW TO OBTAIN REPORTS**

10. Are there any other comments you would like to add?
  Thank you very much for your time!

DRIVER'S LICENSE, REAL ID, POLICE, AND DAY LABORERS

1. How has the state of Minnesota responded to increases in the numbers of immigrants and refugees over the past ten years? What policy changes have you observed?

2. How have US concerns over security and prevention of terrorism affected state policies toward immigrants in Minnesota?

3. **IF NOT MENTIONED:** How has Minnesota responded to the REAL ID Act and changes in regulations regarding identification documents that are accepted for drivers' licenses, bank accounts and credit? **PROBE FOR SPECIFIC REGULATIONS**

4. Which groups have been actively advocating for restrictive policies?

5. Which groups have been advocating for less restrictive policies?

6. How would you characterize relations between the police and major immigrant groups in Minnesota? Does this vary greatly from city to city and in rural areas?

7. Are you aware of calls for the police in Minnesota to be "deputized" to identify and report undocumented immigrants in particular communities? **(IF YES:** Where?)

How have the police themselves responded to these requests? **PROBE FOR SUPPORT OR OPPOSITION FROM POLICE GROUPS**

8. In some states there have been local controversies over groups of Latino day laborers seeking work. Has this occurred in Minnesota? **(IF YES:** Can you say more about this? **PROBE FOR LOCATIONS AND INCIDENTS)**

9. How have community members reacted in these communities? How have the police reacted?

10. Are there particular reports that we should read on any of the topics we have just discussed? **GET SPECIFIC INFORMATION ON HOW TO OBTAIN REPORTS**

11. Are there any other comments you would like to add?

Thank you very much for your time!

HOUSING

1. How has the state of Minnesota responded to increases in the numbers of immigrants and refugees over the past ten years? What policy changes have you observed?

2. Can you comment on issues related to access to affordable housing for immigrants in Minnesota?

3. How has the state responded to these needs?

4. What are some specific changes in programs or funding related to access to housing for immigrants?

5. What are examples of successful housing programs and policies for immigrants in Minnesota? (BE SURE TO GET NAMES AND LOCATIONS)

6. How has Minnesota responded to federal budget cuts that affect the access of low-income individuals to housing (and therefore also affect immigrants who are in low-income categories)?

7. Other than access to affordable housing, are there other housing problems faced by immigrants in Minnesota?

8. What "report card grade" would you give to the state of Minnesota in responding to the health needs of immigrants? A, B, C, D, or F.

9. Are there particular reports that we should read that describe state programs or policies on this topic? GET SPECIFIC INFORMATION ON HOW TO OBTAIN REPORTS.

10. Are there any other comments you would like to add?

Thank you very much for your time!

APPENDIX B

OP-ED ARTICLE IN THE *MINNEAPOLIS STAR TRIBUNE*, JANUARY 9, 2006

For good reasons, police aren't meant to be immigration agents. If they were, it would erode trust and interfere with the duties of an already overburdened force.

By Katherine Fennelly

Gov. Tim Pawlenty's call for creation of a "Minnesota Illegal Immigration Enforcement Team" could undo years of gains in building trust among immigrant communities, police and service providers in Minnesota.

It is no accident that many police organizations across the United States have come out in opposition to the kind of policies that the governor is proposing. Minnesota has been a leader in community policing—a strategy that depends upon the establishment of trust between law enforcement and community members. Deputizing state and local officials to seek out undocumented immigrants will immediately erode this hard-earned trust, with the result that immigrants who are victims of or witnesses to crime will be reluctant to come forward.

Policies that require police to seek out undocumented individuals and to check visa status and place of birth are also likely to reverse progress that has been made in preventing racial profiling. The Minnesota statute prohibiting racial profiling states that "the legislature finds that the reality or public perception of racial profiling alienates people from police, hinders community policing efforts, and causes law enforcement to lose credibility and trust among the people law enforcement is sworn to protect and serve."

Although the governor's proposal calls for police checks after persons have been pulled over or cited, it is one that casts aspersion and presumes guilt on the part of immigrants in general, and Latinos in particular.

The enforcement of immigration policy is a federal, not a state responsibility. This has been wisely recognized by both the Minneapolis and St. Paul city councils in ordinances that in no way limit officials' ability to investigate suspected criminal activity. In fact, one could argue that adding immigration responsibilities to an already overburdened police force will make it less likely that they will have time to identify and arrest criminals, regardless of where they were born.

Most undocumented residents come to Minnesota to work, or to join working family members who are cleaning our hotels, hospitals and offices, picking our crops, packaging our meat, assembling our consumer products, washing our dishes and building our houses.

Unfortunately, the federal government issues far fewer employment-based visas than are needed to meet the enormous demand for this type of labor. It is our policies of recruiting workers without issuing legal visas that turn law-abiding individuals into "illegal aliens." Rather than criminalizing them, the governor should be supporting the call for rational immigration reform that meets the country's economic and social needs.

CHAPTER 6

NEBRASKA'S RESPONSES TO IMMIGRATION

Lourdes Gouveia

NEBRASKA'S CONTEXT OF RECEPTION:
THE ROLE OF POLICY AND COMMUNITY RESPONSES

INTRODUCTION

In the midst of the fiery debate regarding undocumented immigration,[1] that old elephant in the room, assimilation, was finally let out of the cage in recent congressional debates and returned to the front seat it once occupied during the early decades of the past century. Public anxieties over increased immigration historically have focused on immigrants' alleged unwillingness to assimilate. The cacophony of new languages, particularly foreign to today's largely monolingual, native-born Americans, often becomes the lightning rod for such anxieties. This is particularly true in new destination communities with little recent exposure to immigration.[2] Such unexamined fears now have materialized in a U.S. Senate bill, declaring English the national language. The dangerous tenor underlying this bill and similar national policy proposals is sure to have a boomerang impact back in the local communities that may have unwittingly informed them.

English proficiency is commonly identified by researchers as a variable associated with immigrant adaptation to host societies. However, the vast research on the subject also makes clear that a much more complex host of factors shapes assimilation trajectories and does so in not always predictable or popularly accepted ways. Second-generation children of poor and racialized immigrant laborers, for example, may

143

be fluent in English and commonly assimilate into their native country. However, when deprived of proactive government policies and compensatory programs that adequately address barriers such as poverty and discrimination, these children tend to assimilate downward, into the lower rungs of American society. Moreover, the negative effect of unaddressed barriers can linger beyond the second generation.[3]

The main purpose of this chapter is twofold: (1) to take stock of the policies and accompanying community responses that the State of Nebraska has crafted to address the challenges and opportunities posed by a growing immigrant population, and (2) to inform policies and programs designed to address those challenges and harness such opportunities. Data for the chapter were obtained by the Office of Latino/Latin American Studies (OLLAS) at the University of Nebraska at Omaha from two major sources: (1) about twenty-four personal as well as e-mailed and telephone interviews with a diversity of experts and (2) archival searches of government, media, and academic sources. Interview protocols consisted of questions about state policy and other actions aimed at addressing the growth in immigrant population in Nebraska, in general, and with regard to the specific policy area in which respondents have unique expertise (employment, health, housing, education, and law enforcement). The chapter's main focus is on state-level policies. To that aim, the author conducted an extensive search of every legislative bill that has been passed since the late 1980s whose content or impetus is associated with the new immigrant wave. However, the chapter also highlights those moments when, in the absence of state-level initiatives, local communities, agencies, and advocates are found to fill the institutional hole.

Space and lack of sufficient data does not allow for a full examination of the differential impact that policies and community responses may have had on every immigrant group in the state. However, given their sheer numbers and historical presence in the United States, it is Mexicans, and to a lesser extent other Latin American groups, that policymakers often have in mind when crafting immigration or immigrant integration policies. This chapter also is largely informed by the experiences of these groups and the author's long-term involvement in research and policy dealing primarily with low-wage, meatpacking workers, the majority of whom are from Mexico and Central America.

The chapter provides a sociodemographic profile of Nebraska's immigrant population, with special attention to Latinos, by far the largest group. The sections following this demographic profile focus on the specific policy areas mentioned above. Space confines us to highlighting some of the most important policy efforts and omissions

TABLE 6.1. INTERVIEWEES' EVALUATION OF NEBRASKA'S IMMIGRANT INTEGRATION POLICIES

NEBRASKA'S IMMIGRANT INTEGRATION POLICIES	PERCENT
Inclusive	17.2
Negligent	44.8
Exclusive	10.3
Others	10.3
No response	17.2

N = 29

at various geographical and political levels and emphasizing state-level policies enacted in the past ten to fifteen years.

The diversity of approaches followed by government policies dealing with new immigration can be generally categorized as promoting "exclusion," "inclusion," or "neglect" of the immigrant population, each with ensuing negative or positive consequences for the long-term integration of immigrants into the state's social and political fabric. The interview protocol utilized for this project asked respondents to evaluate the state along those lines. Their responses are found in Table 6.1.

IMMIGRATION POLICY AND COMMUNITY RESPONSES: A BROAD OVERVIEW

Nebraska experienced two major immigration waves during the 1900s, one at each end of the twentieth century. Southern European laborers arrived in the early 1900s to work on the railroads and in a flourishing meatpacking industry. Immigrants from Latin America, and to a lesser extent Asia and Africa, began arriving in earnest by the early 1990s and have continued to come in large numbers as the twenty-first century begins. Active recruitment by a new breed of meatpacking plants has been the major trigger of this latest migration stream, albeit immigrants arriving in Nebraska today are also filling jobs at the middle and, to a lesser extent, the upper end of the employment scale. In 2006, as earlier, immigrants are the labor engine of the state's agrofood economy and are therefore found in significant numbers in rural, not just urban, areas. In 1910, 14.8 percent of the total Nebraska population was foreign-born white and 67.6 percent of those lived in rural areas. In 2000, the foreign born made up only 4.4 percent of the total state population and 33 percent lived in rural areas, the majority of which are home to large meatpacking plants and an overwhelmingly Latino labor force.[4]

Despite differences in the national origins, proportion, and timing of these two labor migration waves, striking similarities can be found in the attitudes and government responses experienced by the poorest segments of these waves. In the early twentieth century, Greeks, Italians, and Poles, among others, were often characterized in the media and academic articles as unwilling to learn English and assimilate into American society.[5] Their growing numbers were considered a threat to workers from ethnic groups enjoying higher social rankings, as was the case with German-origin groups who had experienced their own share of discrimination in an earlier period. An *Omaha Daily News* editorial published around 1919 captured this sentiment against the Greeks, a group that eventually fled Nebraska under fear of persecution: "Greeks are a menace to the American laboring man—just as the Japs, Italians, and other similar laborers are."[6]

Official policy responses to the "immigrant problem" during the first part of the twentieth century were rather muted, contradictory, and sporadic when compared to the more persistent and vitriolic attitudes found among some segments of the general public. Nebraska did pass a law in 1919, later overturned by the U.S. Supreme Court, declaring English the official language of the state and forbidding the teaching of foreign languages in Nebraska schools. The proviso, believed to have been aimed at German immigrants, was nevertheless inscribed in the 1920 Nebraska constitution, making Nebraska the second state in the nation to declare English its official language. Efforts to ratify a constitutional change to eliminate the provision that specifically forbids teaching foreign languages in private schools failed in a 2002 referendum. Voters mistakenly feared a yes vote would amount to official support for bilingual programs.[7]

In the early part of the twentieth century, Nebraska also joined other states in establishing the "Americanization" programs popular at the time. While Native Americans, and to some extent Germans, were exposed to the most oppressive elements of this Americanization effort, immigrants in Nebraska as a whole tended to encounter a rather benevolent program administered by local neighborhood organizations such as Social Settlement. The program focused mainly on English language instruction and citizenship classes. There is also scattered evidence of collaborative efforts between the state and social service organizations and the schools to offer free health and dental clinics as well as adult education classes for immigrant parents.[8] In the end, Nebraskans seemed to recognize that these foreign-stock workers were critical to the economic vitality of a largely under-populated and depopulated state.

The reception afforded to new immigrants in recent years, especially to those from Latin America, also has been contradictory. It has varied from community to community, vitriolic among some segments of the public, and rather passive or haphazard but seldom utterly restrictionist in official state or local policies. On the contrary, as I shall detail later, the Nebraska unicameral legislature has passed or attempted to pass a series of legislations aimed at welcoming immigrants and facilitating their integration into economic and other local institutions. Local governments in rural counties dependent on meatpacking have been largely proactive in facilitating the arrival and integration of a labor force they understand is their lifeline in the aftermath of the farm and rural crises of the 1980s. In fact, media coverage and analyses of census data continuously point out that international migration has literally saved the state and many rural communities from losing population since the 1990s, something they cannot afford.[9]

While there has been some minimal activism against school bond issues and immigrant-driven housing patterns at the local levels, particularly in rural areas, these have been rare and have often failed. It is conceivable that the state's populist history and persistent labor needs have fostered what some advocates and students of local immigration believe is a somewhat positive context of reception for new immigrants. As a civil rights attorney steeped in local history put it:

> In Nebraska, there isn't anything politically entrenched around how we treat minorities. If anything is entrenched it is [the idea] that this is a state built by immigrants and newcomers. . . . You don't go out there and make it sound like you are beating up on people who have come here to work and live in Nebraska because it is an option they decided upon to better their family life. For what other reason did our grandparents come here?[10]

Unfortunately, the country's increasing fears about lax border security and rising numbers of unauthorized migrants are beginning to affect the tenor of political discourses at the local level and, to some extent, the state's policy environment. In the 2000 primary elections, for example, three of the four Republican candidates for the U.S. Senate, as well as the Democratic candidate, Ben Nelson, were anything but shy in telling their rural and urban constituencies that immigrant workers were needed in Nebraska. They advocated easing immigration laws to allow more of them to come legally to the United States. They also came out in support of temporary worker programs, even exempting some immigrant-dependent industries from immigration caps, and looked favorably at a citizenship path for temporary and unauthorized workers. In addition, all candidates, as well as the state's governor at the time, Mike Johanns, currently the U.S. secretary of agriculture, expressed their disapproval of something called Operation Vanguard,[11] an industry-by-industry, employment-enforcement strategy aimed at removing unauthorized migrants from the workplace in non-border areas, which the Immigration and Naturalization Service (INS) unsuccessfully piloted in Nebraska's meatpacking plants starting in December 1998. It continued until the months prior to the primary election of 2000.[12]

The immigration story was dramatically different in the recent primaries held in May 2006. By this time, the two candidates who had also competed in the 2000 primaries, Senator Ben Nelson, a Democrat, and former attorney general Don Stenberg, a Republican, made border enforcement and fences the centerpiece of their immigration proposals, while their earlier pro-immigration rhetoric was all but forgotten.[13] Nebraska residents lately have become increasingly animated by the "enforcement first" rhetoric that has characterized the Nelson campaign, while the other Nebraska senator, Republican Chuck Hagel, is repeatedly berated in the media for what some insist on labeling an "amnesty" immigration proposal.[14]

To be sure, many other contradictory and divergent views abound across issues and among politicians trying hard to navigate carefully the torrential waters of immigration and its diverse constituents. The entire Nebraska congressional delegation, including U.S. Representative Tom Osborne, has recently supported harsh anti-immigrant legislation in the U.S. Congress such as HR4437, the Border Protection, Antiterrorism, and Illegal Immigration Control Act of 2005. The bill will make it a crime to be in the United States illegally or provide assistance to undocumented immigrants. Yet during his recent bid to win the Nebraska GOP gubernatorial primary, Osborne took a strong stand in favor of LB239, a state bill granting qualifying children of unauthorized migrants the right to pay in-state college tuition rates.[15] The in-state tuition bill was unsuccessfully vetoed by the current governor, Dave Heineman, who, like all other candidates in the 2006 elections,[16] has sought to make illegal immigration a focal point of his campaign. "Illegal immigration," he stated in a recent mailing, "puts a burden on our taxpayers."[17] Heineman defeated Osborne for the GOP nomination for governor and is all but assured a victory in the November 2006 general election.

Conversely, Senator Hagel has achieved national stature and is currently leading a Senate compromise on comprehensive immigration reform that will include a guest worker program and earned legalization for unauthorized migrants. At the state level, a considerable number of Nebraska state senators have been proactive in a number of efforts aimed at facilitating immigrant integration. A Republican senator cast the decisive vote that allowed the Nebraska unicameral legislature to successfully override the governor's veto of the in-state tuition bill.

There is, however, an increasingly visible segment in Nebraska that seems emboldened or even newly constituted by the anti-immigrant climate brewing around the country and, arguably, some of the high-profile enforcement stands taken by some of our representatives in Congress. Immigrants are generally portrayed by this group as primarily Mexican and undocumented. The litany of complaints hurled against them is rather predictable (they do not want to assimilate or learn English, they abuse the generous public benefits system to which they are not entitled, and lately, they bring diseases into the country). In a Nebraska Public Radio program in which I participated, my opponent, an emeritus professor from the University of Nebraska Medical Center, sounded all these alarms, plus called Mexico a "hellhole" and the culture of Latin American immigrants "degenerate."[18]

Anti-immigrant voices in Nebraska have become more salient and more vicious in the weeks surrounding the large pro-immigrant marches held around the country on April 10 and May 1, 2006. On April 10, the state was in the headlines of major national news organizations when a surprising number of pro-immigrant individuals marched in rural and urban towns alike (15,000 was the last count in Omaha). As in the rest of the nation, the majority were immigrant and native-born Latinos protesting House Bill HR4437 and supporting a comprehensive immigration reform that would include a citizenship path for unauthorized migrants currently in the state.[19] A smaller number, about 3,000, marched on May 1 and delivered similar messages to the various congressional offices. As another advocate put it, "The marches did not so much change the respective positions of people per se, but [they] did also facilitate the coming out of the woodwork of a lot of the anti-immigrant forces who otherwise were just hunkered down."[20]

Until recently, anti-immigrant groups have been all but absent in Nebraska, even when compared to neighboring Iowa, which has very few. The only signs of organized anti-immigrant efforts have been billboards paid for by national organizations such as the Federation for American Immigration Reform (FAIR) that occasionally have been spotted along Interstate 80, near towns such as Grand Island and Lexington, where meatpacking plants hire large numbers of Latino immigrants, many of whom are unauthorized. More recently, however, a group calling itself Nebraskans Fed Up with Illegal Immigration organized its first protest in front of the Omaha Mexican Consulate on May 20, 2006. About ninety people showed up. Another small group, composed of residents of Omaha and surrounding nonmetropolitan areas, met at a local library on May 17 to organize a chapter of the Minutemen Civic Defense Corps, which is known for sending armed groups to patrol the U.S.-Mexico border. According to the leader, they plan to launch a series of local actions, such as surveillance of companies suspected of hiring undocumented workers and pressure on landlords not to rent to unauthorized migrants.[21]

A recent *Omaha World-Herald* article also recounted how both U.S. senators from Nebraska are receiving record numbers of calls, the majority against immigration. "You are acting stupid," a rural caller said to Senator Hagel, "close our borders." "Immigrants bring disease," said another from Omaha.[22] Letters to the editor have been running about the same, with anti-immigration letters far outnumbering those who favor less-restrictionist stands. On the other hand, some polls suggest that Nebraskans, like the rest of the nation, feel as conflicted about immigrants today as they have in the past. While 74 percent of Nebraskans surveyed agreed with the national majority that enforcement should come before other immigration reforms, less than half (47 percent) were in favor of forcibly requiring undocumented immigrants to leave the country. An even larger number (61 percent) support an immigration law that welcomes immigrants as long as terrorists, criminals, and those who will abuse the welfare system are kept out.[23]

The policy choices Nebraskans stand to make in the next months and years will determine whether the state adopts a more exclusive, inclusive, or passive approach to immigrant integration.

The role of a much denser and better-organized network of immigrant organizations, advocacy groups, and community social agencies retooling themselves to support immigrant rights and more fully integrate their immigrant workforce is an important counterweight to the exclusionary impulses found in other circles.[24] Until very recently, such community responses have been mostly concentrated, but not singularly present, in the larger urban communities such as Omaha and Lincoln. Their well-documented successes in influencing government policy changes, such as stopping Operation Vanguard, encouraging the formation of diversity and welcoming programs, and raising levels of

TABLE 6.2. WORLD REGION OF BIRTH OF FOREIGN BORN, NEBRASKA, 2004

FOREIGN-BORN POPULATION EXCLUDING POPULATION BORN "AT SEA"	TOTAL	PERCENT
Europe	9,581	11.5
Asia	21,477	25.8
Africa	5,447	6.5
Oceania	359	0.4
Latin America	44,754	53.8
Northern America	1,608	1.9
Total	83,226	100.0

Source: Office of Latino/Latin American Studies calculations, based on the 2004 American Community Survey, U.S. Census Bureau.

unionization in Nebraska's food-processing industry, also defy easy generalizations about contexts of reception in new destinations as well as urban versus rural communities. Finally, a very important development for all of us to watch will be whether the historical immigrant marches held in the streets of large and small Nebraska communities in spring 2006 will evolve into a sustained political movement that will shape local immigration and immigrant integration policies in novel ways.

IMMIGRANTS IN NEBRASKA: A BRIEF SOCIODEMOGRAPHIC PROFILE

In 2004, the U.S. census estimated Nebraska's foreign-born population at 83,226, or about 5 percent of the state's population. The majority of these immigrants arrived between the early to mid-1990s. Another 25,576 immigrants entered the country in 2000 or later. The great majority of these immigrants (53.8 percent) are of Hispanic and Latino origin, primarily Mexican, but increasing numbers of Central and South Americans have made Nebraska their new destination.[25] The next largest groups were made up of Asians with nearly 26 percent, Europeans with 11.5 percent, and Africans with 6.5 percent (see Table 6.2 and Figure 6.1, page 152).

Nebraska's foreign population grew faster than any other of the ten midwestern states between 1990 and 2000; however, the foreign born still made up a small fraction, about 5 percent, of Nebraska's total population in 2004.[26] But such aggregate measures fail to capture the true

impact of new immigration to the state. Analysts point out that newly released census estimates once again reveal that Nebraska's positive
international immigration has offset its negative domestic immigration
since the 1990s and fueled much of its economic growth.[27] While
70 of the state's 93 counties lost population over the past five years,
immigrant-receiving communities continue to grow, albeit at a slower
pace than in previous years.[28] Omaha is the state's most important
immigrant destination, and during the past five years it has added an additional 8,691 foreign born.

While the majority of the foreign born are concentrated in
metro areas, about a third have settled in non-metro destinations. The rapid demographic shifts Nebraska has experienced in
the past fifteen years or so can best be captured at this sub-state
level. Some non-metro Nebraska communities, for example, saw
their population swell upwards of 1,300 percent between 1990
and 2000 as a result of immigration. This was the case of rural

FIGURE 6.1. FOREIGN-BORN POPULATION BY WORLD REGION OF BIRTH, NEBRASKA, 2004

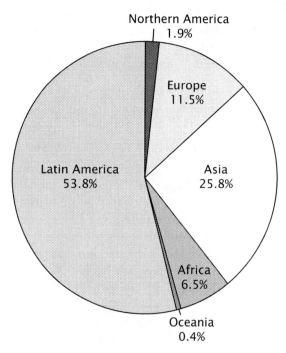

Source: Office of Latino/Latin American Studies calculations, based on the 2004 American
Community Survey, U.S. Census Bureau.

TABLE 6.3. PERCENTAGE CHANGE IN WHITE ALONE, NOT HISPANIC/LATINO, AND HISPANIC/LATINO POPULATIONS IN SELECTED NEBRASKA CITIES, 1990–2000

| CITY | WHITE ALONE, NOT HISPANIC/LATINO | | HISPANIC/LATINO | | PERCENT CHANGE IN WHITE ALONE, NOT HISPANIC/ LATINO POPULATION IN 2000 (BASED | PERCENT CHANGE IN HISPANIC/ LATINO POPULATION IN 2000 (BASED |
	1990	2000	1990	2000	IN 1990)	IN 1990)
Omaha	276,218	293,876	10,288	29,397	6	186
Bellevue	26,968	36,916	1,213	2,609	37	115
Columbus	19,171	19,209	167	1,395	0	735
Fremont	23,261	23,570	165	1,085	1	558
Grand Island	36,732	34,960	1,887	6,845	−5	263
Hastings	22,192	21,790	268	1,343	−2	401
Kearney	23,415	25,525	667	1,118	9	68
Lexington	6,231	4,635	329	5,121	−26	1457
Lincoln	179,302	198,087	3,764	8,154	10	117
Norfolk	20,748	20,834	299	1,790	0	499
North Platte	20,994	21,725	1,355	1,596	3	18
Schuyler	3,873	2,893	164	2,423	−25	1377
Scottsbluff	10,460	10,548	2,720	3,476	1	28
South Sioux City	8,704	8,074	545	2,958	−7	443

Source: Lourdes Gouveia and Mary Ann Powell, with Esperanza Camargo, "Educational Achievement and the Successful Integration of Latinos in Nebraska: A Statistical Profile to Inform Policies and Programs," Office of Latino/Latin American Studies, University of Nebraska at Omaha, 2005.

communities devastated by the farm and rural crises of the early 1980s that sought to recover their economic vitality by attracting new meatpacking plants or expanding old ones.[29] As Table 6.3 makes clear, the Latino population, overwhelmingly of foreign stock, moved into a number of communities that had experienced serious population losses among non-Latino whites between 1990 and 2000. By 2000, towns such as Lexington or Schuyler, whose Latino population did not exceed 5 percent in 1990, were, respectively, 51 percent and 45 percent Latino.

Fueling this growth is not simply new arrivals, but a large number of children born to immigrant parents—the second generation. The Latino population in Nebraska is very young (about 44 percent of Latinos were nineteen years old or less in 2000 and only 14.5 percent were forty-five years or older in 2003).[30] Nebraska's population is aging rapidly and has one of the slowest child population growth rates in the country (about 5 percent in 2000).[31] In fact, were it not for the increase in Hispanic children in recent years, the state would have shown a continuous decline in its child population. In 2004, the latest year with available figures, the number of births increased for the tenth straight year and was the highest recorded since 1982. This growth is mostly attributed to the surge in the number of births among Latinos.[32] In 2004, a much larger proportion of Latinos (20.6 percent) than whites (13.2 percent) or African Americans (14 percent) were in their twenties, an age band commonly associated with peak levels of fertility.[33]

While persons from Africa make up a smaller percentage of Nebraska's foreign born than Latinos, Asians, and Europeans, their numbers have been increasing steadily. This is largely due to the resettlement of Somali and, most important, Sudanese refugees. In fact, Nebraska has the largest concentration of Sudanese refugees in the nation, estimated at about 8,000 by local Sudanese leaders. There are no accurate counts of the African population. The majority resides in the two largest metropolitan areas, Lincoln and Omaha, and some estimate that between 5,000 to 6,000 Sudanese now make their home in the latter.[34] In 2000, about 500 Sudanese were estimated to be living in Grand Island, a metropolitan town of 42,940.[35] A smaller, but not insignificant number of people from both groups also made their way to smaller meatpacking communities such as Norfolk, home to a Hormel meatpacking plant. In 2004, about 1,500 African immigrants, primarily Sudanese, were estimated to reside in Norfolk, a town of about 24,000 people. The Hormel plant was bought by Tyson and has recently closed, prompting a massive exodus among these workers. While there is much talk in new destinations, including Nebraska, about new immigrant children straining local school resources, the concern expressed by Norfolk's school superintendent, Randy Nelson, is of a different sort. In a recent newspaper story, he lamented the loss of up to $1.8 million in state aid to his district that may result from this population exodus.[36]

Individual characteristics of immigrants partly determine their integration prospects; however, they vary by nationality and social class, among other things. Such differences must be taken into account when designing policies that address potential barriers to the productive integration of immigrants and, most important, their children. The majority of immigrants to Nebraska are Mexican and Central American laborers with low levels of education and high levels of poverty, and they are concentrated in low-income occupations.[37] In 2004, 42.2 percent of the total foreign born had not completed high school.[38] The percent among Latino foreign born is significantly higher—in 2000, it stood at 71.8 percent.[39] On the opposite site of the educational spectrum,[40] the foreign born in Nebraska were more likely to have completed a graduate or professional degree than the native born—12 percent and 8 percent, respectively, in 2004.

Poverty levels among the foreign born are higher than for the native born (18.4 percent and 10 percent, respectively). However, for naturalized citizens, the rates are equal to those of the native born, while for Latinos the rate is much higher—in 2000, it stood at 20.4 percent.

The rate of naturalization has been increasing in Nebraska but, as in the rate for the nation, it is lower among poorer Latino groups. In 2004, 46 percent of the foreign born, but only 38.9 percent of Latinos were naturalized.[41] Poverty, high rates of unauthorized migrants, and low levels of English language fluency are commonly associated with lower naturalization rates, as is a high possibility of returning to one's home country.

Finally, English proficiency levels for the foreign born vary significantly by the language spoken at home, which is another way of saying that they vary by the class differences associated with those nationalities. As a whole, among the foreign born who speak a language other than English and are five years old or over, 26.6 percent speak English very well and 55.5 percent speak English less than very well. Among Spanish-speaking foreign born, the proportions are 20.9 percent and 79.1 percent, respectively.[42]

As the U.S. Senate has voted to declare English the national language, it becomes particularly important for researchers to clarify for the American public the factors that contribute to, or conspire against, learning English or acquiring other traits associated with sociocultural, economic, or political incorporation. Among such factors is a real dearth of focused and coherent policies, as well as accessible and affordable programs in Nebraska that are aimed at eliminating these language and socioeconomic barriers, especially for the majority of Latino immigrant workers as well as Sudanese refugees.[43]

IMMIGRANT EMPLOYMENT AND LABOR CONDITIONS IN NEBRASKA

Nebraska's perennial labor shortages, found at both ends of the employment spectrum, provide the relevant backdrop for understanding the formation and impact of the second largest immigration wave in the state's
history. The state's unemployment rate remained below 3 percent during
the entire decade of the 1990s, when immigration was at its highest. Today, Nebraska's 3.4 percent unemployment rate (as of April 2006) is the
seventh lowest in the nation.[44]

By far the biggest demand for immigrant labor, documented and undocumented, has come from the lower-wage, labor-intensive meat processing industry, a mainstay of the state's economy. The overwhelming
majority of these workers are Latinos. A ten-year examination (1988–
97) of industrial concentration of Latinos in the Midwest helps document this pattern. From that review we learn that the "food and kindred
products" industry, a subcategory of manufacturing, which contains
meatpacking workers, was the only industry in the Midwest that met
the definition of a "Latino industrial niche" during each of the ten years.
Moreover, foreign-born Latinos are more than twice as likely as native-
born Latinos to be employed in this and, to a lesser extent, nine other industrial niches.[45]

As their numbers and diversity have increased, however, immigrants
have begun to fill jobs in a wider array of labor markets. Table 6.4 shows
the location of the foreign born across broad industry categories. While
space does not allow for more detailed tables, it is already clear that
the foreign born are much more likely than the native born to be concentrated in industries employing large numbers of lower-wage workers,
as is the case with manufacturing and food services. However, somewhat smaller proportions of immigrants are also found in industries associated with higher-skilled workers such as professional and scientific
management and administrative services. The last column on the right
shows how these proportions are shifting for immigrants arriving after
2000. Specifically, the number of immigrants in manufacturing and food
services is declining, while more are found in the higher-end industries.
This is due to the fact that, since 2000, a larger number of higher-edu-
cated immigrants have made their way to the state, rather than due to
upward mobility experienced by traditional labor migrants.

Where immigrants work varies by nationality or region of origin,
which is also highly correlated with educational and skill levels. As Table
6.5 (page 158) suggests, Mexican, Guatemalan, and Salvadoran foreign

TABLE 6.4. INDUSTRY BY NATIVE BORN AND FOREIGN BORN, NEBRASKA, 2004

INDUSTRY	PERCENT NATIVE	PERCENT FOREIGN BORN	PERCENT FOREIGN BORN, ENTERED U.S. 2000 OR LATER
Agriculture, forestry, fishing and hunting, and mining	5.8	1.9	3.1
Construction	6.9	6.9	11.1
Manufacturing	8.3	32.7	20.5
Wholesale trade	4.3	2.4	1.0
Retail trade	12.1	5.2	6.0
Transportation and warehousing, and utilities	6.2	3.2	2.3
Information	2.1	0.3	0.3
Finance, insurance, real estate, and rental and leasing	8.1	2.4	0.3
Professional, scientific, management, administrative, and waste management services	7.9	8.4	7.0
Educational, health and social services	22.0	16.7	16.8
Arts, entertainment, recreation, accommodation, and food services	7.5	13.5	28.3
Other services, except public administration	4.9	3.3	2.1
Public administration	4.0	3.1	1.2
Total	100.1	100.0	100.0

Source: Office of Latino/Latin American Studies calculations, based on the 2004 American Community Survey, U.S. Census Bureau.

born are much more likely than immigrants from other Latin American and non-Latin American countries to be found in the manufacturing industry (of which meat processing is the largest sector in Nebraska), construction, and lower-paid service industries. Asians are found at both ends of the industry scale. Their presence in manufacturing today is less likely to be connected to meatpacking than when the industry first

TABLE 6.5 INDUSTRY BY REGION OF BIRTH OF FOREIGN BORN, NEBRASKA, 2000

INDUSTRY	PERCENT ASIA	PERCENT MEXICO	PERCENT GUATEMALA	PERCENT EL SALVADOR	PERCENT OTHER CENTRAL AMERICA, CARIBBEAN, SOUTH AMERICA	PERCENT SUDAN	PERCENT OTHER AFRICAN
Agriculture, forestry, fishing and hunting, and mining	1.3	4.7	0.7	2.5	0.0	0.0	0.7
Construction	0.9	11.3	12.7	0.6	4.8	0.0	2.3
Manufacturing	32.3	52.9	60.9	82.3	11.0	22.9	17.9
Wholesale trade	2.9	3.9	4.4	0.6	2.0	0.0	3.4
Retail trade	5.8	3.9	1.0	6.0	7.8	0.0	0.0
Transportation and warehousing, utilities	2.2	1.3	4.7	0.0	3.1	0.0	2.2
Information	2.1	0.7	0.0	0.0	0.0	0.0	4.6
Finance, insurance, real estate, and rental and leasing	3.6	1.6	2.0	0.9	3.3	0.0	6.8
Professional, scientific, management, administrative, and waste management services	6.8	3.4	0.0	1.7	7.6	38.5	7.1
Educational, health, and social services	25.7	4.7	1.8	3.4	44.3	0.0	40.4
Arts, entertainment, recreation, accommodation, and food services	10.1	8.1	8.3	1.7	7.9	0.0	13.9
Other services, except public administration	3.7	3.0	1.6	0.6	5.6	38.5	0.7
Public administration	2.7	0.5	2.0	0.0	2.5	0.0	0.0
Total	100.0	100.0	100.0	100.0	100.0	100.0	100.0

Source: Office of Latino/Latin American Studies calculations, based on the 2000 Census, Public Use Microdata Sample: Nebraska, U.S. Census Bureau.

began expanding into rural Nebraska communities. At that time, Vietnamese and Laotian refugees were heavily recruited by meatpacking companies such as IBP, although their numbers were never as significant as those of Latino workers.[46] Conversely, newer arrivals such as Sudanese and Somali refugees (included under "other African," in Table 6.5) have often found or been placed in meatpacking jobs upon their resettlement to Nebraska. A similar course was followed by Asian refugees, who have now moved on to better employment. In fact, Sudanese community members often express frustration about their inability to access good jobs early on, despite the relatively high educational credentials of some of their members.[47] I expect the Sudanese will follow a path similar to other refugee communities and even some Mexican and Central American immigrants, whose first Nebraska job was in meatpacking, regardless of educational credentials.

The employment hierarchy becomes even clearer when looking at the kinds of occupations in which immigrants are highly represented or underrepresented. Table 6.6 (page 164) clearly shows that Mexican, Guatemalan, and Salvadoran foreign born, as well as the Sudanese, are highly represented in production occupations but virtually absent from management. Conversely, immigrants from Asia and other Latin American countries, as well as "other African," are much more likely than these other groups to be found in the "management, professional, and related occupations" category.

IMMIGRANTS IN NEBRASKA'S MEATPACKING INDUSTRY

After experiencing a severe profitability crisis and employment contraction during the previous decade, by the 1980s the meatpacking industry had begun to expand again under the leadership of new companies such as IBP. It was also transformed from an urban to a rural industry, close to cattle and away from old union strongholds.[48] Meatpacking's expansion proved fortuitous for a state—and particularly its smaller communities—that had been devastated by the farm crises of the mid-1980s. State and local officials often intervened quite decisively in support of new economic development strategies centered on "value-added" agriculture. More often than not, "value added" referred to labor-intensive meat processing facilities.[49]

The farm crises had exacerbated Nebraska's population exodus that had begun decades earlier. Native-born workers also had exited a crisis-ridden meatpacking industry during the 1970s as old plants closed down or reduced employment and benefits. Luring those workers back into the industry would prove all but impossible; seldom do workers return to an industry they have exited. More important, this new breed of packers hinged their profit-making strategies on, among other things, reorganizing work tasks in a way that would allow them to hire an unskilled, and therefore lower-wage, workforce. Real wages in meatpacking in 1990 were about half what they were in the early 1970s. In the absence of, or lack of support for, unions in smaller communities, the new workforce would labor in an environment characterized by fewer worker benefits, faster line speeds, higher injury rates, and shorter career paths.[50]

The combination of all these factors made it clear that labor would have to be imported from somewhere. Meatpacking plants hired full-time recruiters and soon relied on the tightly woven immigrant networks to create a workforce literally from scratch. As has been well documented elsewhere, the state, as well as local governments and leaders, contributed to the recruitment of, and subsidized training costs associated with, this new labor force.[51] Today, Latino workers constitute between 80 percent and 90 percent of any given meatpacking plant's labor force. Local Latino leaders and researchers estimate that unauthorized migrants make up anywhere between 25 percent and 50 percent of individual meatpacking plants' workers.

Meatpacking employers clearly have benefited from and been the major contributor to this influx of workers. For small meatpacking towns there are certain costs as well as benefits associated with the sudden presence of a large employer that seeks to import nearly 100 percent of its labor force, the majority of whom are linguistically, ethnically, and culturally distant from the pre-existing population.[52] While no single study adequately summarizes the aggregate costs and benefits of this new immigration, there have been several case studies, countless media stories, and at least one economic analysis examining these mixed results.[53]

Lexington has been one of the most studied meatpacking towns in the state, beginning with the work of this author and her colleagues. Our work documented the strain on local schools, the struggle of non-profit social agencies trying to provide housing and basic necessities for newly arrived workers, and an initial wave of crime associated with age as well as contingents of California-based criminal groups that sought to take advantage of this vulnerable population. By the same token, we documented benefits such as a healthy increase of sales taxes, the revitalization of downtown businesses (most of which were boarded up at the end of the farm crisis), and the fact that the immigrant presence created additional jobs for native-born or older residents while taking virtually none from them.[54] A labor study conducted by two Nebraska economists further highlighted these benefits. Immigration, the study concluded, had boosted property values and tax revenues in Lexington as well as increased wages for nonimmigrants.[55]

IMMIGRANT LABOR'S IMPACT BEYOND MEATPACKING AND RURAL NEBRASKA

Benefits to employers derived from the presence of large numbers of immigrant workers are no longer confined to the meatpacking industry nor to the small towns that first triggered their move to Nebraska. Hispanic workers can be found in dairy farms, egg processing, livestock operations, retailing, and small manufacturing. Today, it is rare to find roofing, landscaping, cleaning, housekeeping, and many other lower-wage businesses in Omaha that do not rely on immigrant workers, especially ones from Latin America.

South Omaha, site of the old meatpacking industry, has been revitalized as Latinos have moved into the empty houses and boarded-up businesses that dotted the district after the meatpacking crisis of the 1970s and early 1980s.[56] Even the meatpacking industry, which claimed to have left the city in order to be closer to cattle, has returned to the area, apparently in order to be close to workers. About a dozen plants have been refurbished or opened anew, and these employ about 4,000 workers today.[57]

As in small meatpacking towns, state and local officials have lavished some of these new immigrant-dependent ventures with generous tax subsidies, even when, according to some immigrant advocates and state senators, they did not qualify. This is the case of Nebraska Beef, established in 1995 by a group of largely unnamed investors who bought an old, decaying packing plant. The owners have received millions of dollars under programs such as LB775 (the Nebraska Employment and Investment Growth Act), a City of Omaha Community Development Block Grant, and—most disputed of all—LB829, the Quality Jobs Act. The latter was intended to provide incentives for companies to locate or expand in Nebraska. However, Nebraska Beef applied for these subsidies only after completing construction of its plant. Advocacy groups such as Nebraska Appleseed have argued quite convincingly that this violates the spirit and letter of the law. In addition, the company has become a sort of "poster boy" for a twenty-first-century version of Upton Sinclair's *The Jungle*. It has been fined repeatedly by Nebraska's

Occupational Safety and Health Administration (OSHA) for safety violations, its managers were indicted for smuggling illegal immigrants, and unions, the clergy, and advocacy groups have denounced the company for conducting a brutal and often illegal campaign to undermine union organizing. This, many argue, further violates the purpose of these subsidies, which are meant to bring quality jobs to Nebraska and must be used for employee training and educational programs.[58]

The business potential of the revived South Omaha community also has been increasingly recognized by city government, as well as a variety of nongovernmental business groups. In 2004, Omaha Mayor Mike Fahey announced plans to build, with the help of private donors, a youth soccer complex to accommodate this growing Latino population after it was unwelcome in pre-existing sports parks owned by the schools. The neighborhood's commercial district has been undergoing a $3.5 to $4 million facelift, financed by the city with federal grants, in an effort to capitalize on the area's "tourist" potential. The effort is especially aimed at residents from other parts of Omaha who may not have ventured into the Latino neighborhoods earlier due, in part, to exaggerated fears about crime.[59]

On the flip side, immigrant day laborers in Omaha, while not that numerous (about forty on any given day), tend to congregate in the Plaza de La Raza, which is located in the middle of South Omaha's commercial center. Current plans do not address this issue, and none of the agencies in the community have been able to address it in any meaningful way. The Chicano Awareness Center offers free referral services and conducts an initial screening of these temporary workers for companies.[60]

Anti-immigrant voices in Nebraska often claim that their "only problem is with the illegals" and, at times, the employers who hire them. Indeed, Nebraska's unauthorized migrant population is estimated to be anywhere between 35,000 and 50,000.[61] Our work and the media have documented numerous instances of employers being less than thorough or purposely negligent when reviewing fraudulent documents.[62] Yet herein lies Nebraska's conundrum: much of the revitalization of business districts, whole industries, and small towns has been spurred by lower-skilled immigrants for whom the U.S. government has not yet created legal work channels. The meatpacking industry, as well as many other Nebraska businesses that employ large numbers of immigrants, have long called for guest worker programs they can access and, more recently, a path to citizenship for many of the families that help stabilize their labor force.[63]

Immigrant workers have responded by mobilizing on their own. Meatpacking unions have experienced a renaissance thanks to immigrant organizers, many of whom are undocumented.[64] The marches in spring 2006 became the latest show of rising immigrant political mobilization levels. One could argue that some of these actions could help prevent wages from falling further and might benefit all workers, not just the foreign born.

Questions remain, however, as to the real impact of immigrant labor, particularly when large numbers of unauthorized migrants are present, on the labor market opportunities and wages of the native born. As many academic and governmental researchers have pointed out, and as the above discussion makes clear, immigrants and natives tend to be found in different labor markets, thus they seldom are in direct competition with one another. When competition does exist, it is likely to occur most among those lower-paid immigrants who are crowded into the same labor markets, or among them and minority workers with high dropout rates, particularly African Americans.[65]

Available evidence does not allow conclusive statements here about job competition between African Americans and Latinos. In Douglas County, a metropolitan area where African Americans are concentrated, however, the phenomenon of ethnic industrial niches seems to hold to some extent, which suggests little competition. In 1990, for example, there were already relatively few African Americans working in food manufacturing (6.8 percent). Their presence in the industry was never huge, and by 2000, the proportion had diminished to 4.6 percent. The reverse is true for Hispanic or Latino workers. Conversely, while both of these groups' shares in the educational, health, and social services diminished between 1990 and 2000, African Americans continued to have a disproportionate presence in this industrial sector (23.7 percent). This is true when compared to either their presence in other sectors, as well as Hispanic or Latinos' presence in the same sector. Less than 10 percent of Latinos are found in this sector, down from 17.6 percent in 1990.[66]

When we look at occupations, the proportion of Hispanics in management, which commands the highest median earnings among broad occupational categories, has steadily decreased while that of African Americans has steadily increased since 1990. In 2004, median earnings for full-time, year-round Hispanic or Latino males were about half ($17,779) of African-American male earnings ($35,635). In fact, while immigrants find an abundance of jobs in Nebraska, the majority of them earn less than $20,000 a year. Once again, however, there are significant differences across national origins. As Table 6.7 (page 164) shows, a larger percentage

TABLE 6.6. OCCUPATION BY REGION OF BIRTH OF FOREIGN BORN, NEBRASKA, 2000

OCCUPATION	PERCENT ASIA	PERCENT MEXICO	PERCENT GUATEMALA	PERCENT EL SALVADOR	PERCENT OTHER CENTRAL AMERICA, CARIBBEAN, SOUTH AMERICA	PERCENT SUDAN	PERCENT OTHER AFRICAN
Management, professional, and related occupations	39.0	5.4	3.0	2.3	42.1	38.5	43.1
Service occupations	14.3	14.3	9.9	6.7	12.4	0.0	18.7
Sales and office occupations	14.6	4.8	5.5	6.0	16.4	0.0	22.7
Farming, fishing, and forestry occupations	1.0	4.9	0.0	2.5	0.0	0.0	0.0
Construction, extraction, and maintenance occupations	1.8	14.6	10.4	0.6	8.7	0.0	0.0
Production, transportation, and material moving occupations	29.3	56.0	71.3	82.1	20.4	61.5	15.6
Total	100.0	100.0	100.0	100.0	100.0	100.0	100.0

Source: Office of Latino/Latin American Studies calculations, based on the 2000 Census, Public Use Microdata Sample: Nebraska, U.S. Census Bureau.

TABLE 6.7. EARNINGS BY REGION OF BIRTH OF FOREIGN BORN, NEBRASKA, 1999

EARNINGS	PERCENT ASIA	PERCENT MEXICO	PERCENT GUATEMALA	PERCENT EL SALVADOR	PERCENT OTHER CENTRAL AMERICA, CARIBBEAN, SOUTH AMERICA	PERCENT SUDAN	PERCENT OTHER AFRICAN
Less than $20,000	49.27	59.3	54.0	56.1	56.0	80.7	50.0
$20,000 to $49,999	38.15	38.4	41.6	42.7	32.4	19.3	48.3
$50,000 to $99,999	10.72	1.9	4.4	1.2	6.4	0.0	0.0
$100,000 or more	1.86	0.5	0.0	0.0	5.1	0.0	1.7
Total	100.00	100.0	100.0	100.0	100.0	100.0	100.0

Source: Office of Latino/Latin American Studies calculations, based on the 2000 Census, Public Use Microdata Sample: Nebraska, U.S. Census Bureau.

of better-educated groups, such as Asians and particularly South Americans and other Latin Americans (about 11 percent in both cases), than of native born (2.2 percent) are estimated to make more than $50,000 a year. This upper tier of immigrant wage earners helps reverse some of Nebraska's "brain drain." However, interviews with Venezuelans and Colombians for another project revealed that they, like the Sudanese, are often frustrated at the slow pace of their economic progress. Some cite factors such as an insufficient number of high-wage jobs available and immigration or other legal impediments to using educational credentials obtained in their country of origin.[67]

KEY STATE POLICY RESPONSES

Not surprisingly, employment is the immigrant issue that has received the most attention from the Nebraska unicameral legislature since the late 1980s and early 1990s, when immigrants began to arrive in large numbers. The state legislature has, according to an advocate who follows it closely, "sought to do some things because they've got some leaders that have tried to move the issue of how state policy impacts new immigrants and certainly the communities where they are living."[68] Importantly, even if not always successful, none of the bills proposed have sought to restrict immigrant rights but, on the contrary, have been crafted in response to concerns over the violation or neglect of those rights.

Table 6.8 (page 166–67) summarizes legislative bills and resolutions that are most directly tied to this issue. Among them are bills and resolutions requesting studies and changes concerning immigrant safety and working conditions, as well as on barriers to their successful incorporation. More recently, senators introduced LR178, a resolution to address growing concerns over the construction industry's use of IRS form 1099 (utilized by subcontractors), which negatively impacts state revenues and undermines workers' safety and labor rights.

Perhaps the most important piece of legislation regarding immigrant workers was a landmark bill spearheaded by these active senate leaders and approved by Governor Mike Johanns in 2003: LB418, the Non-English Speaking Workers Protection Act.[69] The bill was aimed at addressing increasing concerns over meatpacking employers' violation of non-English-speaking workers' rights. It brought together elements from an earlier bill, LB20, that, for example, required employers to provide those workers with written statements outlining the terms and conditions of their jobs, and to make available to those workers a bilingual employee to

TABLE 6.8. NEBRASKA LEGISLATIVE BILLS ON IMMIGRANT EMPLOYMENT

No. Legis.	Year	LB No.	LR No.	Introduced by	Description	Date First Read	Final Action
93th	1993–1994	757		Landis	Create the Workplace Safety Consultation Law. To implement the requirement for safety committees to examine workplaces.	1993	Approved by the governor
94th	1995–1996	20		Chambers	To provide duties for employers of non-English-employers of non-English-speaking employees and penalties for those who fail to provide bilingual translators and written statements specifying terms of employment.	1/5/95	Approved by the governor
95th	1997–1998	455		Wesely	For an act relating to revenue and taxation. To provide restrictions on employment of unauthorized aliens for purposes of tax incentive programs.	1/16/97	Failed
96th	1999–2000		282	Vrtiska, Chairperson; Chambers, Dierks, Hilgert, Preister, Schimek.	To initiate a study of the regulation of the immigrant workforce through federal programs operated by the Immigration and Naturalization Services (INS).		
		1363		Connealy, Bourne, Bromm, Chambers, Cudaback, Dierks, Hilgert, Jensen, Kiel, D. Pederson, Preister, Price, Robak, Smith, Stuhr, Suttle, Tyson, Aguilar.	Create the Task Force on the Productive Integration of the Immigrant Workforce Population; to provide for a Meatpacking Industry Worker Rights Coordinator; to provide powers and duties; to create a fund; and to provide a termination date.	1/19/00	Approved by the governor on April 10, 2000
97th	2001–02	415		Stuhr, Connealy, Kremer, Schimek, Vrtiska.	For an act relating to farm labor contractors. Change farm labor contractor provisions. To amend the Farm Labor Contractors Act, 48-1707, 48-1709, 48-1711, 481712, and 48-1714.	1/9/01	Indefinitely postponed

No. Legis.	Year	LB No.	LR No.	Introduced by	Description	Date First Read	Final Action
		931		Stuhr	For an act relating to labor. To change the Farm Labor Contractors Act provisions. Provide a bilingual employee who shall be available at the worksite for each shift a non-English-speaking worker is employed if the farm labor contractor has a workforce of ten or more non-English-speaking workers who speak the same non-English language. The bilingual employee shall be conversant in the non-English language spoken by such workers.	1/10/02	Approved by the governor on April 19, 2002
98th	2003–04	178		Connealy, Synowiecki, Combs	To study the state's laws regarding immigration and employment of non-citizens. The study shall include the practice of Nebraska employers using Form 1099 contract labor and how it affects state revenues, worker safety, and workers' rights.	3/03	
		418		Speaker Bromm, Connealy, Aguilar, at the request of the governor	For an act relating to labor. To name the Non-English Speaking Workers Protection Act.	1/15/03	Approved by the governor on April 2, 2003
99th	2005–2006	590		Preister	For an act relating to the Nebraska Worker's Compensation Act. To exempt injuries caused deliberately or by the willful negligence of the employer from coverage under the act.	1/18/05	Indefinitely postponed

Source: Adapted by the Office of Latino/Latin American Studies from the Nebraska Unicameral Legislature Web site, available online at http://www.unicam.state.ne.us/.

explain such terms and refer workers to safety net community services. Major impetus for this bill came from a sustained campaign by a workers' committee and advocacy groups to denounce conditions in Nebraska's meatpacking industry.[70] Media coverage of these conditions helped nudge Republican Governor Johanns into issuing an equally historic Meatpacking Industry Workers' Bill of Rights, now included in LB418. This bill of rights lists eleven different rights workers should be aware of, with the right to organize as number one. To give it real traction, however, LB20 sponsors required the governor to introduce a full-time meatpacking industry worker rights' coordinator under the Nebraska Department of Labor.

Assessments as to the real impact of the bill vary, and its enforcement is highly uneven. However, most agree that being the only bill of its kind in any state, it is indeed historic. Also, while it may not have fundamentally changed working conditions within the industry, the fact that the governor listed the right to organize as number one tended to empower workers to continue their organizing struggle with particular zeal. Finally, the coordinator's position has been a very positive outcome of this bill, as it does allow workers to report abuses and obtain useful advice.

IMMIGRANTS' HEALTH AND SOCIAL SERVICE ISSUES

> You know, that is one of the biggest problems—shortfalls—we have as far as Nebraska is concerned. We try to respond but at the same time, we are pretty restricted by federal guidelines. So it is a problem that a lot of times it is left up to local entities and communities to come up with their own deal. In Grand Island, we have a community free clinic for people in that arena, and it's worked quite well. We don't get any federal or state funding.[71]

This quote is a state senator's answer to the question of how the State of Nebraska has responded to increases in refugees and immigrants, especially regarding health and health care issues. Nearly every one of the individuals interviewed about this subject agreed that: (1) the state has been slow to respond but is beginning to pay more attention to the issue; (2) community organizations have, in turn, shown impressive leadership and picked up the slack for state neglect; but (3) community clinics serving immigrants and refugees are unevenly situated and concentrated in more populated communities or regions; and (4) growing health care problems are neither confined to the state nor to immigrants.

Evidence gathered for our study revealed heightened awareness and increased attention to these concerns by health professionals and researchers across the state. Just during the past two to three years, researchers from the state's major medical centers have produced a number of important reports that, mainly through indirect evidence, contribute to our understanding of this issue.[72] Much of this recent attention has focused on Latinos, the state's largest immigrant and minority population. On May 18, 2006, the University of Nebraska Medical Center (UNMC) teamed up with Pfizer Pharmaceuticals to sponsor a conference entitled "Latino Health Issues for Primary Care Providers: Achieving Better Health Outcomes," the first of its kind in Nebraska.

At the state level, the Office of Minority Health, which functions within the state's Department of Health and Human Services, has also paid increased attention to the immigrant population. The agency was founded in 1991, largely out of concern for the growing AIDS epidemic and how it affects minorities, particularly African Americans. Annual conferences have incorporated specific sessions on the immigrant population since the mid-1990s. However, the office has yet to produce data that are sufficiently disaggregated to reveal an accurate picture of issues uniquely tied to foreign-born status and nationality. The data instead are broken down according to more conventional racial and ethnic categories in which immigrants and nonimmigrants are grouped under categories such as "Hispanic Americans" or "African Americans."

According to our interviewees, some of the most successful efforts, at least in terms of raising awareness through better data collection, appear to be occurring among emerging private/public-sector coalitions. These groups are taking a fresher look at the social and economic complexities of Nebraska's demographics and incorporating them into their research initiatives and recommendations to the state legislature. In 2003, for example, Governor Mike Johanns appointed a twenty-eight-member "Health Insurance Policy" coalition that included representatives from state government, the legislature, the business and insurance sectors, and advocacy and health care organizations. In its first two years, with funding from the U.S. Department of Health and Human Services, the coalition or its subsets produced several presentations and reports. The research was carried out by UNMC and was based on a combination of telephone surveys and focus groups. Especially from the latter we can glean some of the richer information regarding immigrants and health care.[73] An interviewee who has coauthored some of these reports stated that:

The findings that the coalition is dealing with pointed out that there are a lot of newcomers in Nebraska who do not understand the U.S. health care system; and a lot of newcomers who may not be or are not documented. So solutions to increase the number of employers who offer insurance or Medicaid and Medicare eligibility really would not help a lot of the newcomers in Nebraska. So the state has opened its eyes to options such as putting federally funded, quality health care centers [QHCC] or QHCC look-alikes in the central part of the state, where demographic information shows us that, especially, the Hispanic population has been booming and increasing very quickly. [74]

As suggested above, local clinics, particularly those that have received federal community health center funding, have been very successful in providing the safety net otherwise absent. One highly successful example is the One World Clinic in Omaha. The clinic was founded in the 1960s by a partnership between the Lutheran Church and Creighton University in order to serve the local Native American population. It was first known as the American Indian Center. As packing plants closed down in the 1970s, the clinic began to serve an influx of Hispanic residents who had lost access to health care. The clinic was renamed the Indian-Chicano Health Center. Today the clinic serves people from thirty-seven countries who speak more than seventeen different languages; in 2003, it again changed its name, to One World.

However, such clinics are largely concentrated in metro areas and, as the respondent above intimated, are absent in the central part of the state where Lexington is located. As regional research has suggested, rural communities suffer from systemic problems, such as a shortage of physicians and qualified interpreters, that tend to discourage existing health providers from serving newcomers.[75] The lack of qualified translators and culturally appropriate providers becomes a particularly severe problem in these rural and smaller communities. Even county-funded initiatives serving newcomers are disproportionately found in metro areas. This is the case of the Douglas County Health Department, which serves Omaha's metro area. The department has been collecting data of its own and, importantly, has hired a slew of bilingual community liaisons and *promotoras de salud* (health promoters).

Having learned much from these initiatives and especially the findings produced by the insurance coalition, some state senators have pledged to create a task force in advance of proposing legislation that would facilitate proliferation of these clinics or "look-alikes" in underserved regions. Ironically, immigrants themselves could alleviate some of the health care provider shortages if the state were to exercise the kind of creative initiatives seen in other countries suffering from similar shortages. "There are many people who have a professional degree who work at a packinghouse, or wash windows, or serve in a restaurant because their accreditation doesn't carry over here or they can't pass the boards necessary to be licensed in their fields here."[76] At least some of these could conceivably be hired as health care workers. Some private colleges have begun to offer courses in health care training that reach a small number of these individuals.

Nebraska's OHSA has led the formation of another coalition that includes Omaha's Mexican Consulate, meatpacking industry representatives, the Nebraska Department of Labor, and the Workers' Compensation Court, among others. Its purpose is to "provide information, guidance, and access to training resources, in an effort to help Mexican citizens working in Nebraska to protect their working conditions and labor rights, including their health and safety." The impetus for this coalition came from the perpetual complaints about high injury rates in the meatpacking and construction industries. OSHA and the meatpacking industry have a separate coalition agreement. The coalition is also part of a larger international agreement signed between Mexico and OSHA in 2004. So far, it is unclear whether there will be any funding and staff to carry out such training and educational campaigns. A major concern among some members of the coalition is that unauthorized migrants may not qualify for these federally sponsored programs.[77]

SALIENT BARRIERS TO IMMIGRANT HEALTH CARE AND RELATED POLICY ISSUES

From published reports and interviews with informed individuals we confirmed much of what the country already knows about barriers to health care among the immigrant population and their various implications in terms of costs and government policy directions. Among such barriers is a lack of health insurance, interpreters, information, and proper documents; the high cost of health care; and lax enforcement of health and safety violations by state and federal agencies.

The majority of immigrants work, but more than a third lacks health insurance. As Table 6.9 (page 172) reveals, 44.78 percent of immigrants from Central America (which includes Mexico) are uninsured. This rate is much higher than that of Hispanics or Latinos as whole, which is about 27 percent. The foreign born as a whole make up about 16.8 percent of the uninsured in Nebraska.[78]

Many employers who hire immigrants do not offer health insurance, especially if these workers have been signed on as independent contractors. Large employers such as meatpacking plants do offer it three to six months after the start date. However, most of the injuries in meatpacking occur during that initial trial period, when workers are unaccustomed to handling knives, easily miss a step on blood-soaked floors and fall, or get injured by carcasses moving at high speed. In addition, as some of these workers have told me and my colleagues during numerous interviews and focus groups, they consider the insurance too costly and the benefits too limited to make it worthwhile to enroll.

Because many newcomers are undocumented, private insurance companies reject their applications. Unauthorized migrants are also ineligible for federal- or state-subsidized health insurance. Moreover, even when families qualify for Medicaid, they underutilize it for fear it may hinder a legalization process down the road. This does not generally apply to refugee groups such as the Sudanese who qualify for Medicaid and are unlikely to compromise their legalization process by enrolling in the program. As Table 6.10 shows, despite widely held views, the foreign born have extremely low rates of Medicaid coverage. About 6 percent of Latinos from Central America are enrolled in Medicaid in Nebraska. National research shows that 70 percent of Medicaid-eligible Latino children are not enrolled.

TABLE 6.9. HEALTH INSURANCE COVERAGE STATUS BY NATIVE BORN AND REGION OF BIRTH OF FOREIGN BORN, NEBRASKA, 2004 (NUMBER IN THOUSANDS)

	PERCENT INSURED	PERCENT UNINSURED	PERCENT NEBRASKA'S TOTAL UNINSURED
Native born	90.0	10.0	83.2
Foreign born	64.5	35.5	16.8
Europe	85.71	14.29	0.5
Asia	90.00	10.00	0.5
Central America	55.22	44.78	15.2
Caribbean	0.00	–	–
South America	100.00	0.00	0.0
Other Areas	85.71	14.29	0.5

Source: Office of Latino/Latin American Studies calculations, based on the Current Population Survey, Annual Social and Economic Supplement, U.S. Census Bureau, 2005.

TABLE 6.10. MEDICAID COVERAGE BY NATIVE BORN AND REGION OF BIRTH OF FOREIGN BORN, NEBRASKA, 2004 (NUMBER IN THOUSANDS)

	PERCENT COVERED	PERCENT UNCOVERED	PERCENT NEBRASKA'S TOTAL UNCOVERED
Native born	10.8	89.2	94.4
Foreign born	5.4	93.5	5.6
Europe	0.0	100.0	0.5
Asia	0.0	100.0	0.6
Central America	6.0	92.5	4.0
Caribbean	–	–	–
South America	–	100.0	0.1
Other Areas	0.0	100.0	0.5

Source: Office of Latino/Latin American Studies calculations, based on the Current Population Survey, Annual Social and Economic Supplement, U.S. Census Bureau, 2005.

Uninsured immigrants who also lack access to community clinics, as is the case in Lexington, often have no choice but to postpone care, return home to heal, or rely fully on nontraditional medicine. Frequently, their only access to formal care is through a hospital emergency room. Such visits raise health care costs and place particular strains on new gateway destination communities.

In 2003, the estimated shortfalls in Medicaid payments for all 94 hospitals in Nebraska were $127.7 million.[79] According to a press interview given by the administrator of public assistance for the Nebraska Health and Human Services, Medicaid reimbursed providers $1.3 million for life-saving emergency care given to thirty-three unauthorized migrants in that year. He added that there were about 122 requests in 2004, but most applications for such emergency care for "aliens" are either disqualified or paid by other sources.[80]

Linguistic barriers create their own funding and access constraints. Local colleges have expanded courses to train translators; however, state government has been fairly absent from this arena. Instead, groups such as the Medical Translating and Interpreting Leadership Committee have provided leadership in this issue, and from them we learn about the state's level of involvement. In one of the focus groups with health care providers conducted by this organization, the discussion about costs of and access to translation was revealing:

The big elephant in the room was the lack of consensus about who was responsible for paying for it. Yet the federal government clearly says that if you receive a dollar of federal money, your agency is responsible. But physicians and providers would say to me, "Oh, no, not me." We had patients going into clinics and the clinic would bill them for the interpreter services. We had others resenting patients. We had private providers refusing to take Medicare patients because they did not want to receive federal funding so that she would not have to deal with interpreters. We also found that reimbursement rates for interpreting were quite low, and Nebraska, as a state, had not applied for the funding because it is a matching program and it gets into your budget issues statewide really quickly.[81]

Among some of the most serious health issues affecting this community and receiving the least attention, mental health services was ranked at the top by our interviewees. This area is also where the absence of bilingual providers is most serious and its consequences most severe.

As in the rest of the nation, Nebraskans ponder if, or outright assert that, immigrants are major contributors to rising health care costs, given their high rates of uninsured. While there is no conclusive evidence, it is clear this issue is much larger than an immigrant problem. As many of the reports cited here point out, most of the uninsured in Nebraska are non-Latino whites and work in smaller businesses that offer no insurance. In addition, as interviewees pointed out, federal budget cuts affecting low-income people's access to health care services are impacting all Nebraskans, not just immigrants.

Individuals interviewed for this project gave Nebraska between a C– and a D+ for its response to immigrants' health care needs. While only one respondent thought state policies were aimed at excluding immigrants, most thought the state was negligent by failing to address the issues head on. No legislation has specifically addressed any of these issues directly. Indirectly, LB 692, approved by the governor on May 16, 2001, has allowed the UNMC and other groups to pay increased attention to the immigrant population in their research and to offer specific recommendations to the legislature.[82] All agree, however, that health care is a highly neglected issue.

HOUSING ISSUES AND POLICIES AFFECTING NEBRASKA'S IMMIGRANTS

Nebraska's rural communities were caught off guard when meatpacking companies announced plans to open large plants that would hire upward of 1,200 workers in some cases. Some of these communities ordered new housing studies. Company employment projections often fell short of actual hires and so did housing. To house workers, the companies leased or subcontracted with trailer courts; communities established transitional or "homeless shelters," for their first time in their history; and workers crowded in small rental houses. In some cases, as in Lexington, Nebraska, the absence of a pre-existing ethnic enclaves and low-income "projects," created a de facto "scattered-housing" approach to addressing the sudden population growth. The state has been somewhat removed from explicit efforts to address the housing issues associated specifically with new immigration. The legislature has not passed any bills that deal specifically with this issue—there are no legislative bills that have directly addressed the impact of new immigration on housing.

The majority of Nebraska's immigrants (57.4 percent) live in rental units, even though home ownership rates among the foreign born, including Latino families of modest means, have been increasing in lockstep with national trends.[83] In fact, researchers correctly point out that living in new immigrant gateways, where housing prices are below national averages, doubles the likelihood of home ownership for immigrants.[84] Whether they rent or own, new immigrants and refugees face a unique set of fair housing issues in Nebraska. The policies aimed at addressing these issues have been less salient and slow to emerge. However, some working in the area of housing discrimination believe the state has finally begun to respond ten to fifteen years after immigrants began arriving in earnest:

> The state of Nebraska I think it's just starting to do that. You have the Department of Economic Development at the state level, and they have been working on some things . . . trying to do research and analysis on fair housing impediments. In the comprehensive plan for different cities like Omaha and Lincoln there wasn't much addressed for new immigrants. However, right now, we just started to see all of that because of the requirements for either CDBG grants or HUD to include fair housing issues.[85]

Among impediments to fair housing identified by the Nebraska Department of Economic Development that most directly affect the newcomer population, we find: (1) a scarcity of affordable housing, (2) discrimination, and (3) local planning and zoning ordinances or, more important, institutionalized "customs and practices" that may or may not be officially sanctioned.[86] Advocates and others working with nonprofit organizations have examined some of these complex issues and point out additional barriers to fair housing that new immigrants face. These include a lack of education about tenant rights and responsibilities, access to credit, predatory lending practices, language barriers, unscrupulous realtors and landlords, and lack of documentation. In answer to the question of whether there were any issues related to affordable housing affecting the immigrant population, a director of a nonprofit housing program said:

> Yes, there are many. One, decent apartments often require, because of Omaha's collective living laws—I forget the exact name of the law[87]— you have to have a police background check before you can rent and that requires a Social Security number. Therefore, without a Social Security number, you are prohibited from some of the better apartment complexes, which means people are left with no choice but to go to the older apartment stock and this kind of converted mansions in older parts of the city. Because of that, people are living, cooking in areas that are just meant really for sleeping. And that, in and of itself, produces overcrowding of people that live in apartment complexes. If someone does have [legal] status, you may find five or six others who don't, which is in violation of rental agreements. [Another] common problem is that associated with trailer homes, because not all the contracts are understood or signed. And then there are the subleases that go on in apartments all the time, but our community only has to be informed of the primary contractor according to U.S. and Nebraska contract law.[88]

Refugees face similar as well as unique sets of housing issues. For example, according to some interviewees, their distrust of government makes them less likely to report abuses on the part of landlords or real estate agents. Alleged differences in cultural practices and larger than average families often conspire against preexisting occupancy ordinances and may provoke discriminatory practices. In a meeting with U.S. Representative Tom Osborne, some argued that they were evicted because their children were roaming around without supervision.[89] One of our respondents, a law enforcement agent, also pointed out the unique problems his small town is encountering regarding the Sudanese refugees:

> If I can be real blunt about this, it's a hygiene issue. These folks don't care if their water is shut off because they are not used to having it. Cockroaches infest their living quarters traditionally. And the Latinos don't like it; they are not used to that. They [the local health department]

have just recently condemned one of the apartment buildings here because of cockroach infestations.[90]

Immigrants living in the smaller meatpacking communities and cities tend to face higher levels of overcrowding, poor housing quality, costs, and discrimination. Local governments are typically less institutionally and politically prepared than their urban counterparts to address these issues. However, experiences vary from community to community, depending on local histories and ensuing attitudes, the degree of proactive leadership and advocacy among governmental and nongovernmental agencies, and even the role university researchers may have had in highlighting some of the issues early enough in the process.[91]

When looking at the three zip codes in South Omaha (68105, 68107, and 68108) where immigrants are heavily concentrated, "overcrowding" and "severe overcrowding" rates are three to four times as high as the city as a whole, particularly among renters. Among renters, overcrowding rates for Omaha and the three selected zip codes are 3 percent and 5.3 percent, respectively. Severe overcrowding rates are 3 percent for Omaha and 8 percent for the three zip codes with heavy Latino concentration.[92] Such rates, however, pale in comparison to meatpacking towns such as Lexington. In Lexington, home to Tyson's second largest meatpacking plant (employing about 2,400 mostly Latino workers), 15.38 percent of the housing units suffer from overcrowding, compared to a 2.7 percent statewide average and 3.7 percent in the three Omaha zip codes. Between 1990 and 2000, Omaha grew 16.14 percent and increased its housing stock by 15.40 percent. During the same period, Lexington grew by 51.66 percent but increased its housing stock by a mere 17.05 percent.[93]

In terms of costs, communities such as Grand Island, home to the state's largest meatpacking plant, employing some 2,600 workers, have experienced the highest price increase for single-family homes in recent years.[94] Speculation in real estate markets that victimize immigrants have been documented sporadically, but never systematically, by researchers and state agencies.

Despite some dire statistics, conditions and availability of low-cost housing in smaller meatpacking communities have improved somewhat since the early 1990s, when immigrant workers began to arrive. Similarly, ordinances aimed at discouraging immigrants from renting or owning in certain parts of the city or particular housing complexes, as was the case in Lexington circa 1990, were slightly more common during these earlier years.[95] While this report does not provide a complete survey of these ordinances, anecdotal and case study evidence suggests that these efforts have often been unsuccessful. In 1998, for example, a proposed change in Schuyler's occupancy ordinance from "family plus four unrelated persons" to "family plus two unrelated persons" failed after several hearings.[96]

More recently, efforts by old-timers to keep immigrants at bay have involved strategies such as rezoning rural or leisure land outside the city limits or an outright exodus from the general area. It is hard to determine whether prejudice against Hispanics or truly objective assessment by older residents regarding their community's deteriorating economic opportunities, schools, and overall quality of life play a more important role in prompting middle-class whites to leave.[97] What research in states such as California has made clear, however, is that the concentration of large numbers of low-wage Latino workers in non-metro communities often results from this exodus. It is the interaction of these two phenomena, not the simple arrival of large numbers of low-wage workers, that can have devastating consequences for the towns the long-term residents leave behind. The quality of housing, specifically, can deteriorate rapidly under such demographic imbalances.[98]

Nebraska's vast land mass and extremely low population density, even in urban areas, is unlikely to fuel the kinds of housing battles seen in other immigrant destinations such as Georgia, New York, or Boston.[99] However, this chapter has barely scratched the surface of the myriad of cumulative issues that, if left unaddressed, can have serious long-term consequences for the economic vitality of immigrant destinations and the state as a whole. Interviewees gave the state relatively low grades in its efforts to respond to the housing needs of immigrants (between a *C* and an *F*). Graded differently, respondents favored the term "negligent" (rather than "inclusive" or "exclusive") when judging government policies' approach toward immigrant incorporation initiatives. Some of the state-level efforts mentioned by respondents were limited to the aforementioned work of the Nebraska Department of Economic Development to identify and document barriers to access to affordable housing, including those faced by new immigrant communities.

There are a number of important new initiatives that suggest a new level of active response to the housing issue. Most of those actions, however, seem to be taking place at the level of individual agencies (federal dependencies or nonprofit), but there is little detectable and focused policy effort at the state level:

Like I said earlier, our agency, it's like the agencies that are required because of funding to look at these issues, we do that already. But like our legislature and the governor, those folks, we need to be able to have some policies that are put in place [at that level]. So I think there is maybe some indifference or negligence. It's like OK, we've heard that these kinds of things are going on, but because we hear about certain things happening in one particular community, but there is no connection that is made to other areas, so there aren't policies that I have heard of, that they are working on for the betterment of the refugees and the immigrant community. The one I have to give credit to was that legislative task force on immigrant integration; that was wonderful.[100]

Among some of the most active local organizations paying increasing attention to the immigrant and refugee housing issues are the Nebraska Equal Employment Opportunity Commission (EEOC), the Omaha Housing Authority, Lincoln's Urban Development Department, Grand Island's Multicultural Coalition, Sudanese resettlement and assistance agencies, and a bilingually staffed South Omaha satellite office of the Family Housing Advisory Services. The latter was chartered by the State of Nebraska in 1968 to assist low-income residents with a variety of housing services and programs. In the early 1990s, it developed a Fair Housing Center, which was instrumental in passing fair housing legislation in Nebraska that, while not aimed directly at immigrants, benefits this population as well.

Finally, a number of private or semiprivate entities such as banking institutions, Fannie Mae, and the Nebraska Investment Finance Authority (NIFA) have been retooling themselves to capitalize on the growing immigrant housing market via increasing educational and loan assistance programs.

IMMIGRANT EDUCATION IN NEBRASKA

Unquestionably, the arrival of large numbers of immigrant workers and their children during a short span of ten to fifteen years has been especially challenging for local schools. Government policies aimed at addressing those challenges will have enormous consequences for the economic progress of both the immigrant community and the state as a whole. The extent to which this mutually intertwined economic destiny is successful hinges in part on intervention programs capable of reversing patterns such as high school dropout rates before they become too entrenched. By 2000, more than 70 percent of Mexican, Guatemalan, and Salvadoran foreign born that were twenty-five years and older had not graduated from high school. Percentages were much lower for Asians (25.2 percent), Sudanese (33.8 percent), and particularly South Americans and other Latinos (12.2 percent), as well as other Africans (6.4 percent) who compared favorably to the rate for native-born Nebraskans who did not graduate from high school (11.7 percent).[101]

Policymakers are faced with the daunting task of quickly moving the second generation onto a college-bound path, a process that previous generations of immigrants were able to pursue at a much slower pace.[102] In fact, policymaking regarding immigrant education has been almost as active as that for immigrant employment in the State of Nebraska. For a summary of legislative bills pertaining to immigrant education, see Table 6.11 (pages 181–83).

THE IMPACT OF IMMIGRATION ON SCHOOLS

About 10 percent of Nebraska's foreign-born population of 83,226 were between the school ages of five and seventeen years old in 2004. Enrollment figures are far more revealing of the true impact this newcomer population and their children (the foreign-stock population) has had on the state's and schools' growth. Unfortunately, Nebraska does not disaggregate school data by foreign born, let alone generational status, using instead conventional, federally based racial and ethnic breakdowns. This constitutes one of the first problems one encounters when attempting to track the impact of the new immigrant population on schools and educational policies.

While not a perfect indicator of the presence of foreign-born students in local schools, percentages of students enrolled in English as a second language (ESL) programs are revealing. In the 2000–01 academic year, 3.7 percent of Nebraska public-school students were English language learners (ELL). By the 2004–05 academic year, the proportion had increased to 5.78 percent. Small meatpacking communities enroll a disproportionate number of ELL students. Schuyler grade schools, for example, enroll more than 30 percent ELL students in any given year (33.8 percent during 2004–05). The Omaha Public School District enroll the largest proportion of ELL students in the state, with the numbers increasing from 7.5 percent to 12.86 percent between 2000 and 2005. Omaha Public School students enrolled in ESL come from sixty-two different countries

TABLE 6.11. NEBRASKA LEGISLATIVE BILLS ON IMMIGRANT EDUCATION

NO. LEGIS.	YEAR	LB NO.	LR NO.	INTRODUCED BY	TITLE	DATE FIRST READ	FINAL ACTION
95th	1997–1998	389		Rod Withem, at the request of the governor	It requires that the University of Nebraska to be among the top 50 percent among the Board of Regents' peer institutions in the employment of women and minority faculty members.	1997	Approved by the governor on May 28, 1997, with line-item veto
		1301		Bohlke	To provide for identification of students with limited English proficiency to harmonize provisions, and to repeal the original section.	1/22/98	
96th	1999–2000		110	Schimek, C. Peterson	Interim study to reauthorize the Select Committee on Gender and Minority Equity.		
		489		Kristensen	To comply with legislative intent contained in the LB 1217, 96th Legislature, Second Session, section 102, which requires a study of the recruitment, development, and retention of minority and women faculty members at the University of Nebraska. This study relates to provisions contained in Laws 1997, LB 389, section 156, requiring the University of Nebraska to be among the top 50 percent among the Board of Regents' peer institutions in the employment of women and minority faculty members by August 1, 2002.	2000	

TABLE 6.11. NEBRASKA LEGISLATIVE BILLS ON IMMIGRANT EDUCATION (CONTINUED)

No. Legis.	Year	LB No.	LR No.	Introduced by	Title	Date First Read	Final Action
		1217		Kristensen, at the request of the governor	Provide for deficit appropriations. To include in the appropriation of $500,000 for FY2000–01 for the recruitment, development, and retention of minority and women faculty members at the University of Nebraska. It is further intended that the legislature study the issue of recruitment, development, and retention of minority and women faculty members at the University of Nebraska	1/12/00	Approved by the governor on March 30, 2000, with line-item vetoes overridden April 3, 2000
		1379		Beutler	Adopt the Minority Scholarship Program to serve as a temporary measure for the purpose of eliminating the statistical disparity between the representation of full time Black, American Indian, and Hispanic minority students in the undergraduate population of the University of Nebraska, the state colleges, and community colleges.	1/20/00	Approved by the governor on March 10, 2000
97th	2001–2002		329	Schimek, Synowiecki, Connealy, Preister, Aguilar	Review Nebraska laws that prevent undocumented immigrants from qualifying for resident tuition.		
		955		Schimek, Aguilar, Beutler, Byars, Connealy, Cudaback, Kruse, Landis, Dw. Pedersen, Preister, Robak, Smith, Synowiecki	Change resident postsecondary tuition provisions.	1/10/02	Indefinitely postponed

No. Legis.	Year	LB No.	LR No.	Introduced by	Title	Date First Read	Final Action
98th	2003–2004	152		Schimek, Aguilar, Byars, Connealy, Kruse, Dw. Pedersen, Preister, Synowiecki	To give undocumented immigrants the opportunity to pay in-state tuition at post-secondary institutions.	1/10/03	
			174	Johnson, Thompson, Bromm, Synowiecki, D. Pederson, Engel, Schrock, McDonald, Cudaback, Beutler, Jensen, Raikes, Erdman, Bourne, Smith, Stuhr, Byars, Kruse, Price, Maxwell, Hartnett, Brashear, Wehrbein	To review public higher education financing in Nebraska to account for demographics.		Enacted
99th	2005–2006	239		Schimek, Aguilar, Combs, Kruse, Preister, Synowiecki	Permit certain students who attended Nebraska high schools to establish residency.	1/10/05	Passed over on the governor's veto on April 13, 2006
			75	D. Pederson	To review the recommendations of key priorities set forth by the LR 174 Task Force in 2003 for the state's system of postsecondary education.	4/11/05	Enacted
		1024		Reikes	Provide for learning communities.	1/10/06	Approved by the governor on April 13, 2006

Source: Adapted by the Office of Latino/Latin American Studies from the Nebraska Unicameral Legislature Web site, available online at http://www.unicam.state.ne.us/.

and speak fifty-nine different languages, although the majority (85 percent) speaks Spanish. Second to Spanish are Nuer and Arabic, spoken by Sudanese refugees.[103]

Given the preeminence of Hispanics/Latinos among the foreign-stock population, enrollment figures showing their present and projected enrollment serve as additional measures of immigrants' impact on the school systems.[104] In the 1990–91 school year, for example, Latinos made up 6 percent of Lexington's student population. By 2002–03, Latino enrollment had increased 1,732 percent, bringing it up to 67 percent of the school population. In 2006, the number is 74.7 percent. In some of the meatpacking communities, the increases have been upward of 3,000 percent during the same period.[105] As Table 6.12 shows, the change in Hispanic/Latino enrollment between 1990 and today is even more dramatic. Population projections suggest that Latinos will make up more than 22 percent of Nebraska's school population in about ten years.

Nebraska's schools enjoy a good national reputation. That has certainly been justified when reviewing the Herculean efforts most school districts have made to address the educational needs of their new student population. That is not to say that all in Nebraska are happy with these school efforts. Some community members harbor great resentment toward newcomers and what they perceive are the major costs and negative impacts they have on the schools. Voters in Schuyler, for example, have four times defeated school-bond initiatives to build a new elementary school. At the moment, trailers are used to address the student population increase.[106]

Small-town school districts struggle most to find qualified ESL teachers. As a palliative answer, local colleges have expanded class offerings for existing teachers and assisted with recruitment among minorities who may wish to teach ESL. Schools in small as well as larger metro communities have established a wide array of special programs to address those needs. These include cutting-edge, dual-language programs in at least two school districts, family resource centers and the teen literacy programs in the Omaha Public School District, bilingual home-school liaisons in several languages in the larger schools, and newcomer and cultural diversity centers across the state.[107] Several of our interviewees mentioned these as examples of successful programs related to the education of immigrant children.

At the state level, the Nebraska Department of Education has expanded some of its technical assistance resources to help schools address issues related to ELL students, such as developing proficiency assessments

TABLE 6.12. PERCENTAGE OF HISPANIC/LATINO ENROLLMENT INCREASE BETWEEN 1990–91 AND 2005–06 ACADEMIC YEARS, IN SELECTED DISTRICTS

DISTRICT	PERCENT LATINO/HISPANIC ENROLLMENT DISTRICT 1990–91	PERCENT LATINO/HISPANIC ENROLLMENT DISTRICT 2005–06	PERCENT LATINO/HISPANIC ENROLLMENT INCREASE BETWEEN 1990–91 AND 2005–06
Bellevue Public Schools	3	7.3	175.9
Columbus Public Schools	0	22.2	5033.3
Grand Island Public Schools	6	34.7	530.0
Kearney Public Schools	3	8.8	221.9
Lexington Public Schools	6	74.7	2018.6
Lincoln Public Schools	2	6.2	320.0
Norfolk Public Schools	2	20.9	1245.2
North Platte Public Schools	8	11.4	33.1
Omaha Public Schools	4	21.2	494.6
Schuyler Central High School	1	52.1	5700.0
Schuyler Grade Schools	6	78.2	1744.4
Scottsbluff Public Schools	5	32.9	8.5
South Sioux City Community Schools	9	51.4	699.6

Source: Lourdes Gouveia and Mary Ann Powell, with Esperanza Camargo, "Educational Achievement and the Successful Integration of Latinos in Nebraska: A Statistical Profile to Inform Policies and Programs," Office of Latino/Latin American Studies at the University of Nebraska at Omaha, 2005. "2005-2006 Membership by Grade, Race, and Gender," accessed May 5, 2006, available online at http://ess. nde.state.ne.us/DataCenter/DataInformation/Downloads/0506/MEMBGRADE.pdf.

required by the No Child Left Behind Act. There also have been efforts to increase understanding of Nebraska's demographic changes, how they impact schools, and what policies are needed to address new students' needs. Most prominent among such efforts has been the organization, in collaboration with the Mexican American Commission, of annual Latino Education Summits. These meetings bring together hundreds of practitioners, researchers, and policymakers concerned with this issue. To my knowledge, the state has not followed up with specific policy initiatives, nor has it organized similar forums to deal with issues faced by other immigrant or refugee groups. The Mexican American Commission, whose offices are in Lincoln, the state capital, is highly involved in policy initiatives with the legislature and participates regularly in hearings. It has spearheaded the creation of several legislative task forces that have, in turn, commissioned studies on the immigrant population such as the one resulting in the Office of Latino/Latin American Studies report referred to earlier.

KEY EDUCATIONAL POLICY ISSUES

Lack of funding to educate the influx of immigrant children into local schools has risen to the top of the state's education policymakers' agenda and evolved into a particularly thorny issue, eventually attracting national attention. As a stop-gap measure, schools have availed themselves of federal grants and other innovative strategies in order to meet these populations' unique needs without delay: "We've been aggressive in looking for grant funds to support our students. In addition, we try to partner with businesses; for example, the First National Bank of Omaha has given us a place to provide educational services to families in South Omaha, at no cost to us."[108] Many of these initiatives also reflect a heightened awareness on the part of schools that serving students requires working with parents to eliminate structural barriers (language, unfamiliarity with the educational system, unwelcoming attitudes), which research shows account for their lower level of participation in their children's school and educational activities.[109]

School funding strategies, however, have now moved beyond the school district level and into the legislature and the courtroom. Two lawsuits were filed—one on June 30, 2003, and the other on August 27, 2004—against the State of Nebraska by more than fifty school districts charging that the state aid-to-education formula under-funds the needs of ELL and poor and minority students as a whole, and it is therefore unconstitutional.[110] As one ESL teacher put it: "The state allocation is about 1.25 for each ELL student. Now, that helps, but it does not cover the total cost of educating our students. We have done studies showing that we should be getting 2.0, meaning that an ELL student is really equivalent to two non-ELL students, because the cost of educating these students is greater."[111]

A parallel strategy has been for many of these same school districts to pursue annexation and district consolidation. The move has encountered fierce resistance from suburban and rural areas. The current governor of Nebraska, Dave Heineman, attempted to veto, and rural voters tried unsuccessfully to repeal, LB126, a law passed in June 2005 forcing the merger of small rural (Class I) school districts with larger K–12 schools.[112] New petitions to place the issue on the ballot for November 2006 are now circulating, and Governor Heineman made the repeal a central issue of his primary election campaign for reelection in May 2006. On the surface, and indeed for many who want the law repealed, the issue is simply about preserving small country schools and the quality education they purportedly provide. However, as a social policy expert we interviewed pointed out, many believe the rural school issue is intertwined with an emerging trend of "white flight" occurring in meatpacking communities. He argues that in places such as Madison and Lexington, long-time residents are moving to the outskirts of town, where they hope to resurrect some of these moribund rural schools and effectively divide the town and its schools along ethnic lines.[113]

The debate over school district consolidation reached its highest point when the Omaha Public School Board voted in 2005 to annex large sections of three suburban school districts (Millard, Ralston, and Elkhorn). The board argued that this move is necessary if the district is going to halt the continuous erosion of its tax base and meet its obligation to the increasing number of ELL and low-income students it serves. More than half the students enrolled in Omaha public schools qualify for low-income subsidies, while less than 8 percent of Millard students fall under that category. Most of Omaha's ELL students are also enrolled in Omaha public schools.[114] Omaha's "One City, One School District" proposal sparked a major and often rancorous debate among its and the suburban districts' superintendents, parents, boards, and student bodies. Suburban districts countered with an informal proposal of their own; it was based on free transportation for and active recruitment of minority children residing in neighborhoods such as South Omaha who may wish to "opt into" these suburban schools. An "Option Enrollment" law that has been on the books since 1989 allowed for free transportation for low-income students wishing to opt out of their school districts, as long as space was available. However, some suburban superintendents had never heard of the law; others argued that the state should pay for transportation, not the schools; some had no extra space; and others had already offered the option with little success. The majority of the students who opt out of Omaha public schools and into suburban schools are non-Hispanic whites. A similar program in Minneapolis resulted in a major loss of students within its core district.[115]

All the discussions became moot when the Nebraska legislature went against the current and introduced LB1024, a law that would split the Omaha Public School District into three districts rather than endorse further consolidation. The districts will be drawn largely along the racial and ethnic divisions separating Omaha's neighborhoods and their corresponding high schools. Particularly surprising to some was that the author of the plan was the highly respected Senator Ernie Chambers, the only African-American senator in the legislature and an avid defender of minority rights. While no friend of suburban schools, which he has often accused of fostering white flight, Chambers had long been frustrated with the Omaha Public School District's inability to end segregation and, also, with minority parents' lack of control over their neighborhood schools. Schools, he argued, were already segregated and the "One City, One School District" proposal did not hold sufficient promise of reversing that trend. Breaking up the district along pre-existing racial and ethnic boundaries would give black, Latino (most of them newcomers), and low-income white parents more control over their children's education, he argued. Although he was referring to black children during recent comments he made to a newspaper, Chamber's argument is consistent with some research on the second generation, which shows that low-income, immigrant children do better in schools attended by a large number of coethnics and supported by their ethnic community:

> You can't tell me what integration is and I can't tell you what it is. And if people are so resistant to it, what is going to happen to this one child? Talk about bullying and mistreatment. Why should a child be subjected to that? It would be much better to bring the education where the children are: Where they have a support system; where they are in familiar surroundings, where it is necessary to seek refuge, they don't have to wait until their parents find transportation somehow.[116]

The funding issue was purportedly addressed through a compromise that allowed for the incorporation of a "learning community," which had been proposed by the chairman of the legislature's Education Committee, Senator Ron Raikes. This overarching bureaucracy will envelop and supposedly equalize funding among all the metro school districts. How all this will actually work is anybody's guess.[117]

The bill received major support from rural and suburban senators and was signed into law by Governor Heineman, who had opposed the "One City, One School District" proposal early in the debate. Many attribute Heineman's win over U.S. Representative Tom Osborne in the Republican primary to his stand on the three key education issues that are partly or totally intertwined with immigrant education: LB126, LB1024, as well as LB239, the bill that made undocumented children of immigrants eligible for in-state tuition. Opponents have called the bill "state-sponsored segregation" and on May 16, 2006, the NAACP Legal Defense and Education Fund (LDF) filed a lawsuit against the state challenging LB1024.[118]

A few other policy issues were highlighted during our interviews, including the need for additional ESL classes for adults in the community. The state has never really addressed this issue, and its importance is now underscored by immigration proposals demanding that immigrants "assimilate" and learn English, but without a clear awareness of the limited opportunities they have to do so. One of the senators we interviewed raised a different issue, which he has been working on with the Omaha Public School District superintendent: "To increase the number of social workers in schools because I don't see this [special needs of immigrant students] as just an isolated educational situation; I also see it as a family dynamic."[119] The implication here is that school failure is highly associated with family structure. While not totally false, in tracking this public discourse for a long time, I have often detected a disturbing bias among policymakers to resort to the simplistic view that immigrant families' lack of educational aspirations are to blame for their children's educational achievement gap. Much research challenges this assumption.[120] The governor's educational summits, where many of these findings are discussed, do not seem to have affected that bias among some high-ranking policymakers.

HIGHER EDUCATION

College graduation rates follow patterns similar to those found in other indicators of social and economic status. In other words, foreign- and native-born Mexicans and Central Americans in Nebraska are much less likely to have finished college than any other population group, except for Native Americans.[121]

The first question posed to our interviewees was if they thought the state was doing enough to address these worrisome trends and special challenges posed by the new immigrant population. Here is one top university administrator's response:

> I think Nebraska has not had a lot of time to respond to fairly dramatic changes, particularly with regard to the Latino immigration. I think their response is to be observed; there hasn't been much response thus far. I wouldn't say none, but not much. The most positive response has been the Nebraska equivalent of the Dream Act that was passed in the last legislative session; of course it didn't pass in the previous session, but that is the most positive response from my perspective. I think there is honest and serious concern about the need to respond, particularly in the K–12 schools, to the increased concentration in certain communities of Hispanic children. We've had some conversations with the K–12 superintendents in greater Nebraska about finding ways to stimulate greater interest in higher education amongst these high school students.[122]

Indeed, LB239, the equivalent of the national DREAM Act proposal, has been the most notable policy action taken by state senators with regard to immigrant education. As mentioned earlier, Nebraska joined just nine other states that have enacted similar laws, and it does not appear that it will meet with any court challenges. However, LB239 does not address remaining barriers such as lack of access to financial aid. The law is silent on that issue, and no one is sure yet whether it will allow the state to offer financial aid to undocumented students.

Governor Heineman's vocal opposition to LB239, as well as his position on some of the other laws discussed above, raises questions for some about his level of commitment to the specific issues facing Latino parents and their children, as opposed to his overall commitment to Nebraska education. He recently was criticized for not including any representatives from the Latino community on a newly formed Nebraska Educational Leadership Council. The council will "encourage educational policies to help prepare our students" to meet the challenges posed by a technologically advanced society. Some of our interviewees viewed the criticism as unfair and argued that Latinos and other minorities, who face the widest gap in meeting those challenges, are represented in a broader and more important group, the P–16 (pre-school through college) initiative steering committee. A representative of the P–16 initiative informed us that "because the Nebraska P–16 Steering Committee is made up of the executives of education, business, and government organizations, the group tends to be dominated by white, mostly male people. The agreement that formed the committee, however, provides for allowing additional members to join the Steering Committee with the approval of the existing committee members." The twenty-eight-member committee approved the nomination of one member of the Latino community, the executive director of the Mexican American Commission.[123]

A related issue, implied by the P–16 representative above, is the lack of sufficiently educated, high-level professionals from the immigrant community in new destination states such as Nebraska. This poses special challenges to higher education and related institutions attempting to introduce proven methods to address educational gaps in this population. As a university administrator put it: "We have a pipeline issue in Nebraska. And it is more serious than in Texas or California and New York where the [immigrant and Latino] population is larger and more developed and longer in existence." However, despite this small pool from which to recruit faculty, representatives to government, and business employees, he agreed the state and the universities could be doing more and be more "creative about this."[124] The report from the Office of Latino and Latin American Studies mentioned earlier confirms the minimal presence of Latino faculty and staff in Nebraska educational institutions.

Finally, we asked interviewees to grade how the state was doing with regard to its role in addressing the growing presence of new immigrants in Nebraska's educational system; they gave the state a D average. When asked if they thought state policies tended to be "exclusive," "inclusive," or "negligent" in its efforts to facilitate educational achievement for new immigrants, most answered negligent.

As with health, and as one of our respondents quoted earlier suggested, maybe we are catching the state at a time when it is just waking to the reality of this population and its potential impact on every aspect of the state's future socioeconomic and political landscape. There is no question that policymakers understand that high dropout rates, accompanied by a brain drain of highly educated Nebraskans, need to be addressed with urgency. What is not yet clear, in this largely non-Hispanic white state, is how much policymakers understand the complexity of factors contributing to those trends among the new immigrant population. The reluctance to call upon, or exercise sufficient political will to expand, the pool of linguistically and culturally appropriate experts is sometimes puzzling. While being a member of the immigrant community does not in itself qualify anyone to speak for that community, some of us believe there is also a fear among well-entrenched people in positions of power of allowing those who enjoy credentials and respect to do so.

LAW ENFORCEMENT AND THE NEW IMMIGRATION

Law enforcement policies directed at new immigrants have not occupied a particularly prominent place in the agendas of Nebraska's policymakers. That is not to say that the state has been devoid of activity in this arena. On the contrary, Nebraska has been an important testing ground for interior enforcement initiatives, particularly with regard to employment and immigrant smuggling. Although formally falling within the purview of the federal government, these initiatives often have been assisted and, at times, encouraged by state and local enforcement agencies. Thus the first issue I examine in this section concerns the approach taken by local law enforcement agencies toward the purportedly undocumented immigrants they encounter or seek out in the course of their work. The issue acquires special significance as the U.S. Congress entertains bills that are likely to expand the immigration enforcement roles of police, highway patrols, and other local agencies.

The second issue I will discuss briefly is Nebraska's driver's license requirements, particularly the changes to them as a result of September 11. Data for this section are drawn from interviews, archival material, previous research, and transcripts from a one-day conference organized by the Office of Latino/Latin American Studies and the Police Professionalism Initiative at the University of Nebraska at Omaha.

LOCAL ENFORCEMENT OF FEDERAL IMMIGRATION POLICY

Nebraska law enforcement agents forcefully maintain, and most immigration advocates agree, that they do not enforce or have any interest in enforcing immigration laws. Playing such a role, they argue, would erode trust within the community and deplete resources needed to pursue serious crimes. If a person is unable to produce identification during a routine stop, the procedure is the same for all:

Just like anyone else, they can be placed under arrest and taken to Central and fingerprinted. We do accept the *matrícula* for traffic stops. If they do not have ID, sometimes we give them a ticket for no operator's license or something. We will not contact ICE on simple traffic stops. The only time we may contact ICE—and ICE follows up anyway because they look at arrest records—is if it is a gun conviction or a gun crime.[125]

We don't care whether they are undocumented, and it may sound kind of cold putting it that way, but if we stop somebody who does not have sufficient identification, we don't care if they are Polish or Mexican if we can determine their identity to a degree that we are comfortable with. We'll issue a citation and release them in lieu of arrest.[126]

Nebraska law enforcement agencies have also not signed memorandums of understanding with Immigration and Customs Enforcement (ICE).[127] However, ICE's presence in the state is ubiquitous, and their agents' cooperation with local and state law enforcement is routine. In this context, the line between legitimate cooperation with ICE during criminal investigations and allowing this federal agency extra opportunities to identify and apprehend individuals with minor or disputable violations can become quite blurred, and it varies from agency to agency and community to community.

And a local police chief agreed with this assessment:

I think some of the folks at the municipal level are a little disappointed that I'm not concerned with somebody that is undocumented, but I guess I'm critical of them, that they are not focused on behaviors instead of where somebody comes from. Frankly, it pisses me off.[128]

Loud claims by a minority of state law enforcement representatives, about immigrant workers causing increased crime in their area, provided some impetus for Operation Vanguard, the work-enforcement action that targeted the entire meatpacking industry in Nebraska in the 1990s.[129] As this short-lived approach wound down in 1999, the Immigration and Naturalization Service (now called Citizenship and Immigration Services) deployed Quick Response Teams (QRTs) along I-80 and around meatpacking communities with large immigrant concentrations such as Grand Island and Omaha. The main purpose of the QRTs was to "strengthen interior enforcement in new destination states and expand the cooperation with state and local law enforcement agencies."

Their focus was to be on "alien smuggling, document fraud, preventing immigration-related crime in the community, and blocking employers' access to illegal workers."[130] Such a constant presence, while it may solve some problems for local and state agencies regarding enforcement of immigration laws, also widens the set of law enforcement circumstances in which these combined teams may overreach and even engage in unwarranted racial profiling and immigration enforcement practices as a routine part of their job:

> What happens is that in the morning, ICE agents [arrive at] an understanding with the Douglas County Corrections where they send agents down to interview individuals. We have what is called a "booking sheet," and they will interview anybody with a Latin surname they suspect.[131]

The relationship of local law enforcement agencies with QRT officers has varied from community to community. In some cases, as in Grand Island at least at the beginning, local enforcement agencies without enough translators would routinely ask bilingual federal officers to accompany them to issue "failure to appear" citations or respond to noise complaints. This inevitably led to arrests for civil immigration violations. Evidence of increased racial profiling cases resulted from this expanded presence of federal immigration agents that readily encouraged highway patrol officers to inquire about legal status during routine traffic stops.[132]

> State Patrol is one that I hear a lot of complaints [about] when they ask too many questions; people get pulled over for a traffic ticket and they end up in deportation proceedings when, typically, they should just get a ticket. That, I think, is an area where it would not take a lot for a state-level official to say: "Your job is to write traffic tickets, not to call ICE or immigration."[133]

Local advocates protested more serious incidences, especially those involving Nebraska's Child Protective Services, a division of the Department of Health and Human Services. One of these involved the deportation of a Guatemalan mother who had been turned in by a teacher for slapping her child. The police opted to take the rare action of arresting the mother for this relatively minor offense and alerted QRT of the arrest.[134]

These events, among others, contributed to the passage of legislation on racial profiling in Nebraska and extended the requirement that the state collect racial profiling data on traffic stops until 2010 (see LB593 and LB1113 in Table 6.13, page 196). Interestingly, as this data became available in video format, researchers have been able to verify the fact that highway patrols continue to ask Hispanics for proof that they are in the country legally "all the time."[135] Additional legislative actions include the introduction of LB1149, aimed at clarifying law enforcement duties, including the need to involve consulates in cases when immigrant children are placed in the custody of Health and Human Services (HHS). Nebraska's HHS has now signed a memo of understanding with the Mexican Consulate, in part to respond to the increasing number of unaccompanied minors showing up in the state. However, the memo of understanding was also in response to advocates' and Nebraska legislators' outrage over the Guatemalan mother's case. Rather than allowing the consulate or family members to assume responsibility for the deported mother's children, HHS terminated parental rights and cleared the way for an American foster parent family, eager to adopt them, to do so. The woman eventually had the case against her overturned and her parental rights restored.

DRIVER'S LICENSE REQUIREMENTS AND IMMIGRANTS

Immigration advocates agree that, for the most part, Nebraska has not gone out of its way to implement laws that would seriously tighten the requirements to obtain a Nebraska driver's license. One recent effort to do so was part of a bill introduced to clarify the language in the license requirements. As an immigrant advocate put it: "That was the closest to an anti-immigrant bill we've ever had in Nebraska."[136] For example, some senators introduced provisions that would have an immigrant's driver's license expire at the same time that his or her immigration documents expired and that required additional documentation from noncitizens. Those provisions were struck down in the final bill, LB559 (see Table 6.13, page 196).

Neither Governor Johanns nor the current governor have supported the idea of allowing immigrants to use the *matrícula consular* (or "Consular ID," issued by the Mexican Consulate) for purposes of identification during traffic stops. However, several Nebraska senators are sympathetic to the clamor from advocacy organizations arguing that the state needs to create some mechanisms that allow unauthorized migrants to drive legally. The discussion took a back seat to the passage of LB239, the in-state tuition bill, but senators agreed to hear arguments during the next legislative session, in 2006–07.

TABLE 6.13. NEBRASKA LEGISLATIVE BILLS ON LAW ENFORCEMENT

No. Legis.	Year	LB No.	Introduced by	Title	Date First Read	Final Action
97th	2001–02	593	Connealy, Aguilar, Beutler, Bourne, Byars, Chambers, Engel, Schimek, Thompson, Wickersham, Hilgert, Dw. Pedersen	Prohibit racial profiling by law enforcement agencies.	1/12/01	Approved by the governor on May 31, 2001
98th	2003–04	559	Baker	Change the Motor Vehicle Operator's License Act.	1/21/03	Approved by the governor on April 15, 2004
99th	2005–06	260	Stuhr, Beutler, Brown, Combs, Fischer, Howard, Hudkins, Landis, McDonald, Price, Redfield, Schimek, Thompson	Create a task force to look at the issue of trafficking persons in Nebraska.	1/10/05	Indefinitely postponed
		1113	Bourne	Reinstates the requirement for Nebraska Law enforcement agencies to collect racial profiling data on traffic stops until 2010.	1/17/06	Approved by the governor on April 13, 2006
		1149	Cornett, Aguilar, Dw. Pedersen	Provide duties for the Department of Health and Human Services relating to foreign national minors in protective custody.	1/17/06	Indefinitely postponed

Source: Adapted by the Office of Latino/Latin American Studies from the Nebraska Unicameral Legislature Web site, available online at http://www.unicam.state.ne.us/.

Most observers agree that local law enforcement agencies maintain a fairly good relationship with new immigrants, albeit this varies by agency and locality. However, at the state level, our interviewees were less positive and most evaluated Nebraska's approach to policies in this area as "negligent" and gave the state a failing grade.

CONCLUSIONS AND FUTURE DIRECTIONS

As a new or revitalized destination state, Nebraska has not shown a clear resolve to address the challenges and opportunities that come with sudden population increases. Table 6.1 (page 145) summarizes that sentiment as expressed by interview respondents. What the data gathered for this chapter suggest is that (1) government and non-government organizations at the local level, where the impact of the new immigration is most directly felt, have devised a plethora of responses in lieu of the state's demonstrated "negligence;" and (2) when state policymakers, specifically state senators, have become involved in immigrant issues, they have done so to facilitate inclusion, not promote exclusion. A respondent compared Nebraska with other states responding to new immigration:

> At the state level, I am not aware of anything they have done. I am more aware of what they've done in certain local communities. I worked in North Carolina for a number of years, which is similar in that they have recently had a major increase in immigrants. North Carolina did respond by creating an office within the state government to address the needs of immigrants and refugees. They had an office on Hispanic affairs that looked at how the different state policies impact immigrants and refugees. I have not seen anything like that in Nebraska. I think they are still in the process of responding. But they could use a little push so they can see the needs or respond in a more comprehensive way.[137]

Researchers have conclusively shown that government policies are a major determinant of immigrant assimilation trajectories. A state that adopts an "indifferent," "neutral," or otherwise neglectful stance toward new immigrants and their settlement process undermines its chances of successfully incorporating these immigrants.[138] This is particularly true with regard to immigrants from modest backgrounds, or labor migrants, who stand to benefit most from policies that facilitate their adaptation to unfamiliar environments. The majority of Nebraska's Latin American or Sudanese immigrants are of modest backgrounds and their receiving heartland environment particularly unfamiliar. For government policies aimed at successful incorporation to be truly effective they must enjoy explicit support from the top of the leadership hierarchy, in this case the governor of the state.

As I conclude this section, Nebraskans' attitudes toward immigrants appear to be changing rapidly and not necessarily for the better. Minutemen wannabes now hold regular protests in front of the Mexican Consulate and are beginning to target Senator Hagel's office because of his support for comprehensive immigration reform. Few of our interviewees hold much hope that the current, and likely to be Nebraska's next governor, Dave Heineman, will provide the kind of leadership that is needed in order for state policies to move from a position of "neglect," to one of "inclusion." As a respondent who is particularly knowledgeable about state policies and politics put it:

> I think there is nothing to indicate from the governor's career or from anything he has said or done, that he is going to be a governor who is helpful to newcomers and new immigrants in Nebraska. This governor has done nothing except willfully seek out political gain from beating up on new immigrants. In the recent governor primary, he specifically used his veto of the in-sate tuition bill as an indication of how "how hard I am going to be [on immigrants,]"or, "I'm the guy who will protect us [the state] from illegal immigrants."[139]

The anti-immigrant rhetoric and policies being trumpeted at the national level are beginning to derail Nebraska's home grown, albeit incipient, efforts to facilitate the successful integration of new immigrants into our local institutions. The fact that unsupportable arguments and irrational polices are having an impact in a state that so clearly benefits from immigrants is worrisome. It also suggests that much of the discomfort is not with illegal immigration. Rather, it is with the "differences" between immigrants and the mainstream majority. It is about race, and class, and Spanish-speaking people we bump into at the check out counters.[140] The failure of policymakers to reverse this downward spiral toward new forms of ethnic conflicts and, worse, their willingness to participate in enforcement-only stances for pure political gain, does not bode well for the state's future.

Notes

Notes to Chapter 2

1. I would like to thank Victoria M. DeFrancesco Soto and Jessica D. Johnson Carew, graduate students in the Department of Political Science at Duke University, for their invaluable research assistance on this project. I would also like to thank Sarah Trent for allowing me to cite interviews from her 2006 seminar paper. I also want to thank Tracy Hadden of the University of North Carolina who created the map of North Carolina.

2. U.S. Census Bureau, 1990 Census of Population and Census 2000 Redistricting File, data available online at http://factfinder.census.gov.

3. Rakesh Kochhar, Roberto Suro, and Sonya Tafoya, "The New Latino South: The Context and Consequences of Rapid Population Growth," Pew Hispanic Center, July 26, 2006.

4. John D. Kasarda and James H. Johnson, Jr., "The Economic Impact of the Hispanic Population in the State of North Carolina," Kenan-Flagler Business School, University of North Carolina, January 2006, p. 1.

5. Ibid., p. i.

6. Jorge Durand, Douglas S. Massey, and Fernando Charvet, "The Changing Geography of Mexican Immigration to the United States: 1910–1996," *Social Science Quarterly* 81, no. 1 (2000):1–16.

7. Roberto Suro and Audrey Singer, "Latino Growth in Metropolitan Areas: Changing Patterns, New Locations," The Brookings Institution, July 2002, available online at http://www.brookings.edu/es/urban/publications/surosinger.pdf.

8. James H. Johnson, Karen D. Johnson-Webb, and Walter C. Farrell, Jr., "A Profile of Hispanic Newcomers to North Carolina," *Popular Government* (Fall 1999): 5–6.

9. Ibid.

10. Kochhar, Suro, and Tafoya, "The New Latino South," p. 13; Kasarda and Johnson, "The Economic Impact of the Hispanic Population in the State of North Carolina," p. 3.

11. Kasarda and Johnson, "The Economic Impact of the Hispanic Population in the State of North Carolina," p. 2.

12. "Fact Sheet: Estimates of the Unauthorized Migrant Population for the States Based on the March 2005 CPS," Pew Hispanic Center, April 26, 2006.

13. U.S. Census Bureau, QuickFacts, available online at http://quickfacts.census.gov/qfd; Ajantha Subramanian, "North Carolina's Indians: Race, Class and Culture in the Making of Immigrant Identity," Global View (Spring 2001): 1, 8–9.

14. David Griffith, *Jones's Minimal: Low-Wage Labor in the United States* (Albany: State University of New York Press, 1993); Raymond A. Mohl, "Globilization, Latinization, and the Nuevo New South," *Journal of American Ethnic History* 22, no. 4 (Summer 2003): 31–66; Sawa Kurotani, "The South Meets the East: Japanese Professionals in North Carolina's Research Triangle," in *The American South in a Global World*, James L. Peacock, Harry L. Watson, and Carrie R. Matthews, eds. (Chapel Hill: University of North Carolina Press, 2005).

15. Deborah A. Duchon and Arthur D. Murphy, "Introduction: From *Patrones* and *Caciques* to Good Ole Boys," in *Latino Workers in the Contemporary South*, Arthur D. Murphay, Colleen Blanchard, and Jennifer A. Hill, eds. (Athens: University of Georgia Press, 2001), pp. 1.

16. William Kandel and Emilio A. Parrado, "Hispanics in the American South and the Transformation of the Poultry Industry," in *Hispanic Spaces, Latino Places: Community and Cultural Diversity in Contemporary America*, Daniel D. Arreola ed. (Austin: University of Texas Press, 2004).

17. Ibid.

18. Cruz C. Torres, "Emerging Latino Communities: A New Challenge for the Rural South," *The Southern Rural Development Center* 12 (August 2000): 1–8.

19. Douglas Massey, Jorge Durand, and Nolan J. Malone, *Beyond Smoke and Mirrors: Mexican Immigration in a Era of Economic Integration* (New York: Russell Sage Foundation, 2002).

20. Sarah Elizabeth Trent, "The Effect of Latin American Immigration on Migrant-Sending Countries," seminar paper, Duke University, May 2006.

21. Raymond A. Mohl, "Globilization, Latinization, and the Nuevo New South, pp. 37, 41, 42; David H. Ciscel, Ellen Smith, and Marcela Mendoza, "Ghosts in the Global Machine: New Immigrants and the Redefinition of Work," *Journal of Economic Issues* 37(2003): 333–41.

22. David Griffith, *Jones's Minimal: Low-Wage Labor in the United States;* Kandel and Parrado, "Hispanics in the American South and the Transformation of the Poultry Industry"; Deborah O. Erwin, "An Ethnographic Description of Latino Immigration in Rural Arkansas: Intergroup Relations and Utilization of Heathcare Services," *Southern Rural Sociology* 19 (2003): 46–72; Greig Guthey, "Mexican Places in Southern Spaces: Globalization, Work, and Daily Life in and around the North Georgia Poultry Industry," in *Latino Workers in the Contemporary South*, Arthur D. Murphy, Colleen Blanchard, and Jennifer A. Hill, eds. (Athens: University of Georgia Press, 2001), pp. 57–67; Rubén Hernández-León and Victor Zuñiga, "Making Carpet by the Mile: The Emergence of a

Mexican Immigrant Community in an Industrial Region of the U.S. Historic South," *Social Science Quarterly* 81 (2000): 49–66; Rubén Hernández-León and Victor Zuñiga, "Mexican Immigrant Communities in the South and Social Capital: The Case of Dalton, Georgia," *Southern Rural Sociology* 19 (2003): 20–45; Rubén Hernández-León and Victor Zuñiga, "Appalachia Meets Aztlán: Mexican Immigration and Intergroup Relations in Dalton, Georgia," in *New Destinations: Mexican Immigration in the United States*, Rubén Hernández-León and Victor Zuñiga, eds. (New York: Russell Sage Foundation, 2005), pp. 244–73.

23. David D. Griffith, "Rural Industry and Mexican Immigration and Settlement in North Carolina," in *New Destinations*, pp. 50–75.

24. Ibid., pp. 62–70.

25. Ibid.

26. Ibid.

27. Kasarda and Johnson, "The Economic Impact of the Hispanic Population in the State of North Carolina,"

28. Ibid., p. 20.

29. Ibid., table 5, p. 13.

30. Claudia Assis and Julian Pecquet, "Hispanics Search for a Better Life Pushes Durham into Poverty," *The Herald Sun*, September 25, 2002, p. A12.

31. James H. Johnson, Jr., "The Changing Face of Poverty in North Carolina," *Popular Government* (Spring/Summer 2003): 14–24.

32. David D. Griffith, "Rural Industry and Mexican Immigration and Settlement in North Carolina," pp. 60–61.

33. Ibid., p. 66.

34. Paula D. McClain, et al., "Black Americans and Latino Immigrants in a Southern City: Friendly Neighbors or Economic Competitors?" typescript, Duke University, 2005.

35. Johnson, Johnson-Webb, and Farrell, "A Profile of Hispanic Newcomers to North Carolina," p. 9.

36. Ibid., p. 10.

37. Center for Public Opinion Polling, Elon University, February 2006 Elon University Poll; April 2006 Elon University Poll.

38. Ibid.

39. Ibid.

40. Individual #716rt02, interview with Shayla C. Nunnally, July 16, 2002. Durham Survey of Intergroup Relations, Durham Pilot Project: St. Benedict the Black meets the Virgin of Guadalupe, Duke University, 2001–05.

41. Michael Easterbrook and Jean P. Fisher, "Illegal Immigration: Who Profits? Who Pays? Health Care," *News and Observer*, March 1, 2006, pp. A1, A8.

42. Karin Rives, "Illegal Immigration: Who Profits? Who Pays? Jobs," *News and Observer*, February 26, 2006, pp. A1, A14, A15.

43. Anonymous, interview with Victoria M. DeFrancesco Soto, February 27, 2006.

44. "Helping Hispanics in Transition: An Interview with H. Nolo Martinez," *Popular Government* (Fall 1999): 13–17.

45. Mary Katherine Appicelli, "Community Building as a Means to Increase Viability and Voice for Latinos in North Carolina," unpublished master's thesis, University of North Carolina, Chapel Hill, 1999.

46. Nolo Martinez is now the assistant director for research and outreach, Center for New North Carolina, University of North Carolina, Greensboro.

47. "Helping Hispanics in Transition: An Interview with H. Nolo Martinez," p. 13.

48. Ibid., p. 16.

49. Ibid., p. 14.

50. Axel Lluch, director, Office of Hispanic/Latino Affairs, interview with Victoria M. DeFrancesco Soto, February 27, 2006.

51. "2004 Report to the Governor Hon. Michael F. Easley," North Carolina Governor's Advisory Council on Hispanic/Latino Affairs, December 2004.

52. Ibid., p. 7.

53. The University of North Carolina System policy, adopted in November 2004, states that undocumented aliens may be considered for admission only if they graduated from a high school in the United States; they may not receive state or federal financial aid; they may not be considered a North Carolina resident for tuition purposes; they must be charged out of state tuition; they will be considered out of state for purposes of the 18 percent cap on out-of-state freshman; and that the program of study will be taken into account in admissions as federal law prohibits states from granting professional licenses to undocumented aliens. (U.N.C. Policy Guidelines 700.1.4[G].)

54. Ibid.

55. David Firestone, "In U. S. Illegally, Immigrants Get License to Drive," *New York Times*, August 4, 2001, p. A1.

56. H1451: Reform Driver's License Issuance Criteria, available online at http://www.ncleg.net/.

57. Ibid.

58. S419: Increased Security for Drivers' Licenses, available online at http://www.ncleg.net/.

59. Office of Minority Health, "Latino Reproductive Health in North Carolina: Demographics, Health Status, and Programs," North Carolina Department of Health and Human Services, August 1999, pp. 25–27.

60. Suzanna Aquirre Young, "Developing, Translating and Reviewing Spanish Materials: Recommended Standards for State and Local Agencies," North Carolina Department of Health and Human Services, Division of Public Health, November 2000, available online at http://www.ncpublichealth.com/pdf_misc/DEVSPAN-web.pdf.

61. "The North Carolina AHEC Spanish Language and Cultural Training Initiative," North Carolina Department of Health and Human Services, Office of Minority Health and Health Disparities, available online at http://www.hhcc.arealahec.dst.nc.us/ahecspaninif.html.

62. "Latino Health Coalition," Center for International Understanding, available online at http://ciu.northcarolina.edu/content.php/initiative/health. htm.

63. B. A. Manson, A. Borg, J. Brewer, M. Lutton, and Y. Torres, "Latina Reproductive Health in North Carolina: Demographics, Health Status and Programs," North Carolina Department of Health and Human Services, North Carolina Office of Minority Health and Health Disparities, 1999, pp. 32.

64. No attempt was made to review all of the various programs the State of North Carolina has put in place to address the health care needs of the Latino immigrant population. I have only highlighted a couple.

65. Kasarda and Johnson, "The Economic Impact of the Hispanic Population in the State of North Carolina," p. 31.

66. Melissa Miles, "Memorandum to Agencies Providing Health Care," July 1, 2004.

67. Michael Easterbrook and Jean P. Fisher, "Illegal Immigration: Who Profits? Who Pays? Health Care," pp. A1, A8.

68. Ibid., p. A8.

69. Axel Lluch interview with Victoria M. DeFrancesco Soto.

70. Ricardo Velasquez, president, Hispanic Democrats of North Carolina, interview with Victoria M. DeFrancesco Soto, May 17, 2006.

71. Tom Pfingsten, "Former Day-Laborer Site Fenced Off in Fallbrook," *North County Times*, May 12, 2006, available online at http://www.nctimes. com/articles/2006/05/12/news/inland/fallbrook/22_33_445_11_06.txt.

72. "Latino Legislative Agenda: Report to the Community," 2003 Legislative Session, El Pueblo, Inc., May 2004.

73. "English as a Second Language: NC's LEP Numbers Since 2000-2001," North Carolina Department of Public Instruction, available online at http:// community.learnnc.org/dpi/esl/archives/2005/06/ncs_lep_numbers.php.

74. Marti Maguire, "Illegal Immigration: Who Profits? Who Pays? Schools," *News and Observer*, February 27, 2006, pp. A1, A6.

75. Jennifer Jones, "Shortage of English-as-a-Second-Language Teachers in North Carolina," National Public Radio, December 9, 2002.

76. "ESL Licensure/University Programs," North Carolina Department of Public Instruction, available online at http:community.learnnc.org/dpi/esl/ archives/2005/07/esl_licensureun.php.

77. Paul Bonner, "NCCU to Offer ESL Training," *Herald Sun*, May 7, 2006, available online at http://www.heraldsun.com/.

78. Maguire, "Illegal Immigration: Who Profits? Who Pays? Schools," p. A6.

79. Kasarda and Johnson, "The Economic Impact of the Hispanic Population in the State of North Carolina," p. 17.

80. Ibid.

81. Kasarda and Johnson, "The Economic Impact of the Hispanic Population in the State of North Carolina," p. 30; Maguire, "Illegal Immigration: Who Profits? Who Pays? Schools," pp. A1, A6.

82. Ibid.

83. "Latino Legislative Agenda 2001," El Pueblo, Inc., January 30, 2002.

84. Ibid.

85. Ibid.

86. "Myrick's Scott Gardner Act Amendment Passes US House by Voice Vote," news release, Office of Representative Sue Myrick, December 16, 2005.

87. Tim Funk, "Myrick Eyes Immigration Court in N.C.," *Charlotte Observer*, March 31, 2006, p. B2.

88. Americans for Legal Immigration Web site, http://www.alipac.us/.

89. Axel Lluch interview with Victoria M. DeFrancesco Soto.

90. Jane Stancill, "Tuition Break Bill Set to Falter: Backlash Targets Illegal Immigrants," *News and Observer*, May 28, 2005.

91. Ibid.

92. Ibid.

93. H1362, available online at http://www.ncleg.net/.

94. S976/H1018, available online at http://www.ncleg.net/.

95. H1495, available online at http://www.ncleg.net/.

96. S814, available online at http://www.ncleg.net/.

97. H1461, available online at http://www.ncleg.net/.

98. "Groundbreaking Program Will Federalize Sheriff Deputies So They May Detain and Remove Illegal Aliens," press release, Office of U. S. Representative Sue Myrick, February 6, 2006; "North Carolina," *News and Observer*, February 26, 2006.

99. "Groundbreaking Program Will Federalize Sheriff Deputies."

100. Axel Lluch interview with Victoria M. DeFrancesco Soto.

101. Given Myrick's general anti-Latino immigrant approach, it is doubtful that the drunken driving deaths were the reason for her activism in the anti-immigration movement, but the events provided additional evidence of the problems caused by illegal Latino immigrants in North Carolina.

102. Gary L. Wright, "DWI Arrest Rate Worries Hispanic Leaders in N.C.," *Charlotte Observer*, May 8, 2005, p. 1A.

103. Jim Shamp, "Grant Funds Look at Hispanics' DWIs," *Herald Sun* (Durham), May 15, 2003, p. B1.

104. "Hispanic DWI a Deadly Reality," *Star News* (Wilmington), November 29, 2005, p. 8A.

105. Wright, "DWI Arrest Rate Worries Hispanic Leaders in N.C."

106. Virginia Bridges, "'Booze It and Lose It': Latinos Are Getting Reminders Not to Drink and Drive over Holiday Season," *Herald Sun* (Durham), December 23, 2003, p. C1.

107. Shamp, "Grant Funds Look at Hispanics' DWIs," p. B1.

108. Eric Bishop, "Campaign Targets Drunken Driving," *News and Observer* (Raleigh), June 29, 2006, pp. B1, B9.

109. "The Nature and Scope of Hispanic/Latino Gangs in North Carolina," North Carolina Governor's Crime Commission, North Carolina Criminal Justice Analysis Center, September 2005, p. 1.

110. Ibid., p. 5.

111. Ibid., p. 11.
112. Ibid., p. 10.

Notes to Chapter 3

1. Iowa Board of Immigration, *Iowa: The Home for Immigrants. Being a Treatise on the Resources of Iowa, and Giving Useful Information with Regard to the State, for the Benefits of Immigrants of Others* (Iowa City: State Historical Society of Iowa, 1970 [1870]). This guide was printed in English, German, Swedish, Dutch, and Danish and was sent by the crateful to Europe.

2. One bumper sticker popular in some Iowa towns is "You Ain't Much If You Ain't Dutch."

3. *New Destinations: Mexican Immigration in the United States,* Victor Zuniga and Ruben Hernandez-Leon, eds. (New York: Russell Sage Foundation, 2005).

4. In this chapter, I will use "Hispanic" when referring to census data for "non-white Hispanics." "Latino" is used as a more inclusive term to include United States citizens who are Hispanics and Latino immigrants. In Iowa, the vast majority of Hispanics in the census are Latino immigrants.

5. "2005 Vital Statistics of Iowa," Iowa Department of Public Health, 2005.

6. "2003 Vital Statistics of Iowa," Iowa Department of Public Health, 2003.

7. Mark A. Grey, "New Hispanics in Old Iowa: Social, Economic, and Policy Consequences of Rapid Ethnic Diversification," presentation to the Pew Hispanic Center, Washington, D.C., July 26, 2005.

8. "Statistics," Iowa Bureau of Refugee Services, Des Moines, Iowa, available online at http://www.dhs.state.ia.us/refugee/bureau/statistics.asp.

9. Mark A. Grey, "New Immigrants in Old Iowa," *Anthropology News* 41, no. 8 (2000): 9.

10. For a case studies of this phenomenon in Iowa, see Mark A. Grey and Anne C. Woodrick, "'Latinos Have Revitalized Our Community': Mexican Migration and Anglo Responses in Marshalltown, Iowa," in *New Destinations,* pp. 133–54, and Mark A. Grey and Anne C. Woodrick, "Unofficial Sister Cities: Meatpacking Labor Migration between Villachuato, Mexico and Marshalltown, Iowa," *Human Organization* 61, no. 4 (2002): 364–76. For a discussion of "postnational" communities, see Robert A. Hackenberg and Robert R. Alvarez, "Close-Ups of Postnationalism: Reports from the U.S.-Mexico Borderlands," *Human Organization* 60, no. 2 (2001): 97–104.

11. Mark A. Grey, "Welcoming New Iowans: A Guide for Citizens and Communities: Building Respect and Tolerance for Immigrant and Refugee Newcomers," University of Northern Iowa New Iowans Program, 2000.

12. Steven Kay, "The Nature of Turnover: Packers Attempt to Reverse a Financial Drain," *Meat & Poultry,* September, 1997, pp. 33–36; Mark A. Grey, "Immigrants, Migration and Worker Turnover at the Hog Pride Pork Packing Plant," *Human Organization* 58, no. 1 (1999): 16–27.

13. "History of the Bureau," Iowa Bureau of Refugee Services, available online at http://www.dhs.state.ia.us/refugee/bureau/history.asp.

14. Ibid.

15. Ibid.

16. Iowa Strategic Planning Council, "Goal 1: Iowa Welcomes a Diverse Population," in *Iowa 2010: The New Face of Iowa* (Des Moines: Iowa Strategic Planning Council, 2000), p. 9–12, available online at http://www.betteriowa.com/whatwedo/2010_pdfs/2010Goal1.pdf.

17. The state contracted with the author to conduct the needs assessments and integration plans with the three pilot communities.

18. The New Iowans Program was renamed the Iowa Center for Immigrant Leadership and Integration in 2005. See their Web site, www.newiowans.com.

19. Pam Belluck, "Short of People, Iowa Seeks to Be Ellis Island of Midwest," *New York Times,* August 28, 2000, p. A1.

20. William Claiborne, "Immigration Foes Find Platform in Iowa, National Groups Fight Governor on Recruiting Workers from Abroad," *Washington Post,* August 19, 2001, p. A3.

21. Jonathan Roos and John McCormick, "Majority: Don't Foster Immigration," *Des Moines Register,* September 3, 2000, p. 1A.

22. Gene M. Lutz, Mary E. Loesch, Melvin E. Gonnerman, and Aaron Maitlan, "Iowa 2001: State Government Survey: Workforce Shortage" University of Northern Iowa, Center for Social and Behavioral Research, 2001.

23. Iowa Workforce Development is the equivalent to the Job Service in other states.

24. Mark A. Grey, with Andrew Conrad, Maureen Boyd, and Anne Woodrick, "Marshalltown New Iowans Pilot Community Assessment: A Report to the Marshalltown New Iowans Pilot Community Steering Committee," University of Northern Iowa, New Iowans Program and Institute for Decision Making, 2001.

25. Christopher Conte, "Strangers on the Prairie: Iowa's Immigrant-Friendly Policies Aren't Wildly Popular among Its Residents. But the State Has Little Choice. It Needs People," *Governing Magazine,* January 2002; Mark A. Grey and Anne C. Woodrick, "'Latinos Have Revitalized Our Community': Mexican Migration and Anglo responses in Marshalltown, Iowa."

26. Mark A. Grey, with Andrew Conrad, Colleen Hovinga, and Anne C. Woodrick, "Mason City New Iowans Pilot Community Assessment."

27. Mark A. Grey and Andrew Conrad, "Ft. Dodge New Iowans Pilot Community Workforce Assessment," University of Northern Iowa, New Iowans Program and Institute for Decision Making, 2001.

28. Christopher Conte, "Strangers on the Prairie."

29. Iowa Code 7.18, Model Community Projects.

30. William Claiborne, "Immigration Foes Find Platform in Iowa, National Groups Fight Governor on Recruiting Workers from Abroad," *Washington Post,* August 19, 2001, p. A3.

31. William Claiborne, "Immigration Foes Find Platform in Iowa, National Groups Fight Governor on Recruiting Workers from Abroad."

32. Iowa Code 1.18, Iowa English language reaffirmation.

33. Until recently, these students were called Limited English Proficiency (LEP) students.

34. Iowa Code, Chapter 280.4, Limited English Proficiency—Weighting.

35. These funds are available from the U.S. Department of Education under Title III: Part A-English Language Acquisition, Language, Enhancement, and Academic Achievement Act as authorized by the No Child Left Behind Act of 2001.

36. Iowa Code, Chapter 280.4, Limited English Proficiency—Weighting, chapter 3.

37. Iowa Department of Education, Bureau of Planning, Research and Evaluation, "Iowa Education Data Spreadsheets 2003–2004.

38. Mark A. Grey, "Secondary Labor in the Meatpacking Industry: Demographic Change and Student Mobility in Rural Iowa Schools," *Journal of Research in Rural Education* 13, no. 3 (1997): 153–64.

39. Available online at http://www.state.ia.us/educate/ecese/is/ell/documents.html.

40. For a summary of the DREAM Act, see the National Council of La Raza Web site, http://www.nclr.org/content/policy/detail/1331/.

41. Survey and Analysis of the Health Needs and Disparities of the Immigrant Population, Bureau of Health Care Access, Iowa Department of Public Health and the Iowa/Nebraska Primary Care Association, 2003, available online at www.ianepca.com.

42. The the Iowa Poject EXPORT Web site, www.iowaprojectexport.org.

43. Michele Yehieli and Mark A. Grey, "A Health Providers Pocket Guide to Working with Immigrant, Refugee, and Minority Populations in Iowa," The University of Northern Iowa Global Health Corps and The University of Northern Iowa New Iowans Program, 2003; see also Michele Yehieli and Mark A. Grey, *Health Matters: A Guide to Working with Diverse Cultures and Underserved Populations* (Boston: Intercultural Press, 2005).

44. Abbie C. Peterson and Mark A. Grey, "Continuity and Change: The *Mexicana* Experience with Health and Healing in Iowa," *International Journal of Global Health and Health Disparities* (forthcoming).

45. "Survey and Analysis of the Health Needs and Disparities of the Immigrant Population," Bureau of Health Care Access, Iowa Department of Public Health, and Iowa/Nebraska Primary Care Association, 2003.

46. These study tours have been arranged by the Iowa Center for Immigrant Leadership and Integration with funding from the Wellmark Foundation and other sources.

47. Donnelle Eller, "Wanted by 2012: 200,000 Workers," *Des Moines Register,* March 19, 2006, p. A1.

48. Ibid.

49. Peter Ortiz, "Filling the Void in Iowa," *DiversityInc Magazine,* April 2006, pp. 27–34.

50. Ibid., p. 34.

51. Ibid.

52. Mark A. Grey, "Storm Lake, Iowa and the Meatpacking Revolution: Historical and Ethnographic Perspectives on a Community in Transition," in *Unionizing the Jungles: Essays on Labor and Community in the Twentieth-Century Meatpacking Industry,* Shelton Stromquist and Marvin Bergman, eds. (Iowa City: University of Iowa Press, 1997), pp. 242—61.

53. Mark A. Grey, "Turning the Pork Industry Upside Down: Storm Lake's Hygrade Work Force and the Impact of the 1981 Plant Closure," *Annals of Iowa* 54 (Summer 1995): 244—59.

54. For an in-depth look at the loss of white privilege in a rural Iowa meatpacking town, see Deborah Fink, *Cutting into the Meatpacking Line: Workers and Change in the Rrural Midwest* (Chapel Hill: University of Northern Carolina Press, 1998).

55. Mark A. Grey, "Bringing Two Worlds Together: Incorporating Latino Immigrants into Muscatine's Workforce: A Report with Recommendations to the Muscatine Economic Development Corporation," University of Northern Iowa Institute for Decision Making, 2000; Mark A. Grey, "Employee Turnover in a Multiethnic Workplace: Swift & Co., Marshalltown, Iowa" University of Northern Iowa Department of Sociology, Anthropology and Criminology, 1998.

56. Mark A. Grey, "Welcoming New Iowans: A Guide for Citizens and Communities," New Iowans Program, 2000.

57. Janet E. Benson, "Households, Migration and Community Context," *Urban Anthropology* 19 (1990): 9–29.

58. Heather MacDonald, "Housing and Community Development in Iowa in 2000: Meeting the Challenges of the Next Decade: A Report to the Iowa Finance Authority and the Iowa Department of Economic Development," January 2003, available online http://planning.urban.uiowa.edu/Iowa2000/Urban_Planning.pdf.

59. These materials are available online at www.ifahome.com

60. "Final Report," New Iowans Study Committee, Iowa Legislative Services Agency, January 2006, p. 1.

61. Ibid., p. 6.

62. As one of the state's experts on immigration and Director of the Iowa Center for Immigrant Leadership and Integration (formerly the New Iowans Program), I was asked by one of the committee cochairs and his staff to help the committee wade through the public testimony and sort out specific kinds of legislation. All committee members received our series of Welcoming New Iowans publications and were made familiar with our activities. I was prepared to not only help them sort through the overwhelming amount of information they received, but I was prepared to offer draft legislation on health disparities, drivers' licenses, and other issues.

But just as the political process overcame proactive efforts to accommodate immigrants with the rise and fall of the Vilsack initiative in 2000–02, the political process squashed any real hope for an informed legislative agenda in 2005. Three days before the final meeting at the capitol, at which I was supposed to speak, the invitation was withdrawn. A staffer informed me that the committee cochairs had met and decided to have no speakers at their final wrap up meeting. The staffer told me that the reason I specifically was no longer invited was because the committee members "did not want to be held accountable by someone who knows what he is talking about in front of the press." In the past, most of the get-tough immigration rhetoric and policy came from Republicans, but in the case of avoiding knowledgeable guests in a public session of the New Iowans Study Committee, Democrats were responsible. Why? Because they felt they had a real chance to take back the senate in 2006 and did not want to take any risks by backing pro-immigrant legislation. Yet another opportunity lost.

I chose not to attend the committee's final wrap up session, but another attendee—an immigration attorney—became so frustrated with the committee's lack of meaningful action that he interrupted the proceedings by shouting, "You are so ill-informed about what's going on that I'm afraid of what's going to happen." He left the room—after being told to shut up by one of the cochairs—saying the "issue was too politicized." He accused the committee of "missing the nuances surrounding the issue of giving undocumented workers drivers' licenses." He was right.

63. Iowa General Assembly, 2006, House File 169, "An Act Repealing the Iowa English Language Reaffirmation Act and Rules of Construction for English Language Laws."

64. Iowa General Assembly, 2006, Senate File 2207, "Relating to the Publication of Official Notices in English Language Newspapers."

65. Iowa General Assembly, 2006, Senate File 2219, "Relating to Human Trafficking and Related Offenses, Including the Provision of Law Enforcement Training and Victim Assistance Programs, Providing Penalties, and Providing for a Study."

66. Iowa General Assembly, 2006, House File 2534, "An Act Relating to Employment Practices and Human Trafficking and Related Offenses and Providing Penalties and Remedies and an Appropriation."

67. Thomas Beumont, "Bill Would Discourage Hiring of Immigrants," *Des Moines Register*, February 10, 2006, p. 3B.

68. Iowa General Assembly, 2006, House Resolution 140, "A Resolution Supporting Efforts to Promote Comprehensive Immigration Reforms that Encourage Legal Immigration, Deter Unauthorized Immigration, Promote Economic Growth, and Ensure Secure Borders."

69. Iowa General Assembly, 2006, Senate File 2219, "Relating to Human Trafficking and Related Offenses, Including the Provision of Law Enforcement Training and Victim Assistance Programs, Providing Penalties, and Providing for a Study."

70. Iowa General Assembly, 2006, Senate File 2340, "An Act Relating to Using a Motor Vehicle to Transport an Illegal Nonresident Alien, and Providing a Penalty."

71. Iowa Administrative Code, Chapter 14, New Iowans Centers, 871—14.2(78GA,SF2428), "Definitions."

72. Iowa Administrative Code, ARC 5087B, Latino Affairs Division [433], Chapter 2: Qualifications of Language Interpreters, 433—2.6(216A), "Approved Proficiency Language Test."

73. Iowa Administrative Code, ARC 5087B, Latino Affairs Division [433], Chapter 2: Qualifications of Language Interpreters, 433—2.7(216A), "QGI Eligibility: Qualified General Interpreter Training Program."

74. Iowa Administrative Code, ARC 5087B, Latino Affairs Division [433], Chapter 2: Qualifications of Language Interpreters, 433—2.8(216A), "QGI Eligibility: Qualified Specialized Interpreter Training Program."

75. "Iowa Interpreter Program: Summary," Iowa Department of Human Rights, Division of Latino Affairs, 2006, available online at http://www.state .ia.us/government/dhr/la/Pages/Interpreter.htm.

76. In my efforts to convince Iowans that accommodating newcomers is critical to the state's long-term economic and social health, I discourage people from using the term "ignorance." I argue that one is uninformed or misinformed and when it comes to immigration, most people are both. What is particularly challenging is fighting both the lack of information and disinformation about immigrants that comes from the political rhetoric among state policymakers. Yet, the ultimate tragedy may be that policymakers are also uninformed and misinformed about immigration but that does not stop them from making immigration policy anyway.

Notes to Chapter 4

1. This report was made possible by support from The Century Foundation. The author wishes to thank her research assistant, Michael Gaddis, for his invaluable efforts in documenting the findings reported here.

2. Demographic information reported in this section is calculated based on data from U.S. Census Bureau, Census 2000 and Census 1990, Summary File 1 (SF1) and Summary File 3 (SF3), and U.S. Census Bureau, American Community Survey 2004, generated by Stephanie Bohon using American Factfinder, available online at http://factfinder.census.gov (accessed April 1, 2006).

3. Georgia Security and Immigration Compliance Act, Georgia Senate Bill 529, signed April 17, 2006, available online at http://www.legis.state.ga.us/ legis/2005_06/sum/sb529.htm.

4. These findings were calculated from data attained from the sources in note 2.

5. Deborah A. Duchon and Arthur D. Murphy, "Introduction: From *Patrone* and *Cacique* to Good Ole Boys" in *Latino Workers in the Contemporary South,* Arthur D. Murphy, Colleen Blandchard, and Jennifer A. Hill, eds. (Athens: University of Georgia Press, 2001), pp. 1–9 .

6. U.S. Census Bureau, American Community Survey, 2004.

7. Audrey Singer, *The Rise of New Immigrant Gateways* (Washington, D.C.: The Brookings Institution, 2004).

8. Georgia J. Borjas and Marta Tienda, "The Economic Consequences of Immigration," *Science* 235 (1986): 645–51; Marta Tienda and Leif I. Jensen, "Immigration and Public Assistance Participation: Dispelling the Myth of Dependency," *Social Science Review* 15 (1986): 372–400; George J. Borjas and Stephen Trejo, "Immigrant Participation in the Welfare System," *Industrial and Labor Relations Review* 44, no. 2 (1991): 195–211; and Julian Simon, *The Economic Consequences of Immigration* (Cambridge, Mass.: Basil Blackwell, 1999).

9. Micki Neal and Stephanie A. Bohon, "The Dixie Diaspora: Attitudes toward Immigrants in Georgia," *Sociological Spectrum* 23, no. 2 (2003): 181–212.

10. Jeffrey S. Passel and Wendy Zimmerman, *Are Immigrants Leaving California? Settlement Patterns of Immigrants in the late 1990s* (Washington, D.C.: The Urban Institute, 2001), p. 24; Randolph Capps, Michael E. Fix, and Jeffrey S. Passel, "The Dispersal of Immigrants in the 1990s," Policy Brief No. 2, The Urban Institute, Washington, D.C., 2002, p. 2.

11. Jeffrey S. Passell, Randolph Capps, and Michael E. Fix, "Undocumented Immigrants: Facts and Figures," The Urban Institute, Washington, D.C., 2004, p. 4.

12. Jeffrey S. Passell, "The Size and Characteristics of the Unauthorized Migrant Population in the U.S.," Pew Hispanic Center, Washington, D.C., March 7, 2006, p. 3.

13. Passel, Capps, and Fix, "Undocumented Immigrants," p. 4.

14. John D. Meadows III, telephone conversation with author, April 7, 2006.

15. John D. Studsill and Laura Nieto-Studstill, "Hospitality and Hostility: Latin Immigrants in Southern Georgia," in *Latino Workers in the Contemporary South*, ed. Arthur D. Murphy, Colleen Blanchard, and Jennifer A. Hill (Athens: University of Georgia, 2001), p. 80.

16. Alea Holman, "Swept Under a Rug: A Look at Immigrant Families in Atlanta," *Southerner*, May 8, 2000, p. 1.

17. Greig Guthey, "Mexican Places in Southern Spaces: Globalization, Work, and Daily Life in and Around the North Georgia Poultry Industry," in *Latino Workers in the Contemporary South*, p. 61.

18. John Lunsford, telephone conversation with author, April 10, 2006.

19. Mitch Seabaugh, telephone conversation with author, April 6, 2006.

20. Cheryl Wienges, interview with author, Jefferson, Ga., April 30, 2006.

21. The Basic Pilot Program is a federally operated electronic database that uses Social Security numbers to verify legal authorization to work.

22. John D. Meadows III, interview with author, April 7, 2006.

23. John Lunsford, telephone conversation with author, April 10, 2006.

24. Mitch Seabaugh, telephone conversation with author, April 6, 2006.

25. Pedro Marin, interview with author, April 24, 2006.

26. John Lunsford, telephone conversation with author, April 10, 2006.

27. A Resolution Recognizing the Great Value of Continued Immigration into the State of Georgia, Georgia Senate Resolution 1426, adopted March 30, 2006, available online at http://www.legis.state.ga.us/legis/2005_06/sum/sr1426.htm.

28. A Resolution Supporting and Commending the Men and Women Who Serve as Patrol Agents in the United States Border Patrol, Georgia Senate Resolution 121, adopted February 10, 2005, available online at http://www .legis.state.ga.us/legis/2005_06/sum/sr121.htm.

29. A Resolution Recognizing the Clarkston Health Collaborative for its Efforts in Promoting the Social, Economic, and Physical Well-Being of the Citizens of the City of Clarkston, Georgia Senate Resolution 778, adopted February 1, 2006, available online at http://www.legis.-state.ga.us/legis/2005_ 06/sum/sr778.htm.

30. A Resolution Recognizing Community Health Centers Day, Georgia Senate Resolution 743, adopted February 1, 2006, available online at http:// www.legis.state.ga.us/legis/2005_06-/sum/sr743.htm.

31. A Resolution Urging the United States Congress and the President of the United States to Pass Comprehensive Immigration Reform in 2006, Georgia Senate Resolution 640, prefiled December 1, 2005, available online at http:// www.legis.state.ga.us/legis/2005_06/sum-/sr640.htm.

32. John Lunsford, telephone conversation with author, April 10, 2006.

33. Sonji Jacobs, "Six Quit Perdue's Latino Board," *Atlanta Journal-Constitution,* April 20, 2006, pp. D1 and D8.

34. Jason Winders, "Vision for a New Georgia a Tad Cloudy," *Athens Banner-Herald,* March 23, 2006, p. A4.

35. Jorge H. Atiles and Stephanie A. Bohon, "*Camas Calientes:* Housing Adjustments and Barriers to Social and Economic Adaptation among Georgia's Rural Latinos," *Southern Rural Sociology* 19, no. 1 (2003): p. 115.

36. Ibid., pp. 97–122.

37. Ibid.

38. The city of Athens covers the entirety of Clarke County, Georgia. Consequently, the government of the city of Athens and Clarke County are incorporated into one. Effectively, county commissioners make the decisions for the city.

39. Cheryl Wienges, interview with author, Jefferson, Ga., April 30, 2006.

40. Jorge H. Atiles and Stephanie A. Bohon, "The Needs of Georgia's New Latinos: A Policy Agenda for the Decade Ahead," Public Policy Research Series 3, Carl Vinson Institute of Government, University of Georgia, 2002, p. 42–44.

41. Cheryl Wienges, interview with author, Jefferson, Ga., April 30, 2006.

42. Stephanie A. Bohon, Heather Macpherson, and Jorge H. Atiles, "Educational Barriers for New Latinos in Georgia," *Journal of Latinos and Education* 4, no. 1 (2005): 44–45.

43. Arguably this is not just a Latino immigrant problem. Georgia is home to undocumented Asian and African immigrants, as well. Nonetheless, the vast majority of undocumented children in Georgia are Latino.

44. Bohon, Macpherson, and Atiles, "*Camas Calientes,*" p. 52.

45. John Lunsford, telephone conversation with author, April 10, 2006.

46. A Resolution Proposing and Amendment to the Constitution, Georgia House Resolution 256, introduced February 17, 2005, available online at http:// www.legis.state.ga.us/legis/2005_06/-sum/hr256.htm.

47. Georgian Senate Bill 171, introduced February 14, 2005, available online at http://www.legis.-state.ga.us/legis/2005_06/sum/sb171.htm.

48. Georgia Higher Education Protection Act, Georgia Senate Bill 368, prefiled December 1, 2005, available online at http://www.legis.state.ga.us/legis/2005_06/sum/sb368.htm.

49. Sarita A. Mohanty, Steffie Woolhandler, David U. Himmelstein, David H. Bor, Susmita Pati, and Olveen Carrasquillo, "Health Care Expenditures of Immigrants in the United States," *American Journal of Public Health* 95, no. 8 (2005): 1431–38.

50. John Lunsford, telephone conversation with author, April 10, 2006.

51. John D. Meadows III, telephone conversation with author, April 7, 2006.

52. Chip Rogers, telephone conversation with author, May 5, 2006.

53. John Lunsford, telephone conversation with author, April 10, 2006.

54. Pedro Marin, telephone conversation with author, April 24, 2006.

55. Pedro Marin, interview with author, April 24, 2006.

56. Georgia House Bill 501, enacted May 2, 2005, available online at http://www.legis.state.-ga.us/legis/2005_06/sum/hb501.htm.

57. Atiles and Bohon, "Meeting the Needs of Georgia's New Latinos," pp. 21–22.

58. Pedro Marin, interview with author, April 24, 2006.

59. Atiles and Bohon, "The Needs of Georgia's New Latinos," pp. 36–38.

60. Ibid.

61. John Lunsford, telephone conversation with author, April 10, 2006.

62. Ibid.

63. Mitch Seabaugh, telephone conversation with author, April 6, 2006.

64. Ibid.

65. Ron Forster, telephone conversation with author, April 12, 2006.

66. John D. Meadows III, telephone conversation with author, April 7, 2006.

67. *Smith v. the State,* 571 S.E.2d 740 (Ga., 2002).

68. Pedro Marin, telephone conversation with author, April 24, 2006.

69. Micki Neal and Stephanie A. Bohon, "The Dixie Diaspora: Attitudes toward Immigrants in Georgia," *Sociological Spectrum* 23, no. 2 (2003): 181–212.

70. D. A. King, "President Bush: Man of the Year in a New America," The American Resistance, available online at http://www.theamericanresistance.com/articles/art2004dec28.html.

71. "Frequently Asked Questions about the Dustin Inman Society," The Dustin Inman Society, available online at http://www.thedustininmansociety.org/info/faq.html.

72. Arthur Rosenberg, "Manual Day Labor in the United States," National Employment Law Project, available online at http://www.nelp.org/docUploads/rosenberg%2E.pdf.

73. Teresa Borden, "Shady Job Agencies Exploit Immigrants," *Atlanta Journal Constitution,* November 30, 2005, p. A1.

74. Marilyn Geewax, "Illegals Case a Landmark," *Atlanta Journal Constitution,* April 27, 2006, pp. E1 and E5.

75. John D. Meadows III, telephone conversation with author, April 7, 2006.

76. Josh McDaniel and Vanessa Casanova, "Pines in Lines: Tree Planting, H2B Guest Workers, and Rural Poverty in Alabama," *Southern Rural Sociology* 19, no. 1 (2003): 86–87.

77. Atiles and Bohon, "The Needs of Georgia's New Latinos," pp. 16–20.

78. Chip Rogers, telephone conversation with author, May 5, 2006.

79. Pedro Marin, telephone conversation with author, April 24, 2006.

80. Keith Whitney, "Newspaper 'Crossed Line,'" Eleven Alive News, March 23, 2006, available online at http://www.11alive.com/news/news_article.aspx?storyid=77664.

81. Pedro Marin, telephone conversation with author, April 24, 2006.

82. "Zamarippa Watch," American Patrol, available online at http://www.americanpatrol.com/GEORGIA/ZAMARRIPA-/MenuZamarripaWatch.html.

83. Mitch Seabaugh, telephone conversation with author, April 6, 2006.

84. Pedro Marin, telephone conversation with author, April 24, 2006.

Notes to Chapter 5

1. I would like to acknowledge invaluable assistance from the immigrant advocates and public policy officials whom we interviewed (see Appendix A), and from the following outstanding graduate students: Mandy Bai, Brynja Gudjonsson, Niki Carlson, Shayerah Ilias, Clare Mortensen, Amy Morris, Burke Murphy, Renee Raduenz, Ben Rau, Kyle Walker, and Corinne Wilson.

2. Minnesota is the nation's largest turkey producer, slaughtering over 46.5 million birds a year, and generating $516 million dollars in sales.

3. Steven A. Camarota and John Keely, "The New Ellis Islands: Examining Non-Traditional Areas of the Immigrant Settlement in the 1990s," Center for Immigration Studies, September 2001.

4. Katherine Fennelly, "Latinos, Asians and Africans in the Northstar State: New Immigrant Communities in Minnesota," in *Beyond the Gateway: Immigrants in a Changing America*, Elzbieta M. Gozdziak and Susan F. Martin, eds. (Lanham, Md.: Rowman and Littlefield, 2006).

5. American Community Survey, U.S. Department of Commerce, Bureau of the Census, 2004.

6. Barbara Ronningen, "Estimates of Selected Immigrant Populations in Minnesota: 2004," Minnesota State Demographic Center, 2004.

7. Judy Keen, "Some Uneasy as Illegals Change Face of Minn. Town," *USA Today*, March 23, 2006, p. 5A.

8. "The Impact of Illegal Immigration on Minnesota: Costs and Population Trends," Minnesota Department of Administration, Office of Strategic Planning and Results Management, December 8, 2005.

9. Dana B. Badgerow, commissioner, Minnesota Department of Administration, cover letter to report "The Impact of Illegal Immigration on Minnesota," prepared by the Office of Strategic Planning and Results Management, December 8, 2005.

10. James Kielkopf, "The Economic Impact of Undocumented Workers in Minnesota," Hispanic Advocacy and Community Empowerment through Research, September, 2000.

11. Conrad deFiebre, "State Ties Steep Costs to Illegal Immigration," *Minneapolis Star Tribune,* December 9, 2005, p. 1A.

12. "Economic Impact of Immigrants," Office of the Legislative Auditor (OLA), State of Minnesota, May 25, 2006.

13. "Pawlenty Takes Aim at Illegal Immigration," *Minneapolis Star Tribune,* January 4, 2006.

14. Bill Salisbury, "Pawlenty Shows a Softer Stance on Immigration: Seven Initiatives Encourage Legal Methods," *St. Paul Pioneer Press,* January 13, 2006, p. 1B.

15. Stan Greenberg, Anna Greenberg, and Julie Hootkin, "The Changing Shape of Minnesota: Reinvigorating Community and Government in the New Minnesota," Greenberg Quinlan Rosner Research, Inc., prepared for the Minnesota Community Project, December 14, 2004.

16. Ibid.

17. Although the DREAM Act did not pass as a separate measure, one legislative analyst noted that the final appropriations bill defines Minnesota residents without mentioning citizenship, and that it might take a court case to determine whether this language opens a path for undocumented students to be eligible for in-state tuition.

18. Grant Makers Concerned with Immigrants and Refugees (GCIR), report on grants classified in a database of the Minnesota Council on Foundations, 2005. The number of grants was determined by searching the database for "immigrant," "newcomers," and "refugees." It is likely to be a significant undercount of grants made to organizations serving the foreign-born since many such grants were only coded for the subject focus, for example, "heath" or "education," rather than for the target population. The foundations making the largest number of grants included the Otto Bremer Foundation (98 grants), the Minneapolis Foundation (36 grants), the Jay and Rose Phillips Family Foundation (28 grants), and the St. Paul Foundation (24 grants).

19. Wendy Amundson, "Philanthropy and Immigration: Changing Practices to Address a Changing Population, Giving Forum," Minnesota Council on Foundations, Fall 2005.

20. "Special Report: Working Towards Diversity III: A Progress Report on Strategies for Inclusiveness among Minnesota Grant Makers," Minnesota Council on Foundations, June 2005, available online at http://xrl.us/msxz.

21. Greenberg, Greenberg, and Hootkin, "The Changing Shape of Minnesota."

22. "Minnesota ABE Impact Report," Adult Basic Education Office, Minnesota Department of Education, 2006.

23. "A+ for Teaching Newest Americans," editorial, *Minneapolis Star Tribune*, May 1, 2006.

24. Katherine Fennelly and Myron Orfield, "Impediments to Integration of Immigrants: A Case Study in Minnesota," in *Suburban Immigrant Gateways: Immigration and Incorporation in New U.S. Metropolitan Destinations*, Audrey Singer, Caroline Brettell, and Susan Hardwick, eds. (Washington, D.C.: Brookings Institution Press, forthcoming).

25. Latinos are both native and foreign-born. The high school graduation rates cited here are not available by place of birth. Katherine Fennelly, "Latinos, Asians and Africans in the Northstar State: New Immigrant Communities in Minnesota," in *Beyond the Gateway*.

26. Deborah Schlick, Affirmative Options Coalition, personal communication with the author, May 22, 2006.

27. "Disparities and Barriers to Utilization among Minnesota Health Care Program Enrollees," Minnesota Department of Human Services, December 2003.

28. "Immigrant Health: A Call to Action: Recommendations from the Minnesota Immigrant Health Task Force," Minnesota Department of Health and Minnesota Department of Human Services, July 2004, available online at http://www.health.state.mn.us/refugee.

29. Wendy Amundson, "Philanthropy and Immigration: Changing Practices to Address a Changing Population," Giving Forum, Minnesota Council on Foundations, Fall 2005.

30. MFIP stands for Minnesota Family Investment Program.

31. "Covering Kids or Moving Backward?" *Minneapolis Star Tribune*, editorial, December 11, 2005.

32. The courts later rejected the implementation of these changes without legislative endorsement.

33. Deena Anders et al., "Immigration Policy and Law in the Post 9/11 Era," paper prepared for a course in immigration and public policy, Hubert Humphrey Institute of Public Affairs, April 2006.

34. Chris Waddington, "Experts Talk on Terror Attacks," *Minneapolis Star Tribune*, November 11, 2001, p. 1B.

35. Jean Hopfensperger, "Federal Raids Target Immigrants in the State," *Minneapolis Star Tribune*, May 27, 2006.

36. See Appendix B for an op ed article by the author on this topic.

37. "Root Causes and Solutions to Disparities for Hispanics/Latinos in the Juvenile Justice System," Hispanic Advocacy and Community Empowerment through Research and the Council on Crime and Justice, May 2005.

38. "Minnesota Racial Profiling Report: All Participating Jurisdictions: Report to the Minnesota Legislature," Institute on Race and Poverty and the Council on Crime and Justice, September 22, 2003, available online at http://xrl.us/jr9u.

39. Anders et al., "Immigration Policy and Law in the Post 9/11 Era."

40. Ibid.; *The Immigration and Nationality Act,* U.S. Code 8 (1952).

41. Ann Ziebarth and Jaehyun Byun, "Migrant Worker Housing: Survey Results from South Central Minnesota," Hispanic Advocacy and Community Empowerment through Research, 2002.

42. The most recent indices are for evaluations up to 2002.

43. The index combines measures of the health of the economy and the people, levels of crime and education, and government services. Kathleen O'Leary Morgan and Scott Morgan, "State Rankings 2005: A Statistical View of the 50 United States (State Rankings)," Morgan Quitno Corporation, 2005

44. John Farrell, "The Changing Shape of Minnesota," Humphrey Institute of Public Affairs, December 2004.

45. Jared Bernstein, Elizabeth McNichol, and Karen Lyons, "Pulling Apart: A State-by-State Analysis of Income Trends," Center for Budget and Policy Priorities and Economic Policy Institute, January 2006.

46. Barbara Ehrenreich, *Nickel and Dimed: On (Not) Getting By In America* (New York: Metropolitan Books/Henry Holt and Co., 2001).

Notes to Chapter 6

1. I have adopted the term "unauthorized migrants" preferred by the PEW Hispanic Center and will use it whenever possible throughout this chapter. I may interchangeably use "illegal" and "undocumented" if I feel they contribute to the clarity of the particular point being made. See Jeffrey S. Passell, "Unauthorized Migrants: Numbers and Characteristics," The Urban Institute, Washington, D.C., 2005.

2. Lourdes Gouveia, Miguel A. Carranza, and Jasney Cogua, "The Great Plains Migration: Mexicanos and Latinos in Nebraska," in *New Destinations: Mexican Immigration to the United States*, Victor Zúñiga and Rubén Hernández León, eds. (New York: Russell Sage Foundation), pp. 23–49.

3. Alejandro Portes, Patricia Fernandez-Kelly, and William Haller, "Segmented Assimilation on the Ground: The New Second Generation in Early Adulthood," *Ethnic and Racial Studies* 28, no. 6 (November 2005): 1000–40.

4. Figures calculated by the Office of Latino/Latin American Studies. Figures for 1910 and 1920 were drawn from the U.S. Census Bureau, "Fourteenth Census of the United States: State Compendium, Nebraska" (Washington, D.C.: U.S. Government Printing Office, 1925), p. 30. Figures for 2000 were calculated from the U.S. Census Bureau, Census 2000, Summary Files 3 (SF3).

5. T. Earl Sullenger and Lillian Hill, "The Immigrant in Omaha," Municipal University of Omaha, 1932.

6. "Racial Tensions in Nebraska in the 1920s," Nebraska Studies.org, available online at http://www.nebraskastudies.org/0700/stories/0701_0130. html (accessed May 20, 2006).

7. Legislative Resolution 20CA proposing the constitutional amendment was passed by the Nebraska Legislature on March 9, 2000. Available online at http://srvwww.unicam.state.ne.us/unicam96.html.

8. "Keeping the Promise: Immigration Proposals from the Heartland," Report of an Independent Task Force, Chicago Council on Foreign Relations, 2004.

9. See for example, Cindy Gonzalez and C. David Kotok, "Immigrants Boost Population," *Omaha World-Herald,* March 22, 2006, pp. 1–2; Joe Duggan, "Changing Faces in Rural Places: Surge in Latino Population Leads to Town's Growth," *Lincoln Journal Star,* March 18, 2001, pp. 1, 6A.

10. Immigrant advocate, interview no. 1, May 17, 2006.

11. Don Walton, "Candidates Agree on Immigration Policy," *Lincoln Journal Star,* October 18, 2000, p. 1B; David Kotok, "GOP Senate Hopefuls Favor Looser Borders," *Omaha World-Herald,* April 28, 2000, p. 19.

12. See Lourdes Gouveia and Arunas Juska, "Taming Nature, Taming Workers: Constructing the Separation between Meat Consumption and Meat Production," *Sociologia Ruralis* 42, no. 4 (2002): 370–90.

13. Don Walton, "Don Stenberg on Immigration," Lincoln Journal Star, April 23, 2006. Candidates' views on immigration are also available at their respective Web sites.

14. For examples, visit the opinion pages of the *Omaha World-Herald* (www.omaha.com), the *Lincoln Journal Star* (www.journalstar.com), the *Grand Island Independent* (www.theindependent.com), and other local papers in the state. Interestingly, the newspaper editorials have generally praised Hagel and criticized Nelson for their positions on immigration vis-à-vis what editors view is the reality of Nebraska's needs for immigrant workers, as well as Nebraska's history of welcoming immigrants.

15. Permits certain students who attended Nebraska high schools to establish residency, Nebraska Legislative Bill 239, signed April 13, 2006. Available online at http://www.unicam.state.ne.us/legal/SLIP_LB239.pdf.

16. Deborah Solomon, "Immigration Debate Reaches Heartland," *Wall Street Journal* online, April 13, 2006.

17. Robyyn Tysver, "GOP Foes Turn Focus to Issue of Immigrant Rights," *Omaha World-Herald,* May 7, 2006, p. 1A.

18. Special Program on Immigration, NET Radio, January 19, 2006, available online at http://www.publicbroadcasting.net/nprn/news.newsmain.

19. Myriam Jordan, "Off the Job, Onto the Streets," *Wall Street Journal,* April 11, 2006, p. 1B; Rachel L. Swarns, "Immigrants Rally in Scores of Cities for Legal Status," *New York Times,* April 11, 2006, p. 1; Cindy Gonzalez, "Immigration Rally Cry: Today We Are Making History," *Omaha World-Herald,* April 11, 2006, p. 1A.

20. Immigrant advocate, interview no. 1, May 17, 2006.

21. Tim Elfrink, "Omahan Tries to Start Minuteman Chapter," *Omaha World-Herald,* May 18, 2006, p. 3B.

22. Jake Thompson, "Hagel, Nelson Inundated. Thousands Express Their Emotions on Immigration," *Omaha World-Herald,* May 22, 2006, p. 1A.

23. "Immigration Views: State-by-State," Rasmussen Reports, May 10, 2006 available online at www.rasmussenreports.com/2006/May (accessed May 19, 2006).

24. These include the nationally renowned Nebraska Appleseed Center for the Public Interest; Omaha Together One Community (OTOC), the interfaith coalition working across racial and ethnic groups that is largely credited for helping organize meatpacking workers; and even academic centers such as ours, the Office of Latino/Latin American Studies at the University of Nebraska at Omaha (OLLAS). OLLAS strives to produce serious and accessible research reports documenting the factors shaping immigration and integration. Across rural communities we have witnessed the slow but increasing organization or reorganization of local social and community agencies, extension services, and chambers of commerce to accommodate the presence of new immigrants in their midst. Importantly, they include the increasing levels of political mobilization of the immigrant population, even the unauthorized, the critical constituencies behind the successes of both unionization and recently held pro-comprehensive reform marches.

25. Cindy Gonzalez, "Non-Mexican Latinos in Nebraska, Iowa, Rising," *Omaha World-Herald,* March 11, 2001. For a demographic profile of Latinos in the state, see Lourdes Gouveia, Mary Ann Powell, with Esperanza Camargo, "Educational Achievement and the Successful Integration of Latinos in Nebraska: A Statistical Profile to Inform Policies and Programs," Office of Latino/Latin American Studies, University of Nebraska at Omaha, 2005, pp. 1–65. For a more in-depth look at South Americans in the state, particularly Colombians and Venezuelans, see Lourdes Gouveia, "Divergent Origins, Converging Destinies? Venezuelans, Colombians and Mexicans in the Heartland," paper presented at the Russell Sage conference, "Migration to the United States: New Sources, New Destinations," New York, February 2, 2005.

26. 2004 American Community Survey, U.S Census Bureau.

27. Joe Duggan, "Immigrants Spur Growth in Nebraska," *Lincoln Journal Star,* April 2, 2006, p. 1D.

28. Cindy Gonzalez and C. David Kotok, "Immigrants Boost Population," *Omaha World-Herald,* March 22, 2006, p. 1A.

29. See Gouveia, Carranza, and Cogua, "The Great Plains Migration, pp. 23–49.

30. Calculated from 2003 American Community Survey, U.S. Census Bureau, in "Nebraska State Fact Sheet," National Council of La Raza (NCLR), www. nclr.org. See also Gouveia, Carranza, and Cogua, "Great Plains Migration."

31. Joe Kolman, "Child Population Slow to Increase," *Omaha World-Herald,* March 25, 2001, p. 1A.

32. "Vital Statistics: Birth Summary," Nebraska Health and Human Services, 2004, available online at http://www.hhs.state.ne.us/ced/vs.htm.

33. Rogelio Saenz, "Latino Births Increase in Nontraditional Destination States," Population Reference Bureau, available online at www.prb.org. Percentages were calculated by OLLAS from the 2004 American Community Survey, U.S. Census Bureau, available online at http://factfinder.census.gov.

34. Jean Ortiz, "Omaha's Sudanese Benefit from Assistance Program," *Lincoln Journal Star,* March 23, 2005, available online at www.journalstar.com.

35. Sarah Schulz, "Members of Sudanese Community Tell Osborne about Issues They Face," *Grand Island Independent,* August 19, 2004, available online at www.theindependent.com.

36. Cindy Gonzalez, "Tyson Plant Closings Have Big Impact on Population of Towns," *Omaha World-Herald,* March 5, 2006, p. 1A.

37. Gouveia, Carranza, and Cogua, "Great Plains Migration."

38. These figures were calculated by OLLAS from the 2004 American Community Survey, "Selected Characteristics of the Native and Foreign-Born Populations," U.S. Census Bureau, available online at http://factfinder.census.gov.

39. Gouveia, Powell, with Camargo, "Educational Achievement and the Successful Integration of Latinos in Nebraska."

40. 2004 American Community Survey, U.S Census Bureau.

41. Ibid.

42. Calculated by OLLAS from ibid.

43. Gouveia, Powell, with Camargo, "Educational Achievement and the Successful Integration of Latinos in Nebraska"; Gouveia, Carranza, and Cogua, "Great Plains Migration"; Schulz, "Members of Sudanese Community Tell Osborne About Issues They Face."

44. "Local Area Unemployment Statistics, 1990–2006," U.S. Department of Labor, Bureau of Labor Statistics, available online at http://data.bls.gov/cgi-bin/surveymost.

45. The authors, following Roger Waldinger, defined industrial niches as "industries that contain a critical mass of ethnic workers as well as a disproportionate share of workers in the industry being members of an ethnic group." See Lourdes Gouveia and Rogelio Saenz, "Global Forces and Latino Population Growth in the Midwest: A Regional and Subregional Analysis," *Great Plains Research* 10, no. 2 (2004): 305–28.

46. Lourdes Gouveia and Donald D. Stull, "Dances with Cows: Beefpacking's Impact on Garden City, Kansas, and Lexington, Nebraska," in *Any Way You Cut It: Meat Processing and Small Town America,* Donald D. Stull, Michael J. Broadway, and David Griffith, eds. (Lawrence: University Press of Kansas, 1995), pp. 84–107.

47. Jennifer Meyer, "Sudanese Struggle to Find Jobs in Nebraska," *La Vista Sun,* November 11, 2005, available online at www.lavistasun.com (accessed March 3, 2006).

48. Gouveia and Stull, "Dances with Cows."

49. Gouveia, "Global Strategies and Local Linkages: The Case of the U.S. Meatpacking Industry," in *From Columbus to ConAgra. The Globalization of Agriculture and Food,* Alessandro Bonnanno, Lawrence Busch, William Friedland, Lourdes Gouveia, and Enzo Mingione, eds. (Lawrence: University Press of Kansas, 1994).

50. *Any Way You Cut It,* Stull, Broadway, and Griffith, eds.

51. Lourdes Gouveia, "Estados, Municipalidades e Inmigrantes Latino-americanos en la Internaciolización del Circuito de la Carne," *Internacional Journal of Sociology of Agricultura and Food* 2 (1992): 116–31; Eric Schlosser,

Fast Food Nation: The Dark Side of the All-American Meal (Boston: Houghton Mifflin, 2001); Lourdes Gouveia and Donald D. Stull,"Latino Immigrants, Meatpacking and Rural Communities: A Case Study of Lexington, Nebraska," Julian Samora Research Institute Report No. 26, Michigan State University, 1997, pp. 1–16.

52. Suzanne Charlé, "The New Nebraskans," The Ford Foundation, New York, Winter 2002.

53. Gouveia and Stull, "Latino Immigrants"; Thomas Sanchez , "The Social Construction of a Rural Latino Immigrant Ethnic Identity: 'The Good Definitely Outweighs the Bad,'" Ph.D. dissertation, University of Nebraska, Lincoln, 2005; Sara Tennessen, "Hispanic Population Growing with Industry: Towns, Immigrants Share in Benefits," *Lincoln Journal Star,* August 26, 2001, pp. 1A, 4A; Associated Press, "Packing Plants Boost Growth in Four Counties," *Lincoln Journal Star,* March 24, 1997, pp. 12–13; Steve Jordon and Mike Riley, "Workers Are Burden, Benefit to Consumers," *Omaha World-Herald,* June 8, 2003, p. 1A.

54. See Gouveia and Stull, "Dances with Cows"; Gouveia, Miguel A. Carranza, and Jasney Cogua, "The Great Plains Migration"; Lourdes Gouveia and Thomas Sanchez, "Incorporation of Latinos/Immigrants in Rural Nebraska Communities: Grand Island and Schuyler," Report to Texas A&M Research Foundation, 2000.

55. Örn Bodvarsson and Hendrik Van den Berg, "The Impact of Immigration on a Local Economy: The Case of Dawson County, Nebraska," *Great Plains Research* 13, no. 2 (2003): 291–309.

56. Christopher Burbach, "The New South," *Omaha World-Herald,* September 2, 1996, pp. 35, 37.

57. Jackie Gabriel, "Si Se Puede: Organizing Latino Immigrant Workers in South Omaha's Meatpacking Industry," M.A. thesis, University of Nebraska at Omaha, 2004.

58. Nebraska Coalition for Quality Jobs, working manuscripts; *Blood, Sweat, and Fear: Workers' Rights in U.S. Meat and Poultry Plants* (New York: Human Rights Watch, 2004).

59. "Adelante South Omaha! Forward South Omaha," press release, RDG Planning and Design, available on line at http://www.rdgplanningdesign.info/news/archives/2005/08/adelante_south.html (accessed May, 5, 2005).

60. Chicago Awareness Center Director, telephone conversation with author, May 18, 2006.

61. Jeffrey Passel, "Unauthorized Migrants: Numbers and Characteristics," Pew Hispanic Center Report, June 24, 2005, available online at www.pewhispanic.org.

62. Gouveia and Stull, "Latino Immigrants"; for media stories see, for example, Deborah Alexander, "Four at Meatpacking Plant Plead Not Guilty to Smuggling Workers," *Omaha World-Herald,* April 10, 2000, p. 21, and Jeremy Olson, "Immigration Raids Target Only the Worst Employers," *Omaha World-Herald,* November 9, 2003, pp. 1–2.

63. "Comprehensive Immigration Reform Is Important to Tyson Foods: How You *Can* Be Heard," flyer, Tyson Foods Inc., Springdale, Ark.

64. Gabriel, "Si Se Puede."

65. See, for example, David Card, "Is the New Immigration Really So Bad?" Working Paper No. 11547, National Bureau of Economic Research, Cambridge, Mass., August 2004; U.S. Congress, Congressional Budget Office, *The Role of Immigrants in the U.S. Labor Market* (Washington, D.C.: U.S Government Printing Office, November, 2005).

66. Calculations by OLLAS based on 1990 and 2000 Population Census, Social and Economic Characteristics: Nebraska, and the 2004 American Community Survey, U.S. Census Bureau.

67. Gouveia, "Divergent Origins, Converging Destinies?"

68. Immigrant advocate, interview no. 1, May 17, 2006.

69. Non-English Speaking Workers Protection Act, Nebraska Legislature Bill 418, signed April 2, 2003, available online at http://srvwww.unicam.state.ne.us/unicam98.html.

70. For a brief history, see Nebraska Appleseed Center for Law in the Public Interest Web site, www.neappleseed.org.

71. Nebraska state senator, interview no. 9, January 30, 2006.

72. Some examples are the reports produced by the Nebraska Health Information Project, which was the result of a unicameral initiative in 1994 and began in 1995 as a partnership between the University of Nebraska Medical Center and Nebraska Health and Human Services. Although prompted by the larger concern to produce accurate data that would inform state health initiatives aimed at all Nebraskans, the timing itself suggested that growth of the immigrant population was at least part of the subtext informing this initiative. For more information, go to www.unmc.edu/nebraska/.

73. Besides the reports mentioned in note 2, see "State Options for Expanding Health Insurance Coverage and Strengthening the Health Care Safety Net," Nebraska Health Insurance Policy Coalition, August 29, 2005, pp. 1–41, available online at http://www.statecoverage.net/statereports/ne3.pdf; Keith Müeller et al., "Health Insurance Coverage in Nebraska: Results from the Nebraska State Planning Grant," Nebraska Center for Rural Health Research, University of Nebraska Medical Center, Omaha, December 2004, pp. 1–42, available online at http://www.unmc.edu/rural/SPG/health-insur-ne-results-updated1.pdf.

74. Health professional, interview no. 33, February 24, 2006.

75. Michelle M. Casey, Lynn A. Blewett, and Kathleen T. Call, "Providing Health Care to Latino Immigrants: Community-Based Efforts in the Rural Midwest," *American Journal of Public Health* 94, no. 10 (October 2004): 1709–11.

76. Advocate and director of nonprofit organization, interview no. 10, April 14, 2006.

77. For information on the coalition, visit the U.S. Department of Labor, Occupational Safety and Health Administration Web site, www.osha.gov.

For information on the specific agreement between OSHA and Nebraska's meatpacking industry, see "OSHA and Meat Processing Industry in Nebraska Work Together to Promote Safety," U.S. Department of Labor, available online at http://www.osha.gov/dcsp/success_stories/compliance_assistance/ne_meatprocessing.html.

78. Müeller et al., "Health Insurance Coverage in Nebraska."

79. Li-Wu Chen et al., "The Cost of Uncompensated Health Care and the Expenditures of Self-Pay Hospital Inpatient Care in Nebraska" Nebraska Center for Rural Health Research, July 2005, pp. 1–33, available online at http://www.statecoverage.net/statereports/ne10.pdf.

80. Cindy Gonzalez, "Illegal Immigrants Add to Burden of Uninsured," *Omaha World Herald,* August 2, 2004, p. 1A.

81. OLLAS transcription of the New Immigrant Orientation Conference, sponsored by The Nebraska Equal Opportunity Commission, Cornhusker Hotel, Lincoln, Nebraska, May 13, 2006.

82. Provide for funding for the Nebraska Lifespan Respite Services Program under the Nebraska Health Care Funding Act, Nebraska Legislature 692, signed May 16, 2001, available online at http://srvwww.unicam.state.ne.us/unicam97.html.

83. Miguel A. Carranza and Lourdes Gouveia, "The Integration of the Hispanic/Latino Immigrant Workforce," final report submitted to the State of Nebraska Mexican American Commission and the Legislative Task Force on the Productive Integration of the Immigrant Workforce Population, May 31, 2002.

84. Demetrious Papademetriou and Brian Ray, "From Homeland to Home: Immigrants and Homeownership in Urban America," Fannie Mae Occasional Papers, Fannie Mae, Washington, D.C., 2004.

85. Equal Opportunity Commission representative, interview no. 63, April 13, 2006.

86. "Nebraska Fair Housing Strategy, 1997–2000," Nebraska Department of Economic Development, Lincoln, 2001.

87. As far as I have been able to ascertain, there is no specific law dealing with this issue. However, the advocate we interviewed has encountered situations in which an immigrant applicant was rejected due to his inability to pass a background check due to a false Social Security number (E-mail communication, June 8, 2006).

88. Advocate and director of nonprofit agency, interview no. 10, April 14, 2006.

89. Reported in Schulz, "Members of Sudanese Community Tell Osborne About Issues They Face."

90. Police chief, interview no. 48, April 25, 2006.

91. See, for example, Rodrigo Cantarero and Blanca E. Ramirez, "A Housing Discrimination Study of Hispanic Residents in Hastings, Nebraska," report submitted to the Nebraska Equal Opportunity Commission (EEOC), May 2003; James J. Potter, Rodrigo Cantarero, X Winston Yan, Steve Larrick, and

Blanca E. Ramirez, "Residents' Perceptions of Housing and the Quality of Life in Schuyler, Nebraska," report submitted to the City of Schuyler, May 2, 1995; Lourdes Gouveia and Donald D. Stull, "Latino Immigrants, Meatpacking and Rural Communities."

92. OLLAS calculations based on U.S. Census Bureau, Census 2000 Summary File 3 (SF3)–Sample Data.

93. "Lexington," in 2006 Profile of Nebraska Demographics, Economics, and Housing, Vol. III (Lincoln: Nebraska Investment Finance Authority, February 23, 2006), pp. III.10.1–12.

94. "2005 Profile of Nebraska Demographics, Economics, and Housing," final report prepared for the Nebraska Investment Finance Authority (NIFA), the Nebraska Department of Economic Development, and the Fannie Mae-Nebraska Partnership Office Portland, Oregon, Western Economic Services, LLC, February 22, 2005.

95. For some of this housing history with regard to Lexington, Nebraska, see Gouveia and Stull, "Dances with Cows."

96. The effort was documented in Thomas Sanchez, "Dissertation Fieldnotes, 2nd Hearing of Housing Ordinance," December 15, 1998. He describes how some residents opposed the ordinance based on the fact that it amounted to discrimination against Latinos and their higher likelihood of having living arrangements that included family and nonfamily members.

97. See, for example, Lourdes Gouveia, "Latinos in Rural America: From Pioneers to New Arrivals," Journal of Latino/Latin American Studies (JOLLAS) 1, Special Issue (Fall 2005): 1–25; Joe Duggan, "Growing Pains in Racially Changing Rural, Small Towns," Lincoln Journal Star, June 10, 2001, p. A1.

98. Elaine Allensworth and Refugio I. Rochin, "Latino Colonization and White Emigration: Ethnic Transformation in Agricultural Communities in California," Journal of Latino/Latin American Studies 1, Special Issue (Fall 2005): 25–66.

99. Charisse Jones, "Crowded Houses Gaining Attention in Suburbs," USA Today, January 31, 2006, p. 5A.

100. Equal Opportunity Commission representative, interview no. 63, April 13, 2006.

101. OLLAS calculations based on "2000 Census Public Use Microdata Sample: Nebraska," U.S. Census Bureau.

102. Alejandro Portes, Patricia Fernandez-Kelly, and William Haller, "Segmented Assimilation on the Ground: The New Second Generation in Early Adulthood," Ethnic and Racial Studies 28, no. 6 (November 2005): 1000–40.

103. Data calculated from Gouveia, Powell, with Camargo, "Educational Achievement and the Successful Integration of Latinos in Nebraska"; "State of the Schools" reports, Nebraska Department of Education, various years,

available online at http//reportcard.nede.ne.us; and Omaha public school handouts on ESL enrollment figures.

104. Due to space limitations, I will not detail this Latino presence in local schools. However, some of this data can be found in Gouveia, Powell, with Camargo, "Educational Achievement and the Successful Integration of Latinos in Nebraska."

105. Data calculated from ibid. and "State of the Schools" reports, Nebraska Department of Education, various years.

106. Sanchez, "The Social Construction of a Rural Latino Immigrant Ethnic Identity."

107. In the larger cities, schools are also able to establish cooperative programs with local agencies dedicated to serving the new immigrant or Latino population. Examples are the Chicano Awareness Center, which places education specialists in four high schools with high Latino enrollment. Lincoln's Hispanic Center and Grand Island's new Multicultural Center are two other examples. Once again, these resources are seldom available in smaller communities. For more on parent involvement and dual-language programs in Omaha public schools, see Juan Casas, et al., "Examining the Impact of Parental Involvement in a Dual Language Program: Implications for Children and Schools," OLLAS Special Report #2, Office of Latino/Latin American Studies (OLLAS), University of Nebraska at Omaha, 2005.

108. ESL coordinator, interview no. 12, March 3, 2006.

109. See Casas et al., "Examining the Impact of Parental Involvement in a Dual Language Program."

110. In 1990, the Nebraska legislature, under pressure by taxpayers and schools to reduce the schools' reliance on property taxes and equalize funding across the state, established a state aid formula that increased funding for public schools.

111. ESL coordinator, interview no. 12, March 3, 2006.

112. Details about LB 126 can be accessed on line at the Nebraska Department of Education Web site, http://www.nde.state.ne.us/FactsLB126_120105.pdf.

113. University administrator, interview no. 19, May 17, 2006. See also Emily Gersema and Paul Goodsell, "Trend in Meatpacking Towns Raises Question of 'White Flight,'" Omaha World-Herald, August 22, 2004, p. 1A.

114. Gouveia, Powell, with Camargo, "Educational Achievement and the Successful Integration of Latinos in Nebraska."

115. Michaela Saunders, "Suburbs Get in Integration Mix: Districts See Option Enrollment as Alternative to OPS Plan," Omaha World-Herald, October 31, 2005, pp. 1–2.

116. Michaela Saunders, "Chambers Up Close: A Q&A with the Senator, Whose OPS Views Are Rooted in His Youth," Omaha World-Herald, April 30, 2006, p. 3B.

117. Henry Cordes, "Sen. Chambers Had Spent Years Preparing for This Big 'Gotcha!'" Omaha World-Herald, April 9, 2006, pp. 1–2.

118. Details of the lawsuit are available online at http://www.naacpldf.org/content.aspx?article=915.

119. Nebraska state senator, interview no. 8, February 20, 2006.

120. See, for example, Casas, et al., "Examining the Impact of Parental Involvement in a Dual Language Program"; M. S. Black, "Historical Factors Affecting Mexican American Parental Involvement and Educational Outcomes: The Texas Environment from 1910–1996," Ph.D. dissertation, Harvard University, 1996; G. R. López, J. D. Scribner, and K. Mahitivanichcha, "Redefining Parental Involvement: Lessons from High-performing Migrant-impacted Schools," *American Educational Research Journal* 38, no. 2 (2001): 253–88.

121. See Casas, et al., "Examining the Impact of Parental Involvement in a Dual Language Program," for a more detailed analysis of this achievement gap and dropout rates among Hispanics and Latinos.

122. University administrator, interview no. 19, May 17, 2006.

123. E-mail communication, May 22, 2006.

124. University administrator, interview no. 19, May 17, 2006.

125. "Law Enforcement and the New Immigration," conference organized by OLLAS and the Police Professionalism Initiative at the University of Nebraska at Omaha, April 7, 2006.

126. Police chief, interview no. 48, April 25, 2006.

127. For a brief history and definition of memoes of understanding, see "Section 287 (G) Immigration Enforcement, fact sheet," U. S. Immigration and Customs Enforcement, available online at http://www.ice.gov/pi/news/factsheets/section287g.htm.

128. Police chief, interview no. 48, April 25, 2006.

129. Lourdes Gouveia and Arunas Juska, "Taming Nature, Taming Workers: Constructing the Separation between Meat Consumption and Meat Production in the U.S.," *Sociologia Ruralis* 42, no. 4 (2004): 370–90.

130. "News Release. INS Enhances Interior Enforcement Strategy," U.S. Department of Justice, Immigration and Naturalization Services, March 30, 1999, available online at www.ins.usdoj.gov (accessed April 12, 2000).

131. Participant at "Law Enforcement and the New Immigration," conference organized by OLLAS and the Police Professionalism Initiative at the University of Nebraska at Omaha, April 7, 2006.

132. Gouveia and Sanchez, "Incorporation of Latino/Immigrants in Rural Nebraska Communities."

133. Local attorney, interview no. 50, May 4, 2006.

134. Advocate and director of nonprofit agency, interview no. 10, April 14, 2006.

135. Personal communication with University of Nebraska-Omaha Ph.D. student, December 2005.

136. Immigrant advocate, interview no. 1, May 17, 2006.

137. Local attorney, interview no. 50, May 4, 2006.

138. Alejandro Portes and Rubén G. Rumbaut, *Legacies: The Story of the Immigrant Second Generation* (Berkley: University of California Press and New York: Russell Sage Foundation, 2001).

139. Immigrant advocate, interview no. 1, May 17, 2006.

140. See Gouveia, Carranza, and Cogua, "The Great Plains Migration."

INDEX

Figures and tables are indicated by *"f"* and *"t"* following the page number.

Administrative law on immigration, 64–65

Adult basic education (ABE), 115, 116–18

AFFIRM (Alliance for Fair Federal Immigration Reforms in Minnesota), 107

AFL-CIO and opposition to immigration, 43

African Americans: attitude toward Latino immigrants, 14, 16–17, 17*t*; workers in Nebraska, 163, 165; workers in North Carolina, 13–14

African refugees: Georgia, 72; Iowa, 36, 38; Minnesota, 101–2, 113, 115, 132, 135; Nebraska, 154, 159, 184

Age of population: Iowa, 35; Minnesota, 135

Agricultural sector. *See* Migrant farmworkers

AIDS, 169

Alexander, Martha, 29

Allred, Cary, 28

American Community Survey on immigrant populations, 72

Americanization programs, 146

American Patrol-sponsored websites, 100

Amnesty programs, 148

Area Learning Centers (Minnesota), 115

Asian immigrants: Nebraska, 157, 159, 165; North Carolina, 8. *See also* Southeast Asian refugees

Assimilation, 143–44

Athens Banner-Herald on Georgia immigration legislation, 78

Athens Grow Green Coalition, 81

Balkan refugees in Iowa, 36, 38

Banking practices of immigrants, 92

Barnes, Roy, 77

Basic Pilot Program to confirm worker's eligibility, 76, 97

Bazan-Mason, Andrea, 28, 30

Black market in "official" documents, 90

Blacks. *See* African Americans

Border Patrol. *See* U.S. Border Patrol

Border Protection, Antiterrorism, and Illegal Immigration Control Act of 2005, 27, 148

Camas calientes describing overcrowded housing, 4, 80–81

229

Hernandez, Juan, 20–21
Higher education and post-secondary
instruction: Georgia, 84–85;
Iowa, 48–49; Minnesota, 116–18;
Nebraska, 148–49, 189–92
Hispanic Advocacy and Community
Empowerment through Research
on racial profiling, 128–29
Hmong. *See* Southeast Asian refugees
Hmong American Partnership, 117
Hombres de paso (employment
agencies that mistreat workers), 97
Homeland Security Department:
approval of state identification
cards and drivers' licenses, 88;
training of local law enforcement
by, 5, 29–30, 91, 193–94
HOPE scholarship, 84
Housing issues: Georgia, 4, 78,
79–82; Iowa, 59–61; Minnesota,
131–33; Nebraska, 174–79; North
Carolina, 12, 26, 29
Howard, Julia, 29
Hubert H. Humphrey Institute
interviews with policymakers in
Minnesota, 103; survey form used
in, 136–40
Hunt, James B., Jr., 19

Illegal Immigrant Fee Act (proposed
bill in Georgia), 86
Immigration and Customs
Enforcement (ICE) and state
enforcement efforts, 5, 29–30,
193–94
Immigration and Naturalization
Service's (INS) Operation
Vanguard, 148, 150, 193
Immigration case law, 92–94
Immigration courts, 27
Immigration Reform and Control Act
of 1986, 76
Industrial employment of immigrants,
9, 10, 156–59, 157t. *See also
specific industries*

Infectious diseases and Mexican
immigrants, 53
Informal work. *See* Day laborers
International Institute of Minnesota,
117
Interpreters: Border Patrol as, 107,
129; Georgia's need for in health
care, 85; Iowa standards for
Spanish-English interpreters, 64–
65; Minnesota's need for in health
care, 123–24; Nebraska's need
for in health care, 173–74; North
Carolina Training for Health Care
Interpreters program, 22
Iowa, 33–66; administrative law
on immigration, 64–65; African
immigrant population in, 36, 38;
Balkan immigrant population
in, 36, 38; Bureau of Refugee
Services, 38; day laborers in, 59;
demographic trends in, 35, 57;
diversity of immigrants in, 33–34;
Division of Latino Affairs, 64,
65; driver's license application
procedure, 54–55; economic
trends in, 58; education issues
in, 46–48; employment issues in,
57–58; Finance Authority (IFA),
60–61; Governor's Task Force
for Indochinese Resettlement,
37–38; gubernatorial re-election
and immigration policy in,
44–46; health care issues in,
3–4, 49–53; higher education in,
48–49; historic context for new
immigration in, 37–38; housing
issues in, 59–61; immigrant influx
in, 35–36; Latino population
in, 33–34, 36, 50–51; law
enforcement in, 55–56; legislation
on immigrant issues (2006),
62–63; legislative hearings on
immigrant issues, 61–62; Office
of Multicultural Health, 51; pilot
community projects in, 39–40,

About the Contributors

GREG ANRIG, JR. is vice president of programs at The Century Foundation, supervising the creation and progress of the foundation's projects. He has written and made media appearances about social insurance, taxes, pensions, and the economy. Before joining the foundation, he was a staff writer and Washington correspondent for Money magazine. He is the coeditor of the books *Social Security Reform: Beyond the Basics* (Century Foundation Press, 1999) and *The War on Our Freedoms: Civil Liberties in an Age of Terrorism* (Public Affairs, 2003).

STEPHANIE A. BOHON is a demographer and associate professor of sociology at the University of Tennessee at Knoxville. She is best known for her work on the growth and needs of Latino migrants in the South, examining the difference between Latino migrant adjustment in traditional and emerging gateways. Her work on immigration and immigration policy has been published in several journals, including *Social Problems, Social Science Quarterly, Rural Sociology, Population Research and Policy Review,* and the *Journal of Latinos and Education*. She is the author of *Latinos in Ethnic Enclaves: Immigrant Workers and the Competition for Jobs* (Routledge, 2000).

KATHERINE FENNELLY is professor of public affairs at the Hubert H. Humphrey Institute, University of Minnesota, and the 2006-2007 Fesler-Lampert Chair in Urban and Regional Affairs. Her research, teaching, and outreach interests include immigration and public policy, leadership in the public sector, the human rights of immigrants and refugees in the United States, and the preparedness of communities and public institutions to adapt to demographic changes. She has been dean of the University of Minnesota Extension Service, a faculty member and department head at the Pennsylvania State University, and a faculty member at Columbia University School of Public Health. She is bilingual in Spanish and English, and has worked and traveled extensively throughout Latin America.

LOURDES GOUVEIA is director of Latino/Latin American studies and professor of sociology at the University of Nebraska at Omaha. She has published numerous articles on the interrelation between the global restructuring of meat processing, the recruitment of Latino immigrant labor, and the implications of these changes for the future of Latino immigrant labor flows and their communities of settlement. She is coeditor of *From Columbus to ConAgra: The Globalization of Agriculture and Food* (University Press of Kansas, 1994).

MARK A. GREY is professor of anthropology at the University of Northern Iowa and director of the Iowa Center for Immigrant Leadership and Integration. He has published extensively in academic journals on immigration in the Midwest. He is the author of Welcoming New Iowans: A Guide for Citizens and Communities, *Welcoming New Iowans: A Guide for Managers and Supervisors, Welcoming New Iowans: A Guide for Christians and Churches* (with Dr. Anne Woodrick), and *Health Matters: A Pocket Guide for Working with Diverse Cultures and Underserved Populations* (with Michele Yehieli). He has won numerous awards for his activities, including the Iowa Friends of Civil Rights Award and the Iowa Council for International Understanding Vision Award.

PAULA D. MCCLAIN is professor of political science, public policy, and African and African American studies at Duke University. She is the immediate past president of the Southern Political Science Association, director of the Ralph Bunche Summer Institute, and codirector of the Center for the Study of Race, Ethnicity and Gender in the Social Sciences. She is a past vice president of the American Political Science Association and a past president of the National Conference of Black Political Scientists. She is the author (with Joseph Stewart, Jr.) of *"Can We All Get Along?" Racial and Ethnic Minorities in American Politics* (Westview Press, 2005). Her most recent articles have appeared in the *Political Research Quarterly, Journal of Politics, American Political Science Review,* and *American Politics Quarterly.*

TOVA ANDREA WANG is a democracy fellow at The Century Foundation and executive director of The Century Foundation's Post–2004 Election Reform Working Group, working primarily on election reform and other issues related to civil rights and liberties. Her commentary on these issues has been published in *The Nation,* the *Los Angeles Times, Newsday,* the *New York Daily News,* the *St. Louis Post-Dispatch,* the *American Prospect, Campaigns and Elections,* and MSNBC.com, among other media outlets.